THE BANK OF ENGLAND

A history from its foundation in 1694

The Charter of the Bank of England, 1694. It bears the Great Seal of William and Mary

THE BANK OF ENGLAND

A history from its foundation in 1694

JOHN GIUSEPPI

Foreword by The Earl of Cromer, MBE

Evans Brothers Limited, London

Published by Evans Brothers Limited,
Montague House, Russell Square,
London WC1

© John Giuseppi 1966
First published 1966

Set in 11 on 13 pt Baskerville
Printed in Great Britain by
W. & J. Mackay & Co Ltd, Chatham, Kent
7/5036   PR 3424

Contents

Foreword by The Earl of Cromer, Governor of
the Bank of England   ix

Preface   xi

1   Antecedents and Foundation   1

2   The Bank Established – Early Difficulties   16

3   The Years at Grocers' Hall 1695–1734   33

4   Threadneedle Street – The First Fifty Years   50

5   'The Old Lady', William Pitt and the French Wars   70

6   The Nineteenth Century I   89

7   The Nineteenth Century II   116

8   The Governorship of Montagu Norman   145

9   Public Ownership and After   184

Bibliography   206

Index   211

Illustrations

The Charter of the Bank of England, 1694   frontispiece

The first page of the Bank's First Cash Book: between pages 68 and 69
A room in the Bank
Sir John Houblon, First Governor
The Silver Tankard of 1697
Three types of Exchequer Bills

1731   Drawing prepared for the Bank
1735   George Sampson's Gatehouse, Forecourt, Great Hall
       and offices
1770   Shows the addition of Sir Robert Taylor's Offices
1788   Showing disappearance of St. Christopher's Church and
       erection of Sir Robert Taylor's Court and Committee
       Rooms
1833   Sir John Soane's work completed

The Threadneedle Street front in 1797   facing page 100
Sir Robert Taylor's statue of Britannia
Bowler Miller, after a painting by Thomas Thompson

The Pay Hall, or Great Hall   101
Daniel Race, from a painting by Thomas Hickey

Sir Robert Taylor's Rotunda   116
Lothbury in 1797

'The Old Lady of Threadneedle Street in Danger'   117
A Bank Volunteer of 1804

Sir John Soane's Lothbury Court   132
Soane's Tivoli Corner

Transfer Day at the Bank   133
Five Pound Note of an early issue

Dividend Day   148
Vignette of Britannia, designed by Daniel Maclise

George Joachim Goschen (Viscount Goschen)   149
The Garden Court

Lord Cunliffe, Governor 1913 to 1918   164
Soane's Bank of England, prior to demolition

Lord Norman   165
Norman caricatured by Low

Lord Catto, Governor 1944 to 1949   180

Cartoon by Lee on the Bank passing into Public Ownership   181
The Bank of England today

Foreword by The Earl of Cromer, M.B.E.,
Governor of the Bank of England

Every schoolchild learns that the Bank of England was founded in 1694 to assist the financing of the war that William III was waging in the Low Countries. Between this fact and the modern role of the Bank there often exists a considerable void in everyman's knowledge.

There are many important works on the Bank but Mr Giuseppi sets out to supply the need for a history of the Bank in a more popular vein. He has drawn on the detailed knowledge he acquired working for many years on the archives of the Bank and tells a living story of the Bank as an institution, enlivening it by many anecdotes concerning the Bank itself, those who have served the Bank and those with whom the Bank has had to do. With a pleasantly fluent pen Mr Giuseppi has related a history full of interest and has filled a gap which needed filling.

C.

7 March 1966

Preface

In this book I have set out to tell, within the covers of a single volume, as much of the story of the Bank of England over its two hundred and seventy years of activity as will, I hope, give the reader an adequate picture of the Bank's contribution to financial, economic and social development in its own country, in the City of London, and in the world in general.

My service in the Bank of England was for many years in the domain of the Bank's archives, and during it I had the privilege of working with the authors of the two most fully detailed histories. Wilfrid Marston Acres, in his *The Bank of England from Within*, published in 1931, wrote in the main from the domestic angle; Sir John Clapham, whose *The Bank of England: A History* was published in 1944 to commemorate the Bank's two hundred and fiftieth anniversary, was the senior economic historian of the day, and fittingly told the story in its economic aspects. In producing a comprehensive account my debt to these two historians is, naturally, immeasurable.

I have told the story in my own way, but I must express my grateful thanks, in the first instance, to the Governor and Company of the Bank for the encouragement they have given me in its compilation, and for permitting me the same facilities of access to the archives as were accorded to my two predecessors mentioned above. I would also say how grateful I am for the very practical help given me by my friends and former colleagues, most of them in the Secretary's Office, and by the Bank Librarian and his staff. It would be right, too, to mention here my gratitude for help given me over the years by successive Librarians at Guildhall, and their assistants.

I must depart from the general anonymity of these acknowledgements to record my special debt to my friend and contemporary in the service,

Mr Frank Dancaster, who has collaborated with me extensively in the writing of this book. Without his help and encouragement, his aptitude for the right phrase and his soundness of judgement I would have found its compilation infinitely more arduous. With his aid and the friendly consideration always shown to me by my publishers it has been a pleasure.

JOHN GIUSEPPI, Esher

January 1966

The illustrations are mainly drawn from the Bank's own collection, and the copyright in reproduction rests with the Bank of England.

Chapter 1

Antecedents and Foundation

When, in 1829, Samuel Shillibeer began running the first public omnibus in London, it started from the Yorkshire Stingo, an inn in the outlying village of Paddington. It finished at the Bank: not this bank or that bank – the Bank.

Because of the density of the traffic, the scarlet monsters of today cannot end their journeys and turn round there. Nevertheless, the same short, rather cryptic word appears as a principal stopping-place on most of the buses traversing the City. And beneath lies one of London's busiest Underground railway stations. This, too is simply labelled Bank.

The bank in question is, of course, the Bank of England. What caused Londoners to name their city's main traffic-ganglion after this particular one among a number of important buildings at or near the site? Why did they not call it Royal Exchange, for example, after a building whose historic associations with the site are considerably older than the Bank of England's.

One's guess is that what caught their imagination was the glint of gold, 'that precious bane', enriching, maddening and destroying, reserved from time immemorial, in all lands, for sacred ceremonial and sacramental uses, for kings' crowns and women's wedding-bands, the metal of the sun itself.

During the greater part of the nineteenth century and the early years of the twentieth, that is, from Mr Shillibeer's day to the first of the Great Wars, the Bank's glory was at its height. A proverbial symbol of safety, it was the most powerful financial institution in the world's most powerful country. Where the kingdom's main highways met, near the foot of London Bridge, it stood, strange but magnificent, a cross between a fortress and a Greek temple. No wonder it impressed the citizens as it loomed through their familiar murk, awe-inspiring in its proportions despite the lowness of its elevation, like some massive beast, still as a rock yet eternally alert, crouching on guard over the nation's hoard.

When it was established in 1694 it was called the Bank of England either by a stroke of genius or of great good luck, for there can be no doubt that the title chosen had a profound and fortunate influence not only upon the development of the Bank itself but on that of all other English banking as well. By every precedent, save one, it should have been called after the city of its foundation. Amsterdam, Genoa and Hamburg are cases in point – Sweden was the exception – but Amsterdam, founded in 1609, had been followed by local banks at, and identified with, Middelburg, Delft and Rotterdam: it was not, except by pre-eminence and repute, the Bank of Holland. Hamburg, founded in 1619 in imitation of Amsterdam, was the Bank of a Free City, while Genoa was the State Bank of the Genoese Republic. In 1682 an attempt was made to found a City of London Bank, but the attempt failed and this may be why the later and highly successful experiment of 1694 omitted any reference to London in its title.

However, we shall probably never know the exact reason why the Bank was named after England rather than its capital, but had it flourished as the Bank of London it is at least probable that the merchants of other trading cities, with Bristol at their head, would soon have sought powers to be similarly incorporated. State-sponsored banks would later have arisen in every town of any size, with the result that banking generally in this country might well have taken a radically different course, while central banking would most certainly have done so.

The foundation of such an institution does not arise from caprice. Its parent country and city have reached a stage in their evolution when a need for it is deeply, though vaguely, felt. A number of attempts may be made to meet this need, but in the end one of them succeeds. Before outlining the immediate historical circumstances which led to the granting of State help towards the incorporation of the Bank of England, it may be best to sketch the earlier history of English banking leading, in particular, to the structure of banking in London at the time of the incorporation.

First of all, what is banking? This is rather like asking, What is religion? – or, What is education? No short definition can be adequate. It is easier to begin by explaining what banking is not. It is not money-lending nor is it pawnbroking, although it is sometimes mischievously compared with these kindred but distasteful trades. A moneylender provides funds for immediate consumption to tide the borrower – in whose breast hope springs eternal – over what he always likes to regard as a period of 'temporary' difficulty. Security for the advance – apart from certain opportunities for blackmail – is negligible if not absent. The interest charged is, in consequence, always high, sometimes even extortionate. A pawnbroker advances money on the security of movables – jewellery, furniture, clothing and the like – and the advance rarely represents anything more than a small fraction of the value of the object pawned. Where men are poor both these trades are rife; they are conducted for the benefit of the lenders alone, who are often the only happy and prosperous members of an otherwise miserable and abject community.

True banking involves the use of credit, or trust, upon which in the last analysis any high civilization depends, and the good banker must take as keen an interest, and pleasure, in the prosperity of his customers as he does in his own. Of his many functions, he perhaps likes best to advance money to finance the expansion of an existing undertaking or the establishment of a new one. The property of the undertaking itself forms his material security, although the last thing he would wish to do would be to realize it. His less tangible, but more real, security lies in his estimate of the integrity and ability of the man to whom he lends – in other words, upon the borrower's credit. He, of course, wants his money back, but would much prefer it to come from expanded profits than from the break-up proceeds of a failed venture. Meanwhile he demands interest for his services, but the rate charged must be a fair one which – the borrower being human – may sometimes irk, but must never cripple.

Trade and commerce begin with barter. The limitations of this system lead to the coining and issue of money – one of the first and most jealously guarded privileges of any State. The need for banking arises when a number of people hold more coin than they require for their immediate outgoings. The primary equipment of a banker is therefore a strongroom rendered as impregnable as possible. Soon, in various more or less widely separated communities, bankers are safeguarding various hoards. Almost at once this leads to a further facility, the transfer of money without the carriage of actual coin and the consequent avoidance of the many dangers inherent in that operation – a facility which should, it would seem, be far more widely taken advantage of, even today, if only for the sake of all the unfortunate wages clerks who are 'coshed' with sickening regularity each weekend.

At intervals depositors wish to draw upon the funds they have entrusted to a banker, either directly or by giving him written instructions to pay someone else. This in due course leads to those familiar

3

conveniences, the drawing or current account and the cheque. The next stage of development is far more complicated and delicate – the advancing by the banker, against proper security, of that proportion of the funds in his custody which he judges may be safely lent without jeopardizing the interests of those who have deposited them. This, it is true, may be called moneylending, since that is what it literally is, but as has already been pointed out, what distinguishes the true banker from the mere moneylender is the fact that he lends only to those he can trust for purposes which ought to be profitable and must be respectable or, at any rate, legitimate. Another function which inevitably adheres to banking during the course of its development is dealing in bullion and precious metals generally.

The problems connected with the safety and transfer of money are most acutely felt by those who handle it most. These, in the earlier stages of a civilization, were the merchants, so it was among them that banking first grew. The mercantile aspect of banking leads to discount – the purchase of bills of exchange before they fall due at somewhat less than their face-value, the difference being the buyer's fee for obliging the seller. Finally comes issue, the provision of acceptable paper-money – paper 'as good as gold', that is, backed by gold or solid, material wealth in one form or another either in the possession of the banker or at his command. This, the last of the banker's functions to develop, was, according to Sir John Clapham, in his book, *The Bank of England: A History*, 'the peculiarity of the Bank of England and its main contribution to the evolution of European banking'.

To turn from an attempted outline of banking to an attempted outline of its history, any examination, however superficial, must take into consideration a circumstance apparently remote but inextricably bound up with the subject. Banking was born, and began growing towards its maturity, when all Europe acknowledged the power and authority of a Universal Church. From the conversion of Constantine to the bloody wars marking the Reformation, this one Church, holy, catholic and apostolic, untiringly asserted its claims to shape, according to the Laws of God, the laws of men, and a great part of Europe's story, during this period, is concerned with the debates, the disputes and, at last, the savage armed struggles over the respective realms of God and Caesar, of Church and State.

Not only did the Church preach and interpret the Faith, it demanded the final word regarding the practical application of Christian principles to the details of daily life and affairs. The Church authorities declared, very rightly, that no Christian must take unfair advantage of his neighbour's needs, and to protect the ordinary man from exploitation, especially during times of famine, when the need for money was greatest, they framed the Usury Laws. These were strictly enforced throughout Europe and limited the rate of interest and fees a banker might charge. But however right the Church authorities may have been, as theologians, in proclaiming one great principle, they forgot, as economic legislators, another almost as great – that a fair day's work deserves a fair day's pay. They confused banking with moneylending: a natural enough mistake, for at the time the wise and fruitful use of deposits for the creation of credit and, hence, of new real wealth, was not fully understood. The only remuneration allowed to a banker was, in effect, charges for his services as custodian and for any transactions he made on behalf of his customers, both being based on the volume of the business performed. These, at the rates fixed, formed an insufficient recompense. The Christian merchant-bankers therefore began seeking their main income from dealings in foreign exchange, while the business of lending money at interest became almost exclusively the province of the Jews – to whom, of course, the laws of the Church did not apply.

In England a Jewish community existed from the Conquest until 1290. They were frugal and industrious, and endowed with their people's seemingly inborn knowledge of the course of 'the river of gold'. They enjoyed a certain measure of protection because they were able to lend money to the Norman and Angevin kings, but when they failed to satisfy exorbitant royal demands, this protection was withdrawn. After a series of massacres, the survivors were banished.

The departure of the Jews hardly disturbed, much less dislocated, the London money market, for the vacuum which would otherwise have been created had already been filled by the Lombards, companies of merchants from Italy who went under this title, though they certainly did not all come from Lombardy. They began to arrive in this country during the reign of Henry III (1216–72), originally, it would appear, as papal agents collecting the taxes due to the Pope. Perceiving many other business opportunities, they settled in London permanently and the colony gradually increased in size as they first reinforced and then supplanted the Jews as lenders. For the appropriate consideration, they would accommodate the very taxpayers whose dues they had come to collect, and they were soon making monetary advances, like the Jews before them, to the English kings. They began trading in the wool produced by the English monasteries and because of their knowledge of Continental business they also acted as money-changers.

As with all trades and professions, there were Lombards and Lombards, or, as R. De Roover in his *Money, Banking and Credit in Mediaeval Bruges*, ingeniously puts it, Lombards and lombards. The smaller fry, to whom he does not award a capital letter, had little or no influence upon the later development of banking in this country. They lent money on movables; in a word, they were pawnbrokers; and their advances merely effected a transfer of purchasing power, the money usually failing to fructify in the hands of the borrower. But when storms rage the high trees fall, while the grasses at their feet go scatheless. The religious wars of the sixteenth century shook the European credit structure to its foundations and the great Lombard banking houses, too deeply engaged in governmental loans, disappeared in a welter of State bankruptcies; meanwhile, the humble 'lombard' continued to dwell safe in his shop, as do his successors to this day, beneath the three golden balls of Lombardy.

As the great Lombard bankers one by one deserted the *nobilissima palatia* which they had built in and about the street still bearing their name, the London merchants took over much of their business. For the first time English banking was mainly in the hands of Englishmen. The practices of the Tudor and Stuart goldsmiths regarding deposit, exchange and loans were adopted in place of those used by the Lombards and the seeds of modern banking were sown.

Recent researches have corrected certain views hitherto widely held, especially in the English-speaking countries, that the contribution of the Lombards to England's present banking structure was not a very considerable one and that their methods were archaic. These methods, admittedly, were different from those of their successors in many important respects, and in a number of cases they were undoubtedly improved upon, but it must never be forgotten that the Lombards came from a land where the use of techniques not entirely obsolete even now had been employed at least as early as the twelfth century; their system of book-keeping was an accurate and flexible one. 'Double entry' – *doppia scrittura* – was invented by an Italian monk of the fifteenth century, and when introduced into England it was called 'the Italian system'. The Lombards were of service to the trade of all the Continent, facilitating in particular the transfer of money from one place to another, for they had correspondents in every city and large market town of western Europe, Germany excepted; and they did much business in bills of exchange – indeed, it was in the development and extension of the bill of exchange that they made their most important contribution. It must be said, however, that their bills were not the same as those drawn nowadays. At that time the bill of exchange was simply what its name implied, being an instrument of credit involving an exchange of some kind. It was never used for the purpose of discounting, still less of re-discounting.

6

The Lombards, then, were masters of a craft which had been prac-tised in their native Italy for a longer period and with greater skill than in any other land, and the City's debt to them, as tutors, is a great and lasting one.

It was in the field of foreign exchange that the absence of the Lombards was most acutely felt. So, in the reign of Elizabeth I, Sir Thomas Gresham set up a 'Burse', a copy of the Bourse at Amsterdam, the home of the Flemish bill-brokers and exchange-dealers. Despite Gresham's efforts, business there failed to prosper. The name of the building was later altered to the Royal Exchange, by proclamation, but in this case the Royal Touch did not cure the Evil. Business still languished, then expired, and the Royal Exchange was taken over as a meeting-place for City merchants. The present building – created in Victorian times – at the apex of the V formed by Threadneedle Street and Cornhill is of little more than symbolic value. Tite's pleasantly dignified hall occa-sionally houses exhibitions of interest to Londoners, in addition to pro-viding them with a useful short cut between the two thoroughfares. It still figures prominently in the news, but only two or three times in a century, when, with full medieval pomp, the accession of a new monarch is proclaimed from its steps to the assembled throng of businessmen, clerks and typists, the modern citizenry who work in the City of London, but dwell anything up to sixty miles away.

The collapse of the Lombard firms thus caused much loss and incon-venience to the City, but it did not create, though it may have increased, its most serious problem of all – a perennial shortage of good strong-rooms. The need for a place suitable for the safe custody of surplus coin and bullion had long been felt. The Royal Mint, then housed in the Tower, was much used by depositors until 1640, when, at the outbreak of the Civil War, Charles I, having failed to raise money by grants from Parliament, seized this treasure. Not unnaturally, the protests were vigorous; they resulted in the return of the treasure, but only on condi-tion that a loan of £40,000 be made to the King. It was a long time before depositors recovered from this shock and henceforward they were wary of trusting any money to the Government.

Meanwhile, alternative places of safe deposit had been gradually provided by the goldsmiths. Among the merchants of London, they had been the most likely to transform themselves into bankers. From the nature of their craft, they had to have well-secured vaults in which to keep their stock in trade and the moment they had placed this security at the disposal of their customers they had taken the first and most essential step on the road to becoming bankers.

By the time of the Restoration there was a large number of goldsmith-

7

bankers in London engaged in every kind of banking business. They accepted deposits at interest, giving receipts, on presentation of which repayment was made; they kept 'running cashes', also interest bearing, but without the formal receipt, and so easily drawn upon: they honoured their customers' 'drawn notes' (the ancestor of the cheque) on these: and their own promises (the goldsmith's 'bill' or 'note'), to pay the depositor or his order, and then the depositor or the bearer, were getting into circulation. They discounted commercial bills, bought and sold bullion and did ordinary money-changing. Furthermore, where Gresham and his Royal Exchange had failed they succeeded, having learned the techniques and acquired the correspondents necessary for the efficient conduct of foreign-exchange business.

They were invaluable to the Government of Charles II, though they doubtless did not forget what his royal father had done in 1640. Their justifiable caution therefore caused frequent irritation to servants of the Crown, not least to the Secretary for the Affairs of the Navy, Mr Samuel Pepys. Yet despite their caution, the Government 'did it again'. In 1672 came the 'stop' of the Exchequer. Nearly £1,000,000 was then owing to the goldsmiths; the Government, having run deeply into difficulties, stopped the payment of interest on part of this sum. The limited nature of the goldsmiths' resources was emphasized by the strain this caused them; most of them, in time, recovered from the setback but the harm done to Government credit was enormous and it continued at a low ebb throughout the remaining years of Stuart rule.

The position was radically altered when the 'Glorious Revolution' of 1688 brought to the throne a Dutchman whose main concern regarding the country over which he had been invited to rule was how much help it could afford him in his native country's war with France; and in considering this subject it is first necessary to take into account a contemporary factor, at first sight only tenuously related but one which, in the end, led to a solution of King William III's urgent problem. This was the long-standing public debate regarding London's need for a bank, on the lines of those at Amsterdam or Hamburg, which would exert a stabilizing influence upon the commercial world. From the times of the Commonwealth numerous schemes had been put forward, but nothing had come of them, the overriding reason probably being the fear that a bank established with royal support might enable a king to raise money without parliamentary sanction; and these discussions might well have continued for many years more, at academic levels only, had not William's dire need for money now been imported into them as a paramount consideration. And even then, as Sir John Clapham has pointed out, the actual establishment of the Bank of England can be regarded 'either as curiously accidental or as all but inevitable'.

From 1690 onwards the various schemes increased both in numbers and in scope; a promoting boom was sweeping the country; admiration for Dutch economic achievements was widespread and the swelling volume of trade had intensified London's need for a banking house which would not be so liable to the bankruptcy, constantly threatening and sometimes overtaking the goldsmiths.

Action was taken at last. Charles Montagu, a Lord of the Treasury and, from 1694, Chancellor of the Exchequer, considered that, of the many schemes put forward, the one sponsored by William Paterson, for the establishment of a proposed 'Bank of England', was the most promising. Paterson seems to have been one of those men whose ideas range some years ahead of their time and who have a streak of the true visionary about them, but in whom intellect outruns intelligence and whose ingenuity may sometimes approach, but never quite reaches, genius. Such men are, in consequence, regarded by the conservative – often with full justification – as being 'not quite sound' or 'too clever', while they arouse the deepest resentment and suspicion in the breasts of the hidebound. Montagu had met Paterson – and his ideas about a 'Fund for Perpetual Interest' – before; and it must be admitted that however feasible this conception of a permanent National Debt may have appeared to Montagu, and nowadays, perforce, appears to us, it must have struck the ordinary prudent businessman of those days as being bold to the point of absurdity.

On this occasion, however, Montagu could hardly fail to be impressed by the standing of the actual promoters, the men prepared to back Paterson's ideas with their own money. Their spokesman was Michael Godfrey, a merchant of great substance, and they were, without exception, members of firms which had become rich and powerful through generations of trading. Among them were members of the leading City Livery Companies, many were Members of Parliament, many were directly associated with the government of the City – of the first twenty-six members of the Court of Directors, six subsequently became Lord Mayor – and, one and all, they were solid in their support of the 'Glorious Revolution', Protestants to a man.

With such backing it may seem curious that the scheme should have been so jealously scrutinized and so hotly contested when, eventually, it came before Parliament. The fact remains that the establishing Act was passed (as Paterson wrote of it later) solely to avoid embarrassment to the Government, which desperately needed the money it promised and could see no other way of getting it.

The opposition from certain quarters was automatic. The Tories could see that the scheme, if put into operation, might very well do all that was expected of it with the unwelcome result, to them, that the position of the Government would be greatly strengthened; the gold-smiths and moneylenders – 'a few usurers and brokers of money', as Paterson contemptuously called them – feared ruin; rival promoters resented the loss of profits which would have come their way had their own schemes been preferred; certain merchants were apprehensive of the formation of what they thought might be a formidable competitor in the field of trade generally; and even among the Whig supporters there were some who still feared that the Bank might make the monarchy financially independent of Parliament.

To put the somewhat unnecessary fears of the merchants at rest a clause was added to the enabling Bill, during its passage through Parliament, forbidding the Bank to trade in 'goods, wares or merchan-dise', while the perhaps more well-founded misgivings among the Whigs were met in a similar way by adding another clause prohibiting the corporation from lending to the Crown, or from purchasing Crown lands, without parliamentary consent. Several other amendments were made to meet the more reasonable of the objections coming from the Bill's natural enemies, the Tories, the goldsmiths and the rival promoters.

But even before the Bill was placed before Parliament strong criticism of certain aspects of Paterson's scheme had come from within the Government itself. Issue was the bone of contention. There can be no doubt that what the promoters had in mind was a bank of issue; their keen eyes had long detected that the most fruitful source of profit to the goldsmith-bankers was in their own 'notes' which passed freely from hand to hand in the limited area where they were recognized – how much greater must the Bank's profits be if they could issue notes which would be recognized and accepted over an area far wider than any the goldsmiths could command. To the Government all this must have looked suspiciously like an attempt to invade that prime monopoly of theirs, the manufacture and control of the actual currency of the realm. It is, of course, a matter of history that when the dust had settled issue did emerge, in Clapham's words already quoted, as the Bank of England's 'peculiarity', but it was on this part of his proposals that Paterson's schemes, in their original form, foundered.

In 1693 Paterson had suggested that the capital sum required by the Government be raised not by a loan for a fixed period but 'upon a fund of Perpetual Interest'. To certain old-fashioned gentlemen who could boast that they had 'never owed a shilling in their lives' or, if they had ever been in debt had got out of it as quickly as they could, this proposed fund must have seemed, in itself, an extremely odd notion indeed; and perhaps they may be forgiven. They could hardly be expected to grasp that what they would have abominated in their private affairs might wear a quite different aspect when applied to public ones. Nor should they be condemned for not immediately perceiving that a nation can, so to speak, be regarded as a public corporation in which the population as a whole can be invited to invest, for the concept of a National Debt was then an entirely novel one.

One million pounds, said Paterson, might be raised by means of his 'Fund' at a cost to the State of £65,000 a year in perpetuity – 6 per cent on the capital sum plus £5,000 for 'management'. The subscribers were to be trustees and 'their Bills of Property should be current', as it is worded in the Journal of the House of Commons (x, pp. 621, 631–2). If this were granted they would be ready 'as a Bank to exchange such current Bills the better to give Credit thereto, and make the said Bills the better to circulate'. Clapham examines this clause and concludes that though the meaning is not perfectly clear the intention is plain enough – the setting up of a bank of issue. The Committee of the Commons, which had been appointed in January 1693 to consider Paterson's scheme among others, approved the idea of the Perpetual Fund, but were against making the bills of property current 'so as to force them on payment on any without their consent'. It looks, says Clapham, as though the Committee thought the proposal was for the issue of bank-notes that must be accepted as legal tender – which, fairly obviously, it was.

So Paterson had to go back to his supporters. A second scheme was put forward in which there was no mention of any bills, whether capable of being 'made current' or not. The revised scheme was brought before the Cabinet by Charles Montagu: it merely proposed that £1,200,000 be raised, to be lent to the Government at 8 per cent, on condition that the subscribers were incorporated and that £4,000 a year be allowed them for management expenses. The Cabinet debated the matter at length and eventually agreed that a Bill embodying the proposals should be submitted to Parliament. Then, in the lop-sided and off-hand fashion occasionally displayed by the English and their governments in the conduct of their affairs, these historic and far-reaching proposals somehow managed to get tagged on to an ordinary Finance Bill. The Act now always known as the Bank of England Act, 1694, actually bears, therefore, this rather longer title:

An Act for granting to their Majesties several Rates and Duties upon Tunnage of Ships and Vessels, and upon Beer, Ale and other Liquors: for securing certain Recompenses and Advantages, in the said Act mentioned, to such persons as shall voluntarily advance the Sum of £1,500,000 towards carrying on the War against France.

11

As a result the Bank was known in its early years as the 'Tunnage Bank'. It also acquired a certain association in the public mind with 'beer, ale and other liquors'. It cannot be said with any certainty whether it was from this time or from a later date, when in the course of its development the Threadneedle Street site absorbed several licensed houses, that a legend arose that the Bank, 'in its Charter', has the right to brew beer. Be that as it may, legends die hard, and from time to time this 'right' still has to be disclaimed by the Bank in response to some curious inquirer.

After the proposals had weathered a stormy reception in Parliament, as already described, the Act received the Royal Assent on 25 April 1694. Under its provisions Commissioners were to be appointed for taking subscriptions to the extent of £1,200,000, of which 25 per cent was payable immediately in cash. (The £300,000 balance of the total of £1,500,000, referred to in the Act's title, was to be raised by annuities.) Opponents of the Bank in the Privy Council tried to get the granting of the Commission postponed, but this attempt was frustrated by the Queen, William being abroad at that time. He had given express orders in the matter and she insisted upon their being carried out. On 15 June, therefore, a Commission was issued under the Great Seal, to which was attached a draft of the proposed Charter. Sir William Ashurst, the Lord Mayor, and a number of City merchants were named as Commissioners; the books were opened at 'Mercer's Chappell' in the Poultry on 21 June; more than £300,000 was subscribed on the first day and the whole sum was completed by 2 July.

The Book of the Subscriptions shows first a sum of £10,000 in the names of the King and Queen, followed by 1,267 individual holdings, although the actual number of entries is greater because many people increased their subscriptions during the time the book remained open. As each vellum sheet was completed it was signed for and sealed by two of the Commissioners and, at the end of each day's takings, the amount subscribed was similarly authenticated. During the ten days or so in which the Book was open forty-six pages in all were completed.

The subscription was open to 'Natives and Foreigners, Bodies Politick and Corporate', but as the books were closed after so short a period there was little opportunity for any corporate body to transact an investment, nor did foreigners have much time in which to do so either.

In all there were eleven contributors of the permitted maximum amount of £10,000. The Earl of Portland; six described as Esquires (a title used with some precision in those days, since it customarily implied the ownership of a manor and the right to bear arms), James de la Brettoniere of London, William Brownlowe of Woodcott, Surrey,

Thomas Howard of Westminster, Thomas Mulsoe of the Middle Temple, Matthew Humberstone and Anthony Parsons, both of London; the remaining four subscribers of the maximum allowed were elected members of the first Court of Directors, viz. Sir John Houblon and his brother Abraham, Theodore Janssen and Sir William Scawen.

This election – of a Governor, a Deputy Governor and twenty-four Directors – was the next business after the subscription had been completed. The draft Charter, incorporated in the Commission, laid down that the qualification for the office of Governor should be the holding of £4,000 stock, for the Deputy Governor, £3,000, and for a Director, £2,000. The Governors and Directors were to be chosen each year, between 25 March and 25 April, by those Proprietors who held not less than £500 stock. Of those persons who had subscribed, 633 were qualified to vote and notice was given to them, in the *London Gazette* of 5 July 1694, to meet in Mercers' Hall on Tuesday, 10 July, at the now unfashionable hour of 8 a.m. to take the oath prescribed and then to record their votes for Governor and Deputy Governor. Scrutiny was to be made on the afternoon of the same day and the result declared. On the following day, Wednesday, the election of Directors would be held, the result being declared on the Thursday.

No record has survived as to how many voted or how the voting went, but as a result of the election the following names were inscribed in the Charter, as constituting the first Court of Directors:

Sir John Houblon, Governor
Michael Godfrey, Deputy Governor

Sir John Huband, Bt.	Thomas Goddard
Sir James Houblon, Kt.	Abraham Houblon
Sir William Gore, Kt.	Gilbert Heathcote
Sir William Scawen, Kt.	Theodore Janssen
Sir Henry Furnese, Kt.	John Lordell
Sir Thomas Abney, Kt.	Samuel Lethieullier
Sir William Hedges, Kt.	William Paterson
Brook Bridges	Robert Raworth
James Bateman	John Smith
George Boddington	Obadiah Sedgwick
Edward Clarke	Nathaniel Tench
James Denew	John Ward

The Charter was sealed at Powis House, Lincoln's Inn Fields, by Sir John Somers, Keeper of the Great Seal, on 27 July, and in the afternoon of that day the Court of Directors met for the first time in Mercers' Hall.

So came into being an institution which was to become a 'stronghold of the Whigs and a bulwark of the Protestant Succession, and would continue to fulfil a useful service to the nation down to the present day', as W. Marston Acres has put it in *The Bank of England from Within*. Its strongest supporters can have had little idea of its future power and influence. The Government hoped it would afford an immediate source of sorely needed funds; the City believed that it would provide banking facilities based on sounder foundations, less liable to bankruptcy, than those with which they had hitherto had to be content. The Bank's strength was engendered from a fusion of the methods by which it satisfied these two separate hopes.

From its inception it aimed at being a State Bank providing funds for the Government, while being at the same time a competitive, profit-making enterprise whence the means for such advances might be found. The more knowledgeable of the projectors had always known that neither of these objects could be achieved unless the Bank could issue its own paper, although it is doubtful whether its supporters in Parliament would have approved of this, had they been as knowledgeable – and, as we have seen, the Committee of the House of Commons, which grasped the implications, rejected Paterson's original scheme upon this very point. In the end, of course, the Bank had its own way, as it had to if it was to accomplish all that its well-wishers, knowledgeable or otherwise, required of it.

Stability, however, rather than extravagant success at money-making, was the chief concern of the first Directors, and that stability was to be rigorously tested during the three years following the first election. In the midst of that turmoil one fact shines clear – that the men in whose hands the government of the newly founded Bank lay were determined to make it work. To work at all it had to pay its way and provide satisfactory dividends to its proprietors, but it is impossible to read its early records without becoming aware that stability was its main consideration. Stability justified its claim to privilege, in that the Bank alone, among the expedients of the time, could provide a regular source of funds by which the revenue could, when necessary, be anticipated and the steadiness of government ensured. That the credit of the State should be sound was essential if the Bank's own credit was to be sound as well.

In retrospect it can be seen how remarkable, for the age and the circumstances, were the wisdom and honesty of these early Directors. The undertaking in their charge gave much promise of success: it was blessed with Government support, a high-sounding name and a guaranteed income from the taxes. Against this, it had no body of real precedents to guide it in the great responsibility it had assumed. Its Directors might have made a 'bubble' of the Bank, gutted it, and decamped, or, yielding to a subtler temptation, have been filled with an inordinate ambition for power leading them into courses calamitous both to the Bank and the country whose name it bore. They did neither, but settled down to the comparatively humdrum task of making the new institution function.

The Directors had sworn upon election that they would be 'indifferent and equall to all manner of persons' and that they would give their best advice and assistance for the support and good government of the corporation: the Governors had sworn that to the utmost of their powers they would, by all lawful ways and means endeavour to support and maintain 'the Body Politique or Fellowship of the Governor and Company of the Bank of England and the liberties and privileges thereof'.

These oaths they kept.

Chapter 2

The Bank Established – Early Difficulties

At any earlier period than the later years of the seventeenth century the foundation of the Bank, upon the lines on which it was established, would have been impossible. After a century-long struggle the Protestant way of regarding Man, and his duty to God and his neighbour, had at last prevailed in England, and while it would be preposterous to call the Bank a religious institution, its establishment was nevertheless largely a direct consequence of this radical change in religious outlook. The Church no longer kept the conscience of both rulers and ruled. As for the rulers, anything which was expedient for the survival and growth of the State was right; as for the ruled, each man, with his private conscience for guide, worked out his own salvation within the laws laid down by the State.

And now the emerging concept of 'economic man' led easily to the belief that 'Man's self-interest was the means of God's Providence'; therefore, provided that he was upright and just in his dealings, there was nothing to prevent the religious man from making as much money as he could. 'The good Christian was not wholly dissimilar from the economic man.' Not that agreement with the new theology was by any means universal. Alexander Pope, for example, in his *Moral Essays*, makes a scathing allusion to the notorious lack of sympathy with those in distress shown by Sir Gilbert Heathcote, one of the original Directors, Governor in 1709 and 1710 and again in 1723 and 1724, and a Member of the Court of Directors until 1733:

> The grave Sir Gilbert holds it for a rule
> That every man in want is knave or fool.

But this was the same Sir Gilbert described upon his tomb at Normanton as 'a kind landlord, a steady friend, an affectionate relation, and one of character unblemished'. Perhaps the strangest thing of all is that the couplet and the epitaph, seemingly so contradictory, are in the circumstances of the age far from incompatible.

The first Court of Directors from the moment they were authorized to start business set to work with a will. The Great Seal having been affixed to the Charter and the Oaths taken before its Lord Keeper, it is with a noting of this event that the Bank's records open. Nevertheless it would seem that such was the eagerness of the Directors, or some of them, to get down to their tasks that, where they could, they had anticipated these formalities. Between their election on 12 July and the opening of the Bank's Minute Book 'A' on the 27th they must have met together constantly, for the actual recording of various decisions suggests that much had been well discussed and settled beforehand.

There is, for example, the matter of the Common Seal. Section 19 of the Act of 1694 laid down that the Bank should have such a seal, yet there is no record of any discussion in the Court itself as to what form it should take. What we do have, however, is an indication that a seal, a silver one, had already been tried and found to be unsatisfactory, for when on the Monday following the opening of the Bank (30 July) the subject is introduced everything is neatly cut and dried:

ORDERED

That the Seale which was now shewn to this Court, cutt in steele, whereof the Impression is hereunto annexed, being Britania sitting and looking on a Bank of mony, with the following inscription (The Seale of the Govern^r. & Company of the Bank of England) be the Comon Seale of the Company in all their Transactions.

As for the silver seal, it was ordered that it be put away in the custody of the Governor, after which no more is heard of it.

The choice of Britannia as a symbol of the Bank, though it may appear today to be appropriate to the point of triteness, perhaps deserves a short digression, for in 1694 she, as the mythological embodiment of this kingdom, was of quite recent birth. It is true that on coins of the Emperors Hadrian and Antoninus Pius she had appeared, bareheaded, holding a spear, and displaying a naked length of sturdy, barbarian leg, but all she denoted was the subjection of one more province of Imperial Rome. After the decline of the Roman Empire there is no known instance of the use of Britannia as a symbol until 1667. In that year, to commemorate the signing of the Treaty of Breda, Charles II ordered a medallion to be struck upon which she again appeared – presumably as the result of antiquarian research. This time, however, it was not as a captive barbarian maid, but as the tutelary goddess of a sovereign state. Serene and stately, seated on a rock by the sea, she bears on her shield the combined crosses of St George and St Andrew. At the King's instance, Frances Stewart, Duchess of Richmond, had sat for the figure to John Roettier, as Pepys records in his Diary on 25 February 1667. '. . . at my goldsmith's did observe the King's new medall, where, in little, there is Mrs Steward's face as well done as ever I saw anything in my whole life, I think; and a pretty thing it is, that he should choose her face to represent Britannia by.'

The Royal Mint then adopted the symbol, in two slightly differing forms, each of which was, in their case, based upon Roman originals. These designs were used on the copper halfpennies and farthings of the 1671 and subsequent issues, so they were well known to the public in 1694.

The Bank's first Britannia followed that on the farthings, which showed the bare leg (though this became modestly covered very early in her career). There were, however, certain alterations in detail – the 'Bank of mony' was introduced and, on the shield, the cross of St George, alone, was substituted for the combined crosses of England and Scotland.

And thus she has remained, in essentials, up to this day. Though new matrices have had to be supplied, at long intervals, the present seal is little different from the first. On the £1 and 10s. notes she is still bare-headed and she retains her spear, disdaining the trident which Britannia of the coinage acquired in 1797. The bank of money is still there, too, though it may be mentioned as a point of interest that this disappeared for a long period during the eighteenth and nineteenth centuries, when successive artists mistook it for a beehive. The supplanting of the symbol of wealth by that of industry was, however, so natural a transition that it seems never to have been questioned.

When the Court first met on the afternoon of 27 July 1694 those Directors who had not attended at the sealing of the Charter in the morning took their oaths before the Governor and the Deputy Governor. The meeting then proceeded to the first matter demanding attention, which was to decide exactly how the banking business was to be conducted. It was resolved that those who deposited money should have the choice of three methods 'and none other'. They might receive 'Running Cash Notes' payable on demand, either in whole or in part, the amounts of part-payments being endorsed on the notes; they might keep a 'book or paper' in which amounts received or paid on their account would be entered up at the Bank; or they themselves might draw 'notes' on the Bank to the extent of their deposits, which the Bank would 'accept'. All these were existing methods practised by the goldsmith-bankers, the three instruments of business utilized being, in embryo, the bank-note, the pass-book and the cheque respectively. No depositor could employ more than one of the three methods specified, though he could change from one to another upon giving notice to the Court of his intention to do so. This decision led to a good deal of cumbersome and unnecessary clerical work; the 'Drawing Office Ledgers' open with a large number of single transactions, each entered separately under the name of the depositor, but it was not long before convenience dictated that he be given the status of a 'customer' with an account in his own name furnishing a running record of each and every one of his transactions. When this happened it became immaterial which of the methods he used and the veto on the use of more than one was abandoned.

On the morning of Monday, 30 July, the Court proceeded to appoint the staff, nineteen of whom were provisionally selected. The first three were the chief officers: John Ince, 'Secretary and Sollicitor', Thomas Mercer, 'First Accomptant', and John Kenrick, 'First Cashier', each at a salary of £200 per annum. These appointments are of some interest in that nearly 250 years were to pass before this arrangement was disturbed, for until the fourth decade of this century the Bank continued to be divided into three main departments administered by a Secretary (John Ince was the one and only 'Sollicitor'), a 'First' or, later, Chief Accountant, and a 'First' or, later, Chief Cashier. The Secretary had as his immediate responsibility the Courts and the Committees, the keeping of their minutes and the general supervision of the premises and staff, both clerical and artisan. The Chief Accountant kept the Bank's own accounts and acted as the registrar of Bank stock; later he had the additional duty of managing the British Government Securities, and a few others, registered at the Bank. The Chief Cashier had charge of the banking business and the note issue. The duties of the 'Stock Side' and 'Cash Side', as the Accountant's and Cashier's departments are familiarly known, still remain fundamentally the same today, but a few years before the Second World War the supervision of premises and staff was taken over from the Secretary by a newly instituted department.

The other sixteen men appointed to the original staff were made up of a Second and a Third 'Accomptant' (£100 p.a. each), a Second Cashier (£100 p.a.), a Third Cashier (£80 p.a.), ten Tellers (£50 p.a. each) and two 'Doorkeepers and Messengers' (£25 p.a. each).

The meeting was resumed in the afternoon, during the course of which it was ordered that a fit place in the Hall be 'fenced off' for the cashiers. As the result of another discussion, it was arranged that eleven of the Directors should view the 'West pawne of the Royal Exchange' and the Grocers' Hall and report which they thought most suitable for the Bank, for it was already realized that Mercers' Hall would prove too small to be a permanent home. The Royal Exchange was evidently unsuitable, for within a short period negotiations were opened with the Grocers' Company for a lease of their Hall. The move to new premises did not take place, however, until 29 December, by which time the staff had been increased to thirty-six persons, in addition to the porters and watchmen.

The long day's business ended with what was doubtless a swift and foregone approval of the seal – already 'Cutt in steele', as we have seen – which was brought in, hardened and polished, by Mr Smith the graver. It was urgently needed, for at the same time the Court ordered that the Bank bills be sealed the next morning in the presence of the Governor or Deputy Governor and two or more of the Committee.

The cause of this urgency is plain. These were the Bank sealed bills, which were intimately bound up with the primary *raison d'être* of the Bank as outlined in the title of the founding Act, that is to say, the handing over to the King's Government of the capital subscribed in order to furnish the sinews of war. By the Act, the issue of such bills was limited to the extent of the capital; they were for amounts of £100 each, bore interest at 2d. per day, were drawn in favour of named individuals and were mainly used for payments into the Exchequer. The first payment so made was on 1 August, when bills for an amount of £112,000 were drawn in favour of persons nominated by the Treasury, as follows:

£80,000 to Lord Ranelagh, for the Army.
£24,000 to Anthony Stevens, for the Navy.
£5,000 to Charles Bertie, for the Ordnance.
£3,000 to Charles Fox and Thomas, Lord Coningsby for 'services of the forces lately employed in the reduction of Ireland'.

Subsequent payments were made, in varying proportions, for similar purposes. The Exchequer issued notched wooden tallies as the only tangible receipts for these loans, and a number have survived to find a place in the Bank's collections of historical relics.

To return to the Bank sealed bills, Sir John Clapham considered: 'much more remarkable than the speed of the Subscription was the speed with which the full sum promised was transferred to the Exchequer'. Treasury Orders for the spending of the funds transferred began on 22 August. By 15 December the General Court of Proprietors was informed that only some £44,000 odd remained to be paid over and that this amount would go in shortly, which it did. The promise to complete the transaction by 1 January 1695 had been more than kept.

A confirmation of the fact that all the capital authorized under the Act was used for the purpose designated – that is, for the prosecution of the war against France – and, moreover, that it was thus used down to the very last halfpenny, may be obtained from an independent contemporary source, contained in the Lansdowne MS. 1215 in the British Museum: 'Apportionment of the Fonds for the Warr in the year 1694 £536,746 : 9 : 3½ for marine services, £663,253 : 10 : 8½ for land services.' The sudden availability of such substantial sums, in what was practically hard cash, had results on both services which were immediate and far-reaching. The Navy and its supply services at the period constituted one of the most comprehensive industries in the country and its administrative machinery was capable of handling its own remittances; nevertheless, the fact that at last it had an adequate amount of what was, in effect, ready money actually to remit led to revolutionary improvements in its fighting abilities. The organization of the Army was more rudimentary.

In September 1694 the Government asked the Bank if its Directors would undertake the task of management of the Army's remittances for the forces in Flanders, and, as the sequel will show, the effects of this on the early history of the Bank were many and profound – and, in one instance, tragic. The Bank realized that this task would be certain to involve it in considerable expenditure, much detailed administration and some rather speculative business, all of them undesirable, especially to so new an institution, but as it had, after all, come into being in order to further the prosecution of the war the Court dutifully agreed – though not without having first prudently ascertained that it could do so 'without any hazard from the Act of Parliament or otherwise'. On 8 October it was arranged with the Treasury that they should remit up to £200,000 within six weeks; a 'Committee for the Remisses' was set up consisting of Michael Godfrey, James Denew, Abraham Houblon and Theodore Janssen; Jacobus de Koning (or de Coninck) was appointed the Bank's agent at Antwerp, who was to pay the money over to Richard Hill, the Government's agent in that city. The whole of one of the Bank's large ledgers is filled with the summarized records of these transactions, from October 1694 to June 1700, when the last of the business was cleared up. The Bank had to make use of a large number of strong firms on the Continent whose bills or whose help it required. In March 1695 correspondents were appointed in Cadiz, Madrid, Leghorn, Lisbon, Oporto, Genoa, Venice, Hamburg and Amsterdam – for practically the whole of Europe was allied against France. In April, at the King's express desire, it was agreed to send a Committee of the Directors into Flanders itself and, at the end of May, Michael Godfrey, Sir James Houblon, Sir William Scawen and Robert Raworth left for Antwerp.

Michael Godfrey was killed by a cannon-ball in the trenches before

Namur on 17 July 1695. It is not really known why he and his fellow Directors were there at all. Clapham says he was present as a mere sightseer, 'to King William's frigid annoyance', but there is some justification for thinking that a much more vital reason took him there. It is not improbable that he was anxious to bring to the King's personal notice a matter which was gravely troubling him and the other members of the Court, both in Flanders and London – the high 'rating', or valuation, of gold in terms of silver by the Government Offices of Account in London.

Silver was then the standard of value, fixed by Parliament, and by a process only too familiar in our own unhappy century, war expenditure had led to an immense credit inflation. Now, in April 1695, the Bank had agreed to remit all public money into Flanders 'for 12 months certain' at 10 guilders per guinea – and the guinea had 'rocketed'. Coined originally in 1663 as a 20s. gold piece, its actual value had soon become 21s., at which it roughly remained until March 1694, when it had reached 22s.; then, in the following November, a few short weeks after the Bank had said they would manage the Army remittances, a steady rise had set in. By June 1695 the price was 30s. The Bank obviously had to take what steps it could to remedy an awkward position which might quickly become an intolerable one and a Treasury Minute of 16 July 1695 records: 'Sir John Houblon and others of the Bank come in. They move about the guineas, complaining of the mischief of the present high rate, that they cannot get any bills to furnish the exchanges.' The Treasury had, however, appreciated for some time the gravity of the situation, as is instanced by the representations they had made to the Lords Justices (the Council of Regency acting in the absence of the King) on 3 July, drawing particular attention to the desire of the Bank and others 'that guineas may be refused at the Exchequer and by the King's Receivers as the only expedient to bring down their price'. It is surely not unreasonable to suppose that, in order to reinforce what was being done in London, Godfrey and his colleagues had gone to Namur with the hope of enlisting the aid of the King himself.

Godfrey's death caused a great loss to the young Bank. He was born in 1658, so was only in his thirty-eighth year when he was killed. He was the son of Michael Godfrey, a London merchant, and a nephew of Sir Edmundbury Godfrey, whose murder on Primrose Hill in 1678, at the time of the 'Popish Plot', had occasioned so much public excitement and still provides a rich vein of ore for those with a taste for mining among the enigmas of history. Energetic and intelligent, he had been one of the foremost promoters of the Bank and one of its most stalwart supporters.

Sir William Scawen, who had been within two yards of the shot that had killed Godfrey, was appointed to succeed him as Deputy Governor. He returned to England in September, and shortly afterwards Sir James Houblon and Robert Raworth were relieved in Flanders by Sir Henry Furnese and James Bateman. Namur was captured from the French on 1 September; there was no further fighting of importance, but the peace treaty was not signed for more than two years, during which the troops had, of course, to continue to be paid.

The business of the 'remisses' was troublesome throughout, risky and far from profitable. Meeting the constant pressure for funds for the Army, especially during the months in 1696 when the English silver money was being recoined, presented what must sometimes have seemed almost insuperable difficulties. The Directors in Flanders must have come to be especially wearied with, as they put it, 'the hazards we have run in passing and re-passing the seas, and the loss we have sustained in our particular affaires by our long absence'. The Government concluded its part in the business in February 1697 by striking tallies for £75,000, to cover losses incurred by the Bank, but that was not the end of the matter so far as it was concerned. It was not until the following year that the Bank was able to clear off a debt of £400,000 which it had been obliged to incur, at the worst period and on stiff terms, by a loan from the Estates of Holland.

The infant Bank was therefore, so to speak, thrown straight into deep and troubled waters from the start, yet it learned not only to keep afloat but to battle triumphantly against a number of adverse tides by reason of an inborn strength, ability, cunning – and integrity. When it was in the very midst of all the intricate and tiresome business of the Flanders remittances, its dearly guarded stability was assailed from other quarters also, notably in regard to the long-delayed and no longer postponable recoining of the nation's silver currency and the attempted setting up of rival banks, but before these matters are discussed certain of the Bank's internal affairs remain to be dealt with.

At a meeting of the General Court on 10 August 1694, the Governor, eighteen Directors and 216 of the Generality being present, it had been agreed that a Committee of fifteen persons, with a quorum of nine, should be chosen to prepare By-Laws and the Proprietors were asked to attend again on 15 August, each bringing a list, in writing, of the fifteen persons of his choice. A scrutiny of these lists on that day gave the largest number of votes (113) to Sir Bartholomew Shower. Michael Godfrey (65 votes) and Nathaniel Tench (56) were the only members of the Court of Directors to be selected, though the list included three who subsequently became Directors – Charles Chambrelan, Sir John

Cope and Nathaniel Gould. The choice of Sir Bartholomew Shower, particularly by a preponderance of votes, is curious, and seems the sort of thing that can happen only among a gathering of the English. Probably he was selected for his legal standing, for it can hardly have been because of his politics. A robust Jacobite, he had been Recorder of London under James II, being replaced in 1688; and after the accession of William and Mary he became 'a rancorous opponent' of their Court as the article on him in the *Dictionary of National Biography* expresses it.

The last meeting of the General Court to be held at Mercers' Hall took place on 28 September. The Governor reported that the Bank was in a flourishing condition, 'and its Creditt daily encreased'; but the Committee had not completed its work on the By-Laws. They were finally submitted, in draft, to a meeting in November and were read a second time on 15 December, when, with certain amendments, they were approved. They remained in force until March 1698, when a fresh set was substituted. These were printed in 1699 and, amended only in detail, served for many years; in fact, much of their substance was embodied in the constitution of the Bank as revised by the public ownership Act of 1946 and the Charter of that year.

Of the seventeen rules in the original draft, drawn up under Sir Bartholomew Shower's chairmanship, the majority were based upon provisions of the Charter or on clauses of the 1694 Act. They call for no particular comment, except for the sixth, which was evidently designed to prevent the Bank from ever falling into the hands of a clique. Under it, it was impossible for more than two-thirds of the retiring Directors to be re-elected in the ensuing year, and it was also designed to limit the tenure of office by the Governor and Deputy Governor to two years. As it happened, this draft By-Law was not agreed to, but a clause to prevent more than two-thirds of an existing Court of Directors being re-elected for the following year found its way into an Act of 1697. This was faithfully observed until 1872; in that year the proportion retiring was changed, and in 1892 the practice was finally dropped. It had necessarily led to the formation of a varying group who, during their 'stand-down' intervals, were known as 'ex-Directors'. In the ordinary way only comparatively junior members of the Court were required to stand down, and once a Director had 'passed the Chair' by serving as Deputy Governor or Governor he became, as it were, an 'elder statesman' who no longer had to submit to what some might have fancied to be the indignity of being called an 'ex-Director'. It also became habitual to elect a new Governor and Deputy Governor every two years – the retiring Deputy Governor usually being elevated to

Governor – and, except in special circumstances, this procedure was followed until recent times.

General Courts were already meeting at Grocers' Hall during the last months of 1694, although the daily business of the Bank was not transferred there until 29 December. From that day Grocers' Hall was the Bank's home for the next forty years. Its first lease was for a term of eleven years; and what was doubtless a consideration in arranging for this particular length of time was the fact that the Government had the power to terminate the Charter on a year's notice at any time after 1705.

The move to Grocers' Hall had no sooner been made than the threat from the 'rival banks' loomed up. The first rumbles of the coming storm were heard in January 1695, when certain City merchants and traders presented a petition to Parliament alleging that the Bank was 'ruinous and destructive to Trade in general' and 'only an advantage to the said Corporation'. In order to defend themselves, the Governors and several Directors attended at the House of Commons on the day appointed for the hearing, but, without being asked for any statement, they had the satisfaction of witnessing the decisive rejection of the petition. This episode, although disturbing, did hold one distinct advantage for the Bank – a number of its enemies had been obliged to come out into the open. In February the Court had the distasteful task of sitting in judgement upon one of its own members, William Paterson, for acting in concert with some of these 'knowne enemies of the Bank', the particular affair upon which he had been thus engaged being a scheme for consolidating the Orphans' Fund of the Corporation of London. The Court decided that Paterson had behaved in a way 'not becoming a Director of the Bank but a breach of his Trust'. He was called upon for a defence, which he supplied by submitting a statement, but without waiting to hear whether his explanation had been accepted or not he sent in his resignation, and on 19 March disqualified himself from office by selling his holding of Bank stock.

His departure, among those who knew him, must have caused little surprise. His gifts were those of the inventor and instigator rather than those of the consolidator and manager; and his fertile brain always germinating this new scheme or that, he must often have felt irritated and impatient with his staider colleagues of the Court – as doubtless, too, they were with him. However, in the eyes of the public, prompted by feelings of generous indignation, a readiness to suspect the worst, or a mixture of both, Paterson had been shabbily treated – the Bank, after all, had been 'his idea'. More serious than that, might he not be leaving the Bank because he had lost faith in it? At all events, his resignation

25

led to a sharp fall in the price of Bank stock. It is still possible to feel some sympathy with the public view and justice requires that the large and important part which Paterson played in the foundation of the Bank should never be overlooked. None the less, he was one of those volatile men whom others find it almost impossible to work with and he was certainly not the Scottish martyr that later interpretations of his resignation attempted to make him. The Bank of England was one only among the multitude of his projects, some successful, like the Bank itself and the Hampstead Waterworks of 1690, others disastrous. Most notorious of the latter was the ill-fated Darien Scheme, an attempt to colonize the isthmus of Panama, which caused untold misery for the unfortunate adventurers, although the fault in this case happened to be none of Paterson's.

It is, then, extremely doubtful if he would ever have been content to devote himself to the day-to-day working of any of his conceptions, but whatever may be the truth of the matter, his 'Orphans' Fund Bank' certainly never gave him a chance to prove this one way or the other. It never developed into a rival of any standing and there is little information available about its transactions. It had apparently started to issue its own notes, since on 29 May 1695 the Court of the Bank decided not to accept them. By February 1700 it had faded out, for by then it is being referred to as 'the late Orphans' Fund'.

A short-lived venture of 1695 was the Million Bank, which combined dealings in lottery tickets and annuities with some measure of banking. This side was apparently unprofitable; the company became virtually an investment trust in Government stocks and in this capacity it survived for a century.

With the advantage of knowing what happened to these rival concerns, we can now see that they were of small account, but lacking that advantage the Court must have felt no small anxiety regarding their potential menace; and there was more than a suspicion that any success they did attain was at the Bank's expense. For example, in the early part of 1695, Godolphin and other prominent Whigs sold their holdings of Bank stock, and word forthwith went round that Godolphin had reinvested the proceeds in the Orphans' Fund.

Another threat, from a possible 'National Land Bank', was altogether more grave. Proposals for setting one up, by a variety of projectors, had been temporarily thwarted by the Bank of England's success in establishing itself. However, the proposals did not lie in abeyance for long. In the fierce struggle just beginning between the landed and the mercantile 'interests' a Land Bank would be the natural answer by the great landowners and the gentry to their antagonists, the professional handlers of money. As Clapham has pointed out, the notion of using land as a basis of credit is far less fantastic than has sometimes been represented and, indeed, is perfectly feasible given the modern organization of the money market. At that period, however, it was not workable, as the event showed, but this was owing more to a lack of the necessary machinery than to any inherent fallacy in the idea itself.

There were four principal projectors of Land Bank schemes, the best known of them being Dr Hugh Chamberlen, derided by his opponents as the 'man-midwife'. His medical career had been a distinguished one and he had been Physician in Ordinary to Charles II. In 1688, however, he was censured by the College of Physicians for mishandling a pregnancy case, and from then on he seems to have transferred his interests to financial experiments. Another projector was John Briscoe, a pamphleteer. The schemes of both Chamberlen and Briscoe were based upon the capitalizing of future rents of landed property. Also in the field was John Asgill, a 'known enemy of the Bank', who had become a trustee of the Orphans' Fund when it had been reorganized by Paterson, and lastly there was Dr Nicholas Barbon, a son of that Puritan worthy whose name once heard is so very difficult to forget – the celebrated 'Praise-God Barebones'. Barbon's chief claim to distinction is that he founded, in 1681, the first fire insurance office in London. The schemes of Asgill and Barbon envisaged the collection of savings, from which advances might be made on mortgage, or what would be known today as a building society.

Early in 1695 all these projectors determined to go ahead with their respective schemes without waiting for parliamentary sanction. Asgill and Barbon entered upon a joint venture for which they opened subscription books on 29 May; a fortnight later, on 11 June, John Briscoe opened a list. Dr Chamberlen started on his venture at about the same time, but the exact date is not known.

So far these three separate and small concerns offered no particular challenge to the Bank, but matters took a far more serious turn when, in January 1696, Asgill and Barbon combined with Briscoe to 'unite in procuring an Act of Parliament for establishing a Bank upon a Fund of Land and Money'. One of the trustees of Briscoe's venture was Paul Foley, Speaker of the House of Commons; while a trustee of the scheme launched by Asgill and Barbon was Edward Harley, brother of Robert Harley, the prominent Tory who was later first Earl of Oxford. It may have been through the interest of these powerful men that the proposals were laid before the House of Commons, though it has never been understood how it came about that a Whig Government, with Montagu of all people as Chancellor of the Exchequer, should ever have

27

lent support to the resultant Bill. Tory support for it was natural enough; as Clapham says, 'country gentlemen were very susceptible to schemes that promised to extract somehow from the land which they held the ready money that they most often lacked'. The Bank was therefore faced with the establishment of a potentially powerful rival with full Parliamentary backing.

Despite strongly expressed Bank opposition and despite its offer to raise, itself, the £2,564,000 which the new concern promised to provide, the Act authorizing the establishment of the Land Bank was passed by both Houses, receiving the Royal Assent on 27 April 1696. It was only when the subscription books were opened at Exeter Exchange on 4 June that the hollowness of the scheme was exposed. The King's name had been put down for £5,000, of which £1,250 was reputedly paid up; in three weeks only £1,600 was added to this and on 1 August all that had been contributed from the whole nation was the contemptible sum of £2,100. The Tories, it is clear, were willing enough to wound the Bank of England, but afraid to strike if that meant risking their own money.

Montagu, whose enthusiasm for the undertaking can never have been great, had succeeded in engrafting on to the Bill a clause which empowered the Government to issue Exchequer bills should the funds promised by the subscription not be forthcoming, a piece of foresight and ingenuity upon his part that helped considerably to overcome a crisis with which the country's economy was now confronted. He had taken a similar precaution when the Bank of England Bill was under consideration, by inserting a clause that any amount in which the subscription was deficient might be made up by the issue of annuities. This, of course, had not been necessary. This present crisis arose from two main causes – from the shock which the Bank's credit had suffered because of the Government's unnecessary support of the Land Bank Act, and, what was far more serious, from the dangers attending a highly necessary legislative action of theirs, the passage, in the preceding January, of the Recoinage Act.

The Recoinage Act, when it came, aimed at the restoration of the silver coinage to its former standard: devaluation was considered inadvisable. It had been preceded by a Royal Proclamation on 19 December that as from 1 January 1696 no clipped crowns or half-crowns were to be accepted except in payment of taxes or as contributions to Government loans and then only until 22 February: shillings were given until 2 March and sixpences until 2 April. The Act itself, which received the Royal Assent on 21 January, provided that the only coins to be remitted were those received by the Government for these purposes. After the dates given, clipped money was to have no currency, except by weight.

The whole matter was not well managed: it was not even honestly managed. To start with, the policy was too drastic and hurried – as the Government found when they had to revise the dates for the acceptance of clipped money. Worse still, with a callous indifference, they threw a great part of the burden of expense on to the shoulders of those least able to bear it, the poor and ignorant, who, not being in the habit of lending to the Government, would be the people most likely to be left with depreciated money on their hands.

In its corporate capacity the Bank was not consulted as to policy, but the views of the Governor, Sir John Houblon, and of a Director, Gilbert Heathcote, had been taken by the Lords Justices. Houblon was in favour of recoinage because he believed that bad silver money was the root cause of high prices and unfavourable exchanges; Heathcote wished the clipped money to be called in at its face-value; both were for restoration as against devaluation. Heathcote suggested a temporary issue of paper to cover the gap in the currency which recoinage would produce, but his suggestion was not followed – unless Montagu's provision, in the Land Bank Act, for the issue of Exchequer bills was due in part to this advice.

Heathcote's forecast of a serious currency gap was speedily proved correct. The time for paying clipped money into the Exchequer was extended until 4 May and by that date about £4 million of old money had been brought in; the issue of new money from the Mint was, however, naturally a slow process and the Bank, which had agreed to receive the deteriorated silver at par value, not only incurred a loss thereby but was soon also finding difficulty in meeting demands for cash.

Hence 6 May saw the first serious run on the Bank, which was only overcome by a partial suspension of cash payments. Macaulay's contention that the run was occasioned by hostility on the part of the goldsmiths is not borne out by the Bank's records, but seems to have been the outcome of the increasing currency difficulties. People generally wanted cash and the Mint could not supply it fast enough to the Bank, while, in addition, notes had been overissued and could be cashed only in part. With the Land Bank pending as well, a number of depositors became anxious for their money, fearing the establishment of a successful rival, an anxiety which the pamphleteers campaigning for that rival were not slow to exploit.

The Bank surmounted the difficulties of 6 May, though for months afterwards its paper was at a heavy discount, reaching its nadir, 24 per cent, early in the following year. And while all this was going on the steady demand for 'remisses' to the Low Countries continued.

The prospect for the Proprietors of getting any return on their money was, for the time being, a poor one; at a General Court held on 13 May the consideration of a dividend was deferred and on 23 May the Directors decided to offer 6 per cent to such persons as were prepared to lend guineas or 'passable money'; on the same day they voted in favour of borrowing from the Proprietors 20 per cent on the nominal amount of their capital, to be repaid with 6 per cent interest after six months. Uncalled capital amounting to £480,000 – 40 per cent of the original £1,200,000 subscribed – was still outstanding, but conditions made any suggestion of a call inexpedient, the Proprietors being informed that the borrowing policy was the best alternative. On 23 June the Directors introduced a fresh device for bringing in cash, the 'Specie Note', a note issued to depositors of new milled silver or guineas, promising repayment on demand in the same specie. On 6 July 6 per cent interest was offered on these notes.

While the Bank was using every possible contrivance to secure cash, the Government were in even greater need of it, and when the Land Bank scheme failed Montagu resorted to his own ingenious expedient, slipped by him into the Land Bank Act, that is, the Exchequer bill; the object of the issue was not only to relieve the shortage of cash but also to provide funds for the Government in the absence of the two and a half millions which the Land Bank scheme had promised but had not provided. Exchequer bills were issued in units of £5 and £10 – less than the average amount of a banker's running-cash note – and were to be met from the Exchequer receipts for the coming year. They bore interest and could not be cashed on demand, but passed from hand to hand by endorsement. As a financial expedient, their only relevance here is that if, as Clapham has pointed out, they had been made a little less formal and if the Bank had not already got its own running-cash notes into general circulation, the regular supplement to silver and gold during the eighteenth century might well have been a Government note issue instead of one by the Bank of England. However, in 1696 it was cash that was generally needed, not additional notes, so public demand for these Exchequer bills was very weak; their circulation, authorized at £1,500,000 in that year, reached £167,000 only.

They did very little, therefore, to ease the position – what both the Bank and the Government needed was the hard cash that simply was not there. During the whole of that difficult summer the Bank did their best to assist the Government, although in one case – an application for an immediate advance of £200,000 for the Army in Flanders – the Court felt that it could not assume responsibility without first referring the matter to the general body of Proprietors. Even so, Montagu was confident that the Bank's customary help would be forthcoming – the day before the General Court met he wrote to William Blaythwayt, the Secretary-at-War: 'The Bank notwithstanding all the hardships and discountenance they have met are yet resolved to venture all for the Government and I hope what they do in our distress will not be forgotten in theirs if ever they are in a greater'. From the start, the Bank, though never the 'Exchequer's City Branch', was always its valuable, and later invaluable, complement, ready with help and advice when asked and, if it thought necessary, its firm but respectful criticism as well.

The General Court met on 15 August. The Governor, Sir John Houblon, delivered a carefully prepared speech, and the £200,000 for the Army was voted unanimously. The Bank, said Sir John, was 'in a very good condition in all respects', though 'suffering from that want of Specie which at this time is the common Calamity of the whole nation'. The support of the Lords of the Treasury for the Bank had been promised and the Court could rely upon their sympathy and help, for they had agreed that 'the welfare of the Bank is the interest of the whole kingdom'.

But there was to be no dividend for the Proprietors in 1696. They had received one of 6 per cent, followed by a second of 4 per cent, in 1695, but as there was nothing for them now, the price of Bank stock, which had been at par in the early part of the year, fell to 60 in October. Gradually the position improved and by the end of the year optimism for the future was evident among the Directors. In commemoration of their emergence from these anxious times they purchased a tankard from the silversmith, William Gamble of Foster Lane. It bore the inscription:

The gift of the Directors of the Bank of England to Sir John Houblon, Governor, Lord Mayor of London, in token of his great ability, industry and strict uprightness at a time of extreme difficulty 1696.

Nothing is known of the subsequent history of this tankard until 1893, when it reappeared at a sale in the United States and was acquired by the New York Clearing House Association. In 1924, as a gesture of international amity, the Association most generously presented it to the Governors and Directors of the Bank.

The year 1697 saw the recovery by the Bank of the prestige and position which the crisis of 1696 had imperilled. By March the cash shortage was greatly eased and the problems set by the recoinage were virtually over. The fiasco of the Land Bank had taught the Government that credit was a vital asset, and that money was not to be had unless there was confidence also. In November 1696 the House of Commons

31

had resolved that during the continuance of the Bank of England no other Bank should be erected by Act of Parliament and a clause to that effect was included in an Act which received the Royal Assent on 1 April. As a result the price of Bank stock rose from 64 to 86 in the course of a week.

The main object of the Government, in this Act, was to restore the public credit by raising the value of its tallies, which by this time were at a serious discount. There was much bargaining between the Directors and a Select Committee of the Commons, as a result of which it was agreed that the Bank should increase its capital by absorbing this floating debt of tallies and orders and the Act authorized them to take subscriptions of which four-fifths might be in tallies or orders and the remaining one-fifth in Bank bills or notes. Interest at 8 per cent was allowed to the Bank on the tallies, the repayment of which was provided for by a salt duty.

The result of the subscription, the books for which were opened at Mercers' Hall, was an increase in the Bank's capital of £1,001,171 10s. This was not treated as a permanent increase, however. These 'ingrafted tallies', as they were called, were not redeemed by the Treasury in one lump sum, but by instalments, and as the Bank received them it passed the money on to the subscribers. By 1707 the debt had, by these means, been extinguished. It was a profitable transaction for those who had bought Exchequer tallies when they were at a great discount – Gilbert Heathcote, for one, is said to have made over £60,000 in this way.

In addition to the clause in the Act which forbade any other 'Corporation, Society, Fellowship, Company or Constitution in the nature of a Bank' to be set up during the continued existence of the Bank of England, this existence was extended for another five years, until the expiry of one year's notice after 1 August 1710. Another clause was one whereby the death penalty was to be imposed for forgery of the Bank's notes – this was a significant step, for the penalty was the same as that for clipping or coining the King's money; and if, as Clapham says, bank-notes were not, as yet, King's money, they must have been getting near to it.

By 15 September 1697 Bank stock was at 98. The year saw a considerable increase in the amount of commercial business transacted; with the advent of peace the conditions for dealing in foreign bills of exchange became easier, and the discounting of inland bills, which had been rather small during the first two years, was much brisker. Above all, the crisis years had given opponents and competitors a far greater setback than any the Bank itself had suffered, besides assuring it a more established position *vis-à-vis* the Government.

32

Chapter 3

The Years at Grocers' Hall 1695-1734

The Bank had started business in a city which symbolized the new age, for London itself had but recently been rebuilt. The Great Fire of 1666 had consumed the medieval town, and as its flames swept away the old buildings it was as if many of the old ways of thought had been swept away with them.

Nevertheless, the City retained many of its medieval characteristics. It was fantastically small, compared even to the 'Wen' which Cobbett was to revile a century or so later, and although, through its port, it looked out upon the trade routes of the world, it was self-contained in a way now hard to conceive, more homogeneous and inward-looking than the smallest of country towns can ever be today. The houses were all dwelling-houses, the larger ones often standing in their own gardens. The great majority were business houses, too. The term 'business house' is still in wide use, though it now signifies a mere corporate abstraction. The Bank's first real home, Grocers' Hall, was in many ways a 'house' in this sense, and it may be mentioned, in passing, that the Bank is still called 'the House' by those who work for it, that the parts of the Head Office occupied by the Governors and Directors are known as the Parlours and that its register of employees is, as it always has been, the 'House List'.

Grocers' Hall was on the northern side of the Poultry and was approached by an alley; it had been rebuilt largely within its medieval walls, and according to that invaluable contemporary guide, Daniel Defoe, was 'a very convenient place and, considering its situation, so near the Exchange, a very spacious, commodious place'. The premises as a whole were so satisfactory, by reason of their central situation and the ample room which they afforded for all the early needs of the Bank, that it did not begin to plan for premises of its own until 1724, and did not leave Grocers' Hall for ten years after that. A carved sign representing Britannia was erected, for which the sum of £7 was paid to one Jonathan Mayne, though only after some demur, for the expense was heavier than had been intended.

A list dated 1704 and headed 'The Habitations of the Servants' shows that, by this time, there were now five members of the staff, in addition to the Gate Porter, occupying quarters at the Hall, which still left plenty of room for business. Later on, residence at the Bank was confined to certain of the Chief Officers and the Head Gate Porter. The number of these was gradually reduced, but the practice continued for more than two centuries, and the last resident officer, Mr (later Sir Ernest) Harvey, then the Deputy Chief Cashier, gave up his quarters over the main gateway in the spring of 1914. A daughter of Sir Ernest's, Mrs Ruth Harper, who was born in the Bank, has told of how she, and an elder brother and sister, had the run of the Bank after closing-time and at week-ends, playing hide-and-seek in the vaults, roller-skating round one and a quarter miles of its corridors and making friendly advances to the Bank Guard, to whom they would take biscuits.

In 1697 the House and Servants Committee ordered that the Gate Porter be fitted out with a 'crimson cloth gowne lined with orange and a large Bamboo cane with a silver head' and this livery has been borne by the Porter on duty at the Gate ever since. The uniform is completed by a cocked hat, adopted at the end of the eighteenth century in place of one of an earlier style which was flatter and 'less imposing'. During its tenancy of Grocers' Hall the Bank employed, in addition to the Gate Porter, two House Porters, from six to eight Watchmen and two 'Messengers and Doorkeepers'. The last-named were in personal attendance upon the Directors and were men of a superior class. Francis Iles, one of the first two appointed, is also described as 'Writer', and George Cooke, who succeeded him as Senior Doorkeeper in 1705, was appointed 'Clerk to the Committee in Waiting' in 1711 at £70 a year, a salary equal to that of a clerk of some years' standing. During the night the Watchmen were on duty, in pairs, in the yard and garden, and were relieved every hour. Each was armed with a sword, a musket and a pistol at his girdle, the fire-arms being charged and primed. Within doors, a further pair had the duty of walking between the Accounting Office and the Money Vault 'carefully observing any noise of fire or thieves'.

At Grocers' Hall the original clerical staff numbered thirty-three, of whom twenty-seven worked in the Cashier's Office. By 1700 the total number employed had grown to sixty-four, of whom thirteen worked in the Accountant's Office and forty-eight in the Cashier's. By 1720 these numbers were thirty-seven and forty-four, respectively, and by 1730 they were thirty-three and fifty-four.

As an examination of these figures will show, it was the Cashier's side which, in the very first years, grew steadily; the work of the Accountant's side did not increase to any appreciable extent until the Bank began to take over the management of more and more Government annuities. The Bank was born under Mars and throughout its history has been much influenced by the red planet. This applies especially to the Accountant's Department; its size has always reflected, more or less, the size of the National Debt, and that, in its turn, has enjoyed, or suffered, its most sudden and spectacular inflations in times of war. Marlborough's campaigns were responsible for the first large increase of the National Debt – and of the 'Stock-side'. Having stood at some £13 million in 1702, it amounted to £36 million in 1714; the War of 1718–21 helped to increase it still further, until, in 1739, it had reached £46 million.

What manner of men were they, the members of the staff in those early years? The answer seems to be, a pretty mixed bag. There was no particularly predominant class of persons from which they could be drawn and the Directors seem to have recruited them whence they could – no one was considered for employment without a Director's nomination. No age limits were imposed. Many of the clerks, throughout the eighteenth century and into the early years of the nineteenth, combined some business of their own with their Bank duties. This they found possible, although the office hours seem rather long by modern standards – when first fixed they were from 8 a.m. to 5 p.m. and attendance was required on every day except Sundays and holidays; it must, however, be remembered that few of the clerks lived at any distance from their place of work and since the 'Holy-dayes' customarily observed by public offices, such as the Custom House and the Excise Office, and by the more substantial business houses then numbered as many as forty, the clerks had very reasonable opportunities for relaxation and for attending to their own concerns.

In the four years of peace which followed the signing of the Treaty of Ryswick in September 1697, the Bank restored its strength and its reserves, which had been so severely threatened by the events of 1696. One of the first steps necessary was to pay off the specie notes, with their high interest rate of 6 per cent, but here the Bank immediately came up against an unforeseen difficulty – no period had been put to the life of these notes and the legal position was not clear. The Bank consulted Sir Edward Northey, the Attorney-General, as Counsel in the matter, and his opinion was that a holder was not bound to come to the Bank for his money. If he chose to do so he could keep the notes as long as he pleased and could claim interest at 6 per cent up to the day he finally demanded payment. Mr Samuel Dodd, a second Counsel consulted, while agreeing with his august brother, approached the subject in a shrewder and more worldly-wise fashion, suggesting it might be 'prudent' for the Bank to try the experiment of giving public notice of calling in the notes, since 'all people are not lawyers and will not advise in such a matter'. Notice was accordingly given in the *London Gazette* of 29 September 1698 that the possessors of these notes should bring them in and receive their money on or before 15 December or else exchange them for Bank sealed bills at 2d. per day interest, payable at demand, 'for that after the said 15th December Interest is to cease on the said Bank Notes'.

Mr Dodd's advice proved to be sound. The public, as they nearly always do, complied with an order which, although of arguable legality, had been given with a sufficient air of confidence and authority. Further specie notes were issued during 1698, but these were made current for one year only, nor was interest allowed, except on notes of £100 and multiples of that sum.

Once the Peace of Ryswick had been signed Parliament had shown a marked aversion from entangling the country further in William's Continental engagements. Nevertheless, threats to the safety of the Protestant Succession could never be disregarded and in 1702 England was again at war. The French had marched into the Spanish Netherlands in February 1701 and on the following 16 September, at the death of the exiled James II, Louis XIV had acknowledged his son James, the 'Old Pretender', as the rightful King of England. William III died on 8 March 1702, but Queen Anne, immediately after her succession, had proclaimed her intention of continuing his policy. Marlborough was sent out to Holland for consultation with the allies and on 4 May war was declared on France and Spain.

Aided by their previous wartime experience and, perhaps, by some rather better luck, the Bank maintained a good position throughout this war, certain vicissitudes apart. This time it was not asked to participate actively in the 'remisses' to Flanders and its provision for funds was not hampered by the difficulties it had met during the former conflict. There was, it is true, a crisis in 1704, when the French invaded Germany; the Directors then found it necessary to issue sealed bills – but not specie notes – bearing interest. Public confidence was, however, restored by the capture of Gibraltar, and shortly afterwards it was strengthened still further by Marlborough's victory at Blenheim on 13 August.

The Bank was, at that time, probably more worried by domestic foes than by foreign ones. In 1704 competition arose once more. The Act of 1697 was not so worded as to prevent a corporation, unless expressly 'in the nature of a bank', from issuing notes of its own. The Sword Blades Company and the Mine Adventurers Company, both of them corporations which had been granted charters for specified purposes, now claimed the powers vested in corporations generally, among which was the right to issue their own bills and notes, and this they proposed to do. The Sword Blades Company favoured running-cash notes bearing an 'impression of Britannia with an anvil before her and two cross swords underneath'; the Mine Adventurers advertised their intention of issuing specie and other bills to their own members. The Attorney-General, consulted by the Bank, was of the opinion that 'Parliament never supposed that a Corporation erected for a purpose could by virtue of it erect a Bank'. This was doubtless true, but, apparently, not of great assistance, and one has the suspicion that the Bank might have done better to consult Mr Samuel Dodd, whose advice had been so helpful in a previous difficulty. However that may be, nothing was done to restrain these rival activities for three years. The Sword Blades Company, emboldened by success, then advertised that they would discount bills and notes and lend money upon securities, upon which the Bank was stung into calling the attention of the Government to this notice. The outcome was a clause in the Act of 1708 extending the Bank's 'exclusive privilege' by forbidding associations of more than six persons from carrying on banking after 24 September of that year. The Sword Blades Company petitioned the House of Commons against the clause: their petition failed, but they did not let this setback interfere with the continuance of their own banking activities.

The Bank's Charter was renewed in 1709. It had by then been established for fifteen years and during all that period its relationship with the Treasury had been growing increasingly stronger. After November 1699 the Bank no longer had the friendship and support of Charles Montagu, but by then the links between the Directors and the Lords Commissioners had been firmly forged. The Treasury was in commission under William and Mary. Under Anne, Godolphin was Lord Treasurer, followed by Robert Harley. Since 1714 the office has always been in commission. It is to William ('Ways and Means') Lowndes that the chief credit must be given for producing a workable system of day-to-day reference. He was Secretary of the Treasury from 1695 until his death in 1724 and was one of England's first great Civil Servants. 'Lowndes', says Clapham, 'was the permanent man with whom the Bank dealt during the thirty years in which it passed from an experiment into a public institution. He, as much as anyone, was responsible for that progress.' His name recurs constantly in the Bank's Minute Books for the early eighteenth century.

The terms of the renewal of the Charter were not arrived at without many negotiations and while these were proceeding there was yet another threat of outside competition. Once the terms were on the Statute Book, however, they assured the position of the Bank till 1733. They provide much evidence of the Bank's increasing power and position. The amount of the authorized capital was allowed to be doubled – it thus became £4,402,343 – and there was no difficulty in raising the money. When the books were opened in Grocers' Hall at nine o'clock on the morning of 22 February 1709 the public response was so great that the list was full by 1 p.m. 'Such was the crowd of people that brought their money' reports a contemporary historian 'that near 1 million more could have been subscribed that day'. The Bank agreed to advance another £400,000 in return for its £100,000 a year; this meant that it would now get 6 per cent on £1,600,000, plus £4,000 for management, instead of the previous 8 per cent on £1,200,000 and the same management fees. The arrangements for the circulation of Exchequer Bills were revised and the terms of their circulation improved. From the Bank's point of view, perhaps the most important clause of all was one which confirmed, and made more precise the provision in the Act of 1708 prohibiting the association of more than six persons for the purpose of carrying on banking. No such partnership was allowed 'to borrow, owe or take up any sum or sums of money on their bills or notes payable on demand or at any time less than six months'. By this the Bank secured a practical monopoly of what was then the most lucrative branch of banking business.

In 1710 the Bank was to undergo a test altogether different from any to which it had hitherto been put. It had successfully overcome a number of financial problems; now it had to deal with a political one. The year opened quietly enough, the only matter of interest being that, in January, the Bank performed one more service for the Government by acting as receiving agents for that year's Lottery. This was the first State Lottery for ten years, an Act of 1699 having declared them a 'nuisance' and made them unlawful. Mercers' Hall was obtained as the Place of Receipt and three Bank officials were appointed as receivers by the Lord Treasurer; similar Lotteries followed in 1711 and 1712.

It was about March 1710 that the Bank's fresh trials began. A creation of the Whigs, it had never known, and had never desired, anything but Whig administrations. Marlborough's victories, in 1705 and again in 1708, had ensured that party's continuation in office, for the country had been going through very difficult times and since those in charge of its affairs had seemed, on the whole, to have dealt well with the various dangers, their position had never been seriously challenged. But now a reaction had set in. The country was tiring of the strains of war. Marlborough had fallen into disfavour with the Queen; some suspected him of aiming at the restoration of the Stuarts and others of even wishing to set himself up as a dictator, on Cromwellian lines, after the Queen's death. A strong section of the clergy also opposed the Government, being alarmed by the support given to the cause of Dissent by an Act for the naturalization of foreign Protestants, and by the introduction into Government of Presbyterianism as a result of the Act of Union with Scotland.

Prominent among these Tory High Churchmen was Dr Henry Sacheverell, who in the previous autumn had preached, and afterwards printed, his two famous, or notorious, sermons at Derby and St Paul's, the latter being delivered on 5 November before the Lord Mayor. In them he had permitted himself to indulge in the dangerous luxuries of invective and innuendo, launching, for example, a thinly veiled insult against Godolphin, the Lord Treasurer, under his widely known nickname of Volpone. He was impeached, and his trial before the Bar of the House of Lords opened on 27 February 1710. The London mob, those staunch champions of the Established Church, were always as ready to run wild against Dissent as they were to raise the cry of 'No Popery', their enthusiasm for religion never dimming a sharp eye for loot. They wrecked the meeting-houses of the Dissenters and supposing the Bank, as Clapham puts it, to be 'full of gold and Whiggery' they threatened to attack it. An appeal for help by the Directors to Whitehall led to the dispatch from St James's of several squadrons of the Horse Guards, at whose approach the mob dispersed.

The Directors were naturally concerned at the prospect of a change in the Government under which they had proceeded so far in the consolidation of their position, but there is no evidence that they ever considered taking any direct steps to counteract the political changes. Nevertheless, as bankers, they had an occupational bias towards stability; when, therefore, in April the Queen changed her Lord Chamberlain and when, in June, it appeared likely that Sunderland, a Secretary of State and Marlborough's son-in-law, was going to be dismissed, Sir Gilbert Heathcote, who was then the Governor, headed a deputation of Directors to express the Bank's views, first to the Dukes of Devonshire and Newcastle, and later in audience with the Queen herself. The interview was almost certainly ill advised, the Tories being quick to seize upon it as indicating an attempt at financial domination. Robert Harley, their leader, wrote sourly that while Heathcote had used 'very strong and earnest terms' to the Dukes he had 'thought fit to alter his speech' when he saw the Queen.

A few days later there appeared a broadsheet, a copy of which is in the Bank's collections. A laboured production, staggering under the weight of its own clumsy sarcasm, it is ostensibly 'The B--k of England's Most Loyal Address to Her M--y' Her Majesty's 'most Audatious, Imperious, Directing and Commanding Subjects' threaten that if she should turn out 'the Low Church Party these peaceful and moderate gentlemen', the Bank will be shut up as the Exchequer was in King Charles the Second's time and then she can 'hoop' for her Assistance. It concludes, 'This is the most true, sense, and harty advice which we present to your most Gracious M--y, from them that has been Instrumental in making You (and now would unmake you) Q--- of G--- B---'. (A reference to the Act of Union, 1707.)

A Treasury historian of recent years, the late Dr W. A. Shaw, has expressed his conviction that this broadsheet was the work of Harley himself. 'Harley', he stated, 'could not write English and he could not reason consecutively. For its illiteracy and its rambling inconsequence I could match it by letter after letter from him in the Treasury records.'

Whatever may have happened at the audience, the Queen continued her changes. Sunderland was dismissed and in August Godolphin was ordered to break his staff of office: he was succeeded as Lord Treasurer by Harley. A new Parliament, predominantly Tory, met on 25 November 1710 – even the City had responded to the prevailing High Church fervour by returning four Tories. The new Ministers were immediately assured by the Bank Directors that they would 'use their utmost endeavours for the support of the Publick Credit and would concur in any measures that their Lordships should think proper for that end'. The Government was quick to respond to this loyal offer with a request for a further loan of £50,000. This the Bank granted, though at the same time they took the opportunity of pointing out that the large advances already made on deposits of tallies with remote redemption dates was the main cause of the prevailing high discount on Exchequer bills.

Despite the polite and correct tone of these exchanges there could be no hiding the fact that there had never been any love lost between the Bank and the Tories, who, at the April election of Governors and Directors in the following year, 1711, attempted to strengthen the foothold they had already obtained in the City by trying to capture the Directorate of the Bank – as they did, also, in the case of the East India Company. Dr Sacheverell had been found guilty by the Lords, and although his punishment was a mild one – his sermons had been ordered to be burnt and he was prohibited from preaching for three years – he had, in consequence, become something of a popular martyr. He now secured a vote by purchasing £500 Bank stock, but his intervention was without effect. The Proprietors came down solidly on the side of the men they knew and trusted. Voting was heavy, the highest ever recorded, and its outcome was the return of the Directors of previous years. Dr Sacheverell, the story goes, 'to his great mortification was hissed at the Bank'. He held on to his £500 stock until December 1714, when he sold it, presumably obtaining some salve for his wounded pride by getting the advantage of the higher prices prevailing in that year.

With the Tories in power, the Pretender in the offing and the Queen's health declining there were occasional losses of confidence in the City which brought about runs on the Bank, one at the end of 1713 and another in January 1714, when a false and deliberately staged report of her death caused a near panic which lasted several days. During this period of confusion the Whigs regained the ascendancy, which they were not to lose throughout the reigns of the first two Georges. On 1 August the Queen did die, and the Elector of Hanover was proclaimed, as George I, King of Great Britain and Ireland.

The year 1715 saw the Pretender's invasion, but as it was suppressed before it became a serious threat, no financial strain was experienced at the Bank. Jacobite plots in London, however, especially that planned for 29 May 1715, menaced not only the Bank's premises but its personalities, too. Three mobs were to assemble at Smithfield, proclaim the Pretender, seize the Bank, set it on fire and assassinate some of the Chief Magistrates, particularly Sir Gilbert Heathcote. Information of this was received in time and the plot was accordingly frustrated. To prevent any future assembly of such mobs, the Riot Act was passed; this gave the magistrates power to call upon the military to disperse any persons to the number of twelve or more 'being unlawfully, riotously and tumultuously assembled to the disturbance of the public peace'. There were certain safeguards to civil liberty; painful memories of the Civil War and the dictatorship of Cromwell inclined the citizens of London to regard the military with a jealous and wary eye and to consider their presence a greater danger to the rights and privileges of the citizens than any threat their own mob might offer. So there was a proviso that the mobs had to remain assembled for an hour, after being ordered to disperse, before action could be taken, and even this concession by those anxious to maintain law and order did not altogether stifle criticism.

The year 1720 saw the South Sea Bubble, the first of those catastrophic breakdowns which have from time to time bedevilled the financial markets of the modern world since they were first set up some three centuries ago. They have presented opponents of an uninhibited market economy with one of their easiest targets for criticism; for some reason difficult to analyse, a spirit of insane optimism and uncontrolled greed possesses the investing public, stock prices are forced up to a point where they can no longer sustain the universal madness, they suddenly collapse and thousands are swept to ruin. The last and greatest of these calamities – the Wall Street crash of 1929 – has the power to make many a man still in business today cringe whenever he remembers it, but nothing can deprive the South Sea Bubble of the 'bad eminence' of being the first in history, and the one which set the pattern for all the others.

Harley had helped to establish the South Sea Company when he came into power in 1711, the year in which he was created Earl of Oxford. As we have seen, he had no love for the Bank and its Directors, though ready enough to accept their aid. He also got some financial support from the East India Company, but the cost of Marlborough's wars had brought the floating debt to such a desperate state that he turned to the idea of repairing the situation by funding a large part of that debt in the capital of a completely new venture, the South Sea Company. He accordingly sanctioned its incorporation, giving it, as a project, an almost entirely fictional monopoly of trade in the most jealously guarded preserve in the world – the Spanish dominions in Central and South America. This right to trade had not, at the time, been granted by Spain; it was not until the Treaty of Utrecht was signed in 1713 that any concession was obtained and even then it consisted only of the right to send one ship a year. However, in the optimistic spirit of the age, it seemed that a vast new area of enterprise was being opened. Subscriptions to the capital of the new Company were easily forthcoming; and in the same way that the Bank had taken over the 'Ingrafted Tallies' in 1697, the Company took over large arrears of navy victualling and transport debentures, and also of army debentures, the holders being only too ready to consent to the funding of their shares in these in return for the golden promises held out by a purely hypothetical monopoly. In fact, the Company's first ship did not make its maiden voyage until 1717 and its next voyage was not until 1723. A second ship was launched in 1718, but before that year had ended war had broken out with Spain once more.

By 1715 the capital of the Company had reached the very high figure of £10 million, the various heavily depreciated short-term Government debts having been converted at their nominal value into long-term South Sea stock. On the security of this capital, the interest on which was furnished by the State, the Company might have borrowed to develop its business – had there been any business to develop. As it was, having nothing else to do with this immense fund of credit, the Company were tempted to gamble with it.

This fundamental unsoundness was not, of course, apparent at the start. Two prominent Bank personalities, Sir Theodore Janssen and Sir James Bateman, were interested in the Company, and between 1712 and 1717 there was much business done with the Bank, who were ready with advances and permitted an overdraft. In 1717 agreement was reached for the Bank to keep the Company's cash; it was to receive the weekly payments from the Exchequer and in return the Company's overdraft might be, at any time, £100,000 at 4 per cent.

These relations continued throughout 1718 and 1719, but it was becoming increasingly apparent to the Bank that the ambitions of the Company presented a serious challenge to its own position. By the autumn of 1719 the Directors of the Company were planning an amalgamation of Company and Bank. In November they propounded a most ambitious scheme for converting the whole of the National Debt, including the various loans made by the East India Company and the Bank. This would have involved an amalgamation of all three institutions. Opposition by the Bank and the East India Company was strong enough to defeat the proposal, but at the start of 1720 the Company offered terms to effect the conversion of the whole debt except that part of it owed to the other two. Parliamentary sanction for this scheme was given and the price of the Company's stock began its spectacular rise. Under the spur of competition the Bank itself had been forced to offer terms for the same object, the rejection of which was undoubtedly a blessing in disguise, for had they been accepted, this might well have resulted in disaster.

With most of the madness and fraud of the 'Bubble year' the Bank, fortunately for its good name, was little involved, standing apart while the Company, all unknown to the public, paid out a million and a quarter in bribes, issuing stock before it was legally entitled to do so in order to get the premiums which enabled it to pay those bribes. The Bank made one mistake, however, when it emulated the Company – which in April had begun to lend on the security of its own script – by declaring, in May, that it would be ready to lend on its own stock. This offer was withdrawn in October.

Speculation ran wild that year and nearly a hundred 'bubble' companies were floated, many of them with the most absurd projects, though in the fever of the time they did not lack subscribers. In June, Parliament – inspired, ironically, by the South Sea Directors themselves – took action against these proliferating companies by challenging their legality. In most cases the promoters were unable to withstand the challenge; their companies consequently failed and many speculators were ruined. In an attempt to save something from the wreck these speculators started to sell their holdings of South Sea stock, thus causing a rapid fall in its price. In September, when the crisis reached its height, the South Sea Directors applied to the Bank for help. Tentative proposals were considered and on 23 September a Committee, composed of Directors from both the Bank and the Company, agreed that the Bank should subscribe into the Company £3,775,000 of the debt owed to it by the Government, receiving in exchange South Sea stock at 400 per cent. Next day the Bank's Court of Directors confirmed the proposal and when books were opened at the Bank to receive subscriptions 'for the support of public credit' large sums were brought in.

But the damage had been done. The Sword Blades Company, who had latterly been acting as the Company's bankers – though it still kept open its account at Grocers' Hall – ceased payment; several goldsmiths also went bankrupt and in the ensuing run on the Bank payments in could not keep pace with what was paid out. Then, in November, the Bank repudiated its agreement with the Company, the Governor giving notice that the arrangement would no longer be proceeded with unless Parliament so ordered.

There has been controversy ever since as to whether this action by the Bank was a common-sense precaution or whether it was an unnecessarily precipitate step and the immediate cause of the Company's collapse. In its later distress the Company naturally blamed the Bank, claiming it had been betrayed, yet it is difficult to see what else the Bank could have done in order to preserve its own safety. Its withdrawal was, as Clapham admits, 'rather unhandsome', but harsh necessity rarely takes any regard of the handsome and, both legally and economically, the Bank's action was justifiable.

It weathered the storm by well-tried methods. It stopped discounting altogether; called up 25 per cent of the loans injudiciously made on its own stock and begged the debtors to return the remainder; called in advances made to the East India Company and other bodies and offered its customers interest-bearing notes, at three months' date, in exchange for ordinary notes and cash. By 1 December it was able to cease issuing these interest-bearing notes. Discounting was resumed, and while the price of Bank stock rose, that of the South Sea Company's stock plunged lower and lower. It is, nevertheless, worthy of note that even so, the year's lowest price, 124 on 24 December, was well above par.

In the following year a Committee of Secrecy appointed by the House of Commons to examine the accounts of the Company confirmed the general suspicion that bribes had been paid in order to procure the passing of the Act, that fictitious stock had been created and that the books had been falsified. The Governors, Directors and Officials were in due course brought before the Bar of the House. They were forbidden to leave the country and it was ordered that their estates be confiscated. John Aislabie, the Chancellor of the Exchequer, was imprisoned in the Tower and those Directors who were members of the House were expelled. Among those whose estates were confiscated was Sir Theodore Janssen, who was lucky in being allowed to retain £50,000 out of his fortune. On this he lived to a great age, dying in 1748. Sir James Bateman, the other Bank Director who had acted as a link between the Company and the Bank, and had served as Sub-Governor of the Company, had died in 1718 before trouble started.

There was a long dispute between the Bank and the Company about the Bank's alleged desertion and betrayal in 1720, which dispute went to arbitration in August 1722. As often happens in such proceedings, the arbitrators decided that the disputants should split the difference. Walpole was then helping the Company to regain some sort of standing and may well have thought that the Bank could afford to make some amends for its excusable but perhaps too drastic action. Business relations between the chastened Company and the Bank were resumed after a decent interval. The Company retained its account at Grocers' Hall and in 1726 was allowed to overdraw up to £150,000. It was sending a ship to South America and was also venturing into whale-fishing and slave-trading with the Spanish colonies; but its ventures continued to be unprofitable and it gave up even the pretence of trading around the middle of the century. Its business became the handling of annuities, for which purpose it found its account with the Bank of much convenience and exercised a regularly authorized right to overdraw up to a limit of £50,000.

Thus with some sort of standing the South Sea Company remained, surviving for well over a century its days of shameful glory. Charles Lamb has told of the South Sea House in its decline 'a melancholy-looking, handsome, brick and stone edifice . . . where Threadneedle Street abuts upon Bishopsgate' with its 'imposing staircases, offices as roomy as the state apartments in palaces – deserted, or thinly peopled with a few straggling clerks' and, in an outmoded but still effective style, apostrophizes with wry affection his one-time place of work: ' – amid the fret and fever of speculation – with the Bank, and the 'Change, and the India House about thee, in the heyday of present prosperity, with their important faces, as it were, insulting thee, their *poor neighbour out of business*.'

'No place in the world has so much business done with so much ease.' Thus wrote Daniel Defoe in 1724 of the Bank at Grocers' Hall; but by modern standards the business done was, of course, quite small and the ways of doing it could certainly have been easier.

From the many surviving records of the period, it is plain that the staff must have had their hands full. The methods first used were copied from the goldsmith-bankers and were unnecessarily complicated – though this is a facile criticism; opposition to changes in time-honoured procedure are not unknown even today and bankers, like everyone else, have to learn by experience. For example, the now obvious device of opening a separate drawing account in a regular customer's name had to be learned: nevertheless, it was adopted within four years of the Bank's foundation. Even then the withdrawal of money continued to be a painfully elaborate ceremony, cluttered, so to speak, with fossil re-mains of the time when the state of a customer's balance could only be ascertained by consulting several different registers. The drawer still had to present himself to the cashier, obtain from him a numbered document, fill this in, sign it, seal it, and return it to the cashier to be authorised for payment. Only then could he take it to the teller and at last get his money. This was the 'drawn note', the forerunner of the cheque. A specially printed form was introduced at Grocers' Hall in 1717, but its use was not insisted upon for nearly a century. Even today a cheque can, in an emergency, be made out on any piece of paper or, indeed, on any surface which will take writing. For security's sake these early forms were printed on chequered paper and presumably came to be known as 'cheques' for that reason, but the American spelling gives a better idea of their purpose – they were a 'check' on whether the drawer was a customer. It was only towards the end of the eighteenth century that the cheque or check, as known today, came into general use.

The issue of the notes variously termed 'Cashier's' or 'Running-Cash Notes' increased steadily. They were on printed forms which bore a Britannia medallion, the numbers, dates and amounts being written in by hand. The issue of notes for fixed sums had, however, always been envisaged and various attempts had been made, but none of these experimental issues had been proof against forgery and all had been quickly withdrawn. It was not until 1725 that it was found safe to make a general issue of notes bearing printed amounts – these were for £20, £30, £40, £50 and £100.

A serious handicap to the circulation of the Bank's notes was the frequency of mail robberies at the time, a risk which cannot be ignored today as events in August 1963 showed. Few real precautions were taken for the safety of the mail: it was carried by postboys, badly mounted and unarmed – the swift, well-guarded mail-coaches were not introduced until 1784, to enjoy some fifty splendid years and more, before the Iron Horse took over. Bank-notes sent by post were frequently stolen and the reputation of the Bank's paper was so high that footpads and highwaymen had little difficulty in cashing them. As the Bank's business grew and, with it, the issue of more and more notes, the Directors did all they could to persuade the public to use bills of exchange instead of entrusting their bank-notes to the postboys. In an attempt to foil the robbers, promissory notes at three days' sight were brought into use in November 1724. These possessed two major safety factors – they were transferable by endorsement and they were not payable until three days after acceptance at the Bank, giving an interval during which payment of a stolen note could be stopped. The experiment had some success, though it was found in practice that the three-day interval was not always long enough. Perhaps the chief point of interest about these promissory notes is that later they developed into the bank post bill. Introduced in 1739, this provided so safe and useful a means of remittance that it continued to evolve, as circumstances changed, and was not discontinued until 1934.

Discounting inland bills was a daily activity from the outset, various regulations being made, as the state of the market demanded, respecting the interest to be charged and what amount of bills might be discounted for any one person. 'Vetting' was the province of a Committee of Directors. Prominent among the early discount customers were a number of members of the Sephardic Jewish Community, among whom, with their connections in Amsterdam and on the Continent generally, dealing in bills of exchange was an important business. But they had no monopoly; names of English firms operating on the Continent appear with an at least equal frequency and often in connection with larger sums.

Under its Charter the Bank had a statutory right to trade in gold and silver. Instructions to the Committee 'to buy gold and silver on the best terms they can for the service of the Bank' appear in the Minutes of the Court of Directors as early as February 1695. In May of that year search was ordered to be made for a 'fit person who understands gold and silver' to be employed in the buying of it; in the next month it was reported that such a person had been found and terms agreed with him. His name does not appear, but in the firm of Mocatta and Goldsmid there is a tradition that they have been the Bank's bullion brokers 'ever since the Bank was established' and it is most probable that this first broker was a member of the Mocatta family. The repository for bullion was for many years called 'The Warehouse', and keeping it supplied was an important and continuous activity.

But even at Grocers' Hall all was not always for the best in the best of all possible worlds. There were black sheep in this decorous and well-behaved fold, tellers who absconded, clerks who, in the words of Sir Edward Northey, Accountant-General, 'by subtle practices, such as false postings, wrong additions and by making alterations and erasures in the Bank books' concealed the fact that they had forged documents and notes, making a transient profit before the inevitable discovery of their malpractices. Nor was it clerks only, for during the days at Grocers' Hall there was one notable scandal of a Director who perpetrated a fraud – an event which, as Acres says, is fortunately unique in the annals of the Bank. This Director was Humphry Morice, M.P. for Grampound, Cornwall, an associate and supporter of Sir Robert Walpole, from whom, as his papers show, he had expectations of considerable political and social advancement. He was a Director for fifteen years and was Governor from 1727 to 1729, a man reputedly of great wealth and of 'great fairness and integrity in his dealings'. He was allowed to discount bills freely and it was not until after his death in 1731 that it was discovered that fictitious bills to an amount of over £29,000 had been discounted by him with the Bank.

In the Bank archives there is a large collection of his private business journals and correspondence; their presence is probably explained by the fact that during his Governorship and in the years immediately following he found it convenient to keep them at the Bank and that they were impounded when his frauds came to light. From these it can be learned that his main ventures were in the Africa trade – gold, ivory and slaves. Slaving, if it was conducted on honest business lines and not piratical ones, was, of course, a trade in which any reputable merchant might then engage. Mr Morice kept a high standard of moral rectitude in his own slave dealings and expected his sea-captains to conform to it. His charges to his employees and their letters to him show that he could be generous in his rewards to those who served him well and that he was angered and grieved by evidence of any fraud, callousness or cruelty, whether to white or black.

No doubt like lesser men, he felt sure that given time he could make good his deficiencies – but he was not given time. He died and his defalcations were discovered. Long-drawn-out litigation followed his death, the Bank endeavouring to obtain restitution from his widow whom he had left very comfortably off. A verdict for £28,993 8s. 1d. was obtained in July 1732, but Mrs Morice put in a bill of complaint and a new trial was ordered. Litigation continued until her death in

1743 as a result of injuries when her coach overturned. Fresh difficulties then arose for the long-suffering Bank, and it was not until 1762 that they overcame the Law's delays to some small extent, receiving about £5,000. Twelve years later they obtained a final payment of £7,000 and then wrote off the balance of nearly £17,000, to 'Profit and Loss', forty years after the discovery of the fraud.

In June 1724 the Bank acquired the property in Threadneedle Street where some ten years later it opened the first premises of its own. The estate, for which £15,000 was paid, consisted of ten messuages, the most important being a large house, occupied by Sir John Houblon from 1671 until his death in 1711, where his widow was still living at the time of the purchase. This house was situated behind four others fronting on Threadneedle Street and separated from them by a courtyard.

When the Bank was negotiating an extension of its lease of Grocers' Hall, in October 1724, certain difficulties had arisen, whereupon the Court of Directors had passed a resolution to build premises on the site it had just acquired. The existing lease from the Grocers' Company granted in 1716 would not expire, however, until 1733, and the negotiations for its extension were not immediately dropped; the Bank were not finding it easy to conclude agreements with the tenants of the Threadneedle Street houses to vacate their premises, and it also had to make suitable arrangements with Dame Mary Houblon, who in the event did not leave her old home until 1731, when she moved to a house on Richmond Hill. She died there at the age of ninety-three on 10 December 1732.

The Court of Directors had not been unanimous in their decision to reject a further agreement with the Grocers' Company, so they referred the question to the General Court, on 20 January 1732, which passed a resolution in favour of the erection of a new building. Short extensions of the Grocers' Hall lease had to be obtained, since even then building delays were not unknown and the new premises were not completed at Michaelmas 1733, as had been expected. It was on 5 June 1734 that the Threadneedle Street offices were opened for the transaction of business, and an association of nearly forty years with Grocers' Hall came to an end.

Chapter 4

Threadneedle Street – The First Fifty Years

So, in 1734, the Bank of England occupied and proceeded to consolidate the foothold or 'bridgehead' it had established on what was, in due course, to become its famous island site – 'the Bank'. At that period three of the principal thoroughfares forming the boundaries of the present building, Threadneedle Street, Bartholomew Lane and Lothbury, approximately traced their modern course. Princes Street, however, followed the banks of the Wallbrook and from half-way down its present length struck off diagonally over the present north-west corner of today's site, to emerge into Lothbury opposite to St Margaret's Church. The area in between was a labyrinth of courts and alleys which was not to be finally swallowed by the Bank until almost another century had elapsed. The premises opened in 1734 had a frontage on Threadneedle Street of a mere 80 feet or so, extending from the church of St Christopher-le-Stocks on the west to the Crown Tavern on the east; the depth of the site was about 300 feet. The tavern lay in a small court approached by an alley from Threadneedle Street.

The houses fronting the street had been pulled down and in their place a massive gateway had been erected, flanked by two porters' lodges. Above the gate were a number of rooms, one of which seems to have been used as the Court Room. A courtyard, known as the Fore-Court, about 75 feet wide by 45 feet deep, lay between the Gate and the Great Hall, or Pay Hall, the principal office of the Bank. This fine structure stood upon the site, and probably to a large extent upon the original foundations of Sir John Houblon's demolished mansion. It remained in being for just 200 years, that is until 1933, when the 'old' Bank was being gutted and rebuilt. Its proportions were sadly marred during its last few years, for the increase of business in the First World War, with the consequent hunger for more office space, had made necessary the construction of a 'temporary' mezzanine floor which, it need hardly be added, remained permanent until the destruction of the Hall itself. Some small idea of its lost beauty may be obtained from the well-known aquatint of 1808, in the celebrated *Microcosm of London,* in which the architecture of the Hall is skilfully and precisely recorded by Charles Augustus Pugin, while the witty brush of Thomas Rowlandson peoples it with figures of contemporary clerks and customers in all their peculiarity.

A feature of Pugin's drawing which quickly catches the eye is a life-sized statue, in neo-classic style, by Henry Cheer, standing against the centre of the east wall. This represented that Protestant hero and patron of the Bank, King William III, long remembered with gratitude and affection by the Governors and Directors, but although gratitude may not die it must inevitably grow less lively with the passing of the centuries, so today King William occupies a position of lesser prominence in the Lothbury Court.

Most of the work which had been conducted in the Hall of the Grocers' Company was transferred to the new Hall, appropriate spaces for the cashiers and tellers being 'fenced off'. An attempt to ameliorate the rigours of the English winter was made at about this time by the erection of a vast charcoal-burning iron stove, though with what success is not known. It is certain, however, that this fearsome apparatus must sometimes had provided as much discomfort, not to say danger, as it did warmth, for it had no chimney. There is a legend that at least on one occasion some innocent 'up from the country', upon being told by a cashier to pass a note 'through the bars' to the teller, mistook his instructions and thrust the note into the glowing heart of the stove instead.

It is very likely – although there is no confirmation in the Bank's records – that Jonathan Mayne's Britannia sign, ordered for Grocers' Hall, was rehung in Threadneedle Street. In a print of 1761, showing the Bank Gateway and St Christopher's Church, a sign hangs between them; its nature cannot be deciphered in the print, but from its position it can relate only to the Bank. Two lamps were also erected, each having 'two spouts' and it was ordered that they be lighted at dusk, and burn till morning, throughout the year. George Harrison was appointed lamp-lighter at £7 a year.

The Bank's move took place during the long reign of peace, from 1721 to 1739, which marked Sir Robert Walpole's term of office. Relations with the Governments were always smooth and easy, both during this period and for a long while afterwards, and were doubtless sweetened by a practice the Bank had of making a New Year's gift of

350 guineas or so to the officers of the Exchequer – a practice which continued till 1797, when William Pitt stopped it.

The actual statutory relations between Bank and Exchequer were mainly concerned with the floating debt of Exchequer bills. Walpole's aim here, as in all his financial transactions, was to reduce the National Debt and to cut the rate of interest on what could not be redeemed. These aims, coupled with the fostering and enlargement of the nation's commerce, were, indeed, his constant preoccupation. In furthering them he could always count upon the support of the Bank's Directors, apart from some not unnatural reservations of theirs regarding the interest rate on any part of the Debt owing to the Bank itself. In every other respect the Directors were more than happy to enjoy this their first real experience of calm, and free from unceasing demands for Government loans which would only be wasted in the sterile fields of war, they quietly and steadily strengthened the Bank's monetary reserves.

Walpole, however skilfully he may have lightened his country's financial burdens, could not, of course, satisfy everybody. A notable critic of his policies was Sir John Barnard, an Alderman who served as Lord Mayor in 1737 and was one of the City's Members of Parliament from 1722 to 1761. The sworn enemy of all stock-jobbers, he spoke and wrote extensively on financial matters. When, for example, Walpole laid proposals before the House of Commons for the repayment of the debt of £1 million owing to the South Sea Company, Barnard argued with much force and ability that the money should be used instead to repay part of the Government's debt to the Bank, while the balance of that debt should be repaid as soon as possible. An extension of the Bank's Charter was due for consideration in the near future: if therefore its loan could be redeemed in full, there would be no need for the continued existence of a body which, in his eyes, used its exclusive privileges to damage trade in general. Walpole procured the rejection of Barnard's proposals without difficulty – even Barnard himself can have had no hope that sufficient funds could be found to implement his suggestion.

From birth, the Bank has never escaped criticism of its policies and methods, ranging from the cogent and informed to the irresponsible, ludicrous and sheerly lunatic. While Barnard was conducting his campaign against them the Directors must therefore have been gratified by one of those occasional tributes which anybody in a position of public responsibility must be glad to receive when it comes from a presumably disinterested source. In the *Daily Gazetteer* of 7 April 1737 there appeared the following encomium:

There certainly never was a body of men that has contributed more to the Publick Safety and emolument than the Bank of England, and yet even this great, this useful Company, has not escaped the invectives of malicious tongues. . . . This flourishing and opulent Company have upon every emergency always cheerfully and readily supplied the necessities of the Nation . . . and it may very truly be said that they have in many critical and important conjunctures relieved this Nation out of the greatest difficulties, if not absolutely saved it from ruin.

Nor must it be taken that Sir John's hostility was typical of the general attitude of the City's fathers. This was usually very favourable towards the Bank; indeed, throughout the eighteenth century there were more often than not one or two Aldermen on its Court, and from time to time a Lord Mayor. For example, Sir John Thompson, the Lord Mayor in 1736 (and, therefore, Barnard's immediate predecessor in that office) was a Director. In the Bank's earliest years the liaison was extremely close, no fewer than nine members of the original Court being Aldermen and five subsequently becoming Lord Mayor. In the latter part of the century the relationship was rather less intimate; even so, two Lord Mayors, Sir Thomas Chitty (1760) and Sir Brook Watson (1796) were also Bank Directors.

When, in 1742, the question arose of the further renewal of the Bank's Charter the negotiations had to be conducted with a new Government, for Walpole's inborn distaste for belligerency had led to his loss of power in the previous year. Having grown fat through a long interval of unaccustomed peace, the country had, two years beforehand, in 1739, felt ready for another bout of arms with one of its traditional European enemies, and popular clamour had compelled Walpole to go to war with Spain. English seamen had, it was alleged, been maltreated and the Spaniards had abused their rights of search for contraband. The interests of British commerce therefore demanded that Spain should be taught a lesson. Walpole's heart was never in the struggle and his evident reluctance, a little later, to embroil the country still further, in the War of the Austrian Succession, had brought about his defeat in the General Election of 1741.

The new Government was formed under Lord Wilmington, and the new Chancellor of the Exchequer was Samuel Sandys, first Baron Sandys, an old enemy of Walpole's. This did not, however, appreciably affect the negotiations for the renewal of the Charter, which had a reasonably easy passage. Despite Walpole's efforts to keep the country out of the War of the Austrian Succession, the new Government were soon fully committed on the side of the Empress Maria Theresa against the French. The exiled Stuarts reacted in a manner only to be expected now that they could once more rely upon French support. An attempt to invade England was made early in 1744, but was foiled by a storm.

Then in the spring of 1745, following the defeat of the English forces at Fontenoy, a Jacobite rebellion broke out in Scotland. Misled by enthusiastic and exaggerated reports that a Stuart restoration would be widely welcomed in England, the 'Young Pretender' set sail from France on 14 July and, eighteen days later, landed in the Hebrides. He quickly gathered some two to three thousand Highland clansmen and, at their head, he entered Edinburgh on 17 September, where he proclaimed his father King. A few days later his Highlanders met and defeated a small force of Hanoverian troops at Prestonpans in Berwickshire.

London was understandably alarmed. Once again there was a run upon the Bank and, once again, the Bank parried it by means of well-tried stratagems, but from the nature of the determined and deliberate attempts to compass the Bank's downfall made on this occasion by its religious and political foes, it seems certain that sentiment in favour of a Stuart Restoration was rather more widespread than has been since allowed by many historians. When, therefore, the excited citizens crowded the Pay Hall clutching their notes and demanding cash in exchange, those fortunate enough to force their way to the front were paid, with no show of unmannerly haste, in the smallest silver coins available, provided always, that is, that when they reached the counter they could find a space not already occupied by friends and agents of the Bank withdrawing large sums and immediately paying them in again.

These, however, were delaying tactics at best; aid for the Bank of a far more effective and weighty kind came from the concerted action of the City's leading merchants, traders and bankers. On 26 September, at Garraway's Coffee House in Change Alley, these, to the number of 1,140, signed a declaration that they were prepared to receive banknotes for all amounts due to them and that they would also use their best endeavours to persuade their creditors to accept payment in the same way. The publication of the declaration and the names of its many influential signatories, in the *London Gazette* of 28 September and 1 October, did so much to allay alarm that the Bank's position was at once relieved, and does not seem to have been threatened thereafter, even on 4 December, on which day the Pretender reached Derby and all London's shops were closed. Within two days the panic had subsided for on 6 December Prince Charles Edward, having attracted little, if any, armed support among the English, began the retreat which was to end in his defeat, on 16 April 1746, on Culloden's bloody field.

Such adventures must be paid for and not only in blood. The Bank advanced £1 million towards the cost of suppressing the Rebellion and for expenses of the war with France. As a result of the attendant negotiations the Bank's capital was now increased to £10,780,000. Nor did the Bank forget its saviours. In gratitude for delivery from a Stuart restoration and all that this might have meant to the Bank, a General Court of the Proprietors, meeting in February 1746, voted a contribution of £1,000 to a fund, opened at Guildhall, for the relief, support and encouragement of His Majesty's forces.

In 1752 an Act was passed which was to give rise to a City term familiar ever since to generations of investors. Under this Act the various issues of 3 per cent annuities established during the reigns of the first two Georges were consolidated into one fund which soon became known as 'Consols'; it was also enacted that the rate of interest on the 4 per cent annuities should be reduced, in 1757, to 3 per cent when this part of the consolidated fund was to be designated 'Reduced 3 per cents'.

The financial position of the country, more especially its rapidly growing international dealings, had prompted a further, and much more important Act of Parliament, passed in 1750, but coming into operation also in 1752. With characteristic insularity and undoubtedly a large measure of pig-headedness arising from her enmity to the papacy, England had not adopted the new and, for most practical purposes, exact Calendar which had replaced that instituted by Julius Caesar and had been promulgated in 1582 by a Bull of Pope Gregory XIII. Thereafter it had been generally adopted by the rest of western Europe. When, 170 years later, England at last had to bow to common sense and the facts of astronomy, the necessary revision was all the more painful; eleven days had to be dropped and the citizen who went to bed on the night of 2 September 1752 awoke to the dawn of the 14th. The Act also removed a further cause of confusion by decreeing that the year was to start on 1 January and not on 25 March as hitherto. Thus the difficulties of dealing with foreign bills and of determining whether their dates should be treated as 'New Stile' (Gregorian) or 'Old Stile' (Julian) was removed. It would, however, be too much to expect that all English systems of reckoning should be adjusted and to this day the Exchequer prefers Julius Caesar to Pope Gregory by starting its tax year on 5 April, which is, of course, the new style date of the old style New Year's Day, 25 March. The vulgar, robbed as they thought of nearly a fortnight of their lives, regarded this sane and necessary measure as a piece of blasphemous tyranny. They were not to be similarly disturbed by an interference with 'God's time' until 1916, when 'Daylight Saving' was introduced.

In 1756, with the outbreak of the Seven Years' War, Europe was once again ravaged – and not Europe alone. The great colonial adventures which had begun in the sixteenth century and were to culminate

at the end of the nineteenth were by now well under way, and when
men fought it was not only on European soil but at the ends of the earth
as well. The war started badly for England with the loss of Minorca
and with defeats on the Continent. In North America also the French
were for the moment triumphant, but under Chatham's guidance the
fortunes of the country were gradually restored, and the defeat of the
French, at Minden in 1759, saw the extinction of their hopes of colonial
expansion in Canada and India.

When Peace was signed at Paris on 10 February 1763, England's
National Debt stood at the then enormous sum of £139 million. In
1727 it had been under £25 million, so in under forty years it had
grown nearly sixfold. All this treasure had been poured out on war,
and a great part of it was represented by Government annuities managed
by the Bank. More and more staff had been needed and their number,
which on the opening of the Threadneedle Street premises had been
just over 100, had doubled by 1760. The Bank's business had been
affected, and increased in other ways also. At the end of the war there
had been many serious bankruptcies on the Continent, with financial
panics at Hamburg and Amsterdam. The inevitable repercussions in
London had threatened the positions of a number of merchants and the
Bank had made advances of nearly £1 million in order that confidence
might be regained. Furthermore, the export of specie for war purposes
had led to a shortage of silver coin. One remedy for this suggested by
the Bank to the Government was that a 7s. gold piece would be of great
utility, and although the suggestion was not adopted, it was remembered,
for when a similar emergency arose, in 1797, pieces of this kind were
coined. The most convenient expedient to meet the silver shortage was,
of course, to provide a larger note issue and one of greater flexibility.
Hitherto, the note of the lowest denomination had been for £20
(though, back in 1751, the Court had approved a suggestion that £10
notes be prepared). Now, in 1759, notes for £10 and £15 were made
available.

Technical improvements greatly diminishing the risk of forgery helped
to make this possible. Up to 1724 the Bank of England note had remained very similar in form and composition to those it first issued, but
in that year a new paper came into use. This was the invention of, and
supplied by, Henry Portal from his country paper mill, Bere Mill,
standing on the bank of the River Test near Whitchurch in Hampshire,
and to this day Portals continue to supply bank-note paper to the
Bank. It was harder and of better texture and in consequence the
watermark possessed a definition and clarity hitherto unobtainable. The
Directors, therefore, could at last implement their long-cherished plan,

so far deemed to be too risky, of printing notes for fixed sums. This they had done in 1725, copper-plates having been engraved for £20, £30, £40, £50 and £100. In 1743 the design had been improved to include the so-called 'sum piece', an elaborate £-sign followed by a verbal denomination spelled in white 'Gothic' lettering upon a black ground – a characteristic feature of the great and historic 'Bank Note' known and loved by us all up to a few short years ago and by our fathers, our grandfathers and half a dozen previous generations. Another addition, at that time, was the incorporation in the body of the note, in a bold black 'Gothic' lettering, of the amount in words. In 1759, therefore, when the need for them became so urgent, it was possible to introduce printed notes for £10 and £15. In 1765 a note for £25 was issued for the first time.

The Bank was beginning to 'burst at the seams'. In 1760 it bought, at auction, the estate of David Scott in Threadneedle Street, consisting of a number of premises to the east of the Bank which included the Crown Tavern, a house occupied by the Sun Fire Office, a mercer's shop and the Bank Coffee House, the tenants being given permission to remain until Michaelmas 1763. This, however, was as much as the Bank could do by its own unaided efforts. Its full needs and desires were made generally known when, early in 1764, it petitioned the House of Commons for power to purchase several further contiguous properties. This request was granted by an Act, passed in March, which enabled it to acquire the rest of the ground, houses and buildings lying between the existing premises and the corner of Bartholomew Lane together with all the property from that corner down to the passage leading from Bartholomew Lane to the 'Warehouse'. The whole of the south-eastern quarter of the present island-site thus passed into the Bank's possession. The Act, which stipulated that both Threadneedle Street and Bartholomew Lane should be widened, also empowered the Bank to acquire a plot of land on the opposite, southern side, of Threadneedle Street, beside the Royal Exchange, the front of which was at this time in Cornhill, and running southward the whole way to Cornhill. Two blocks of buildings, known as Bank Buildings, divided lengthwise by a new street joining the two thoroughfares and called Bank street, were later erected on this land.

The erection of the eastern section of Bank Buildings was, in fact, the first part of the Bank's extensive new building programme to be put in hand, Robert Taylor, who was knighted in 1782, being employed as the Architect and Surveyor. As for the Bank site itself, by 1770 a noble Rotunda had arisen, surrounded by four light and spacious vaulted Halls, one to the north, one to the south and two to the east, these last two being connected by a vestibule, the style of the four Halls being an imitation of Gibbs's church of St Martin-in-the-Fields. Westwards, between the Rotunda and the Fore-Court, another vestibule had been constructed, with a Treasury to its north and a strongroom to its south. For the façade of this new east wing Taylor imitated a building by Bramante in the Belvedere Gardens at Rome, attractive in itself but too slight in its proportions to harmonize effectively with the massive Gatehouse which, with the Pay Hall, had been constructed by George Sampson in 1733–4. When, therefore, under Sir John Soane, who was Architect to the Bank from 1788 to 1833, the containing walls were reconstructed between 1823 and 1825, they were considerably heightened.

All this work had no sooner been begun than the Bank, by another Act, acquired still more ground. Progress in the opposite direction, westwards along Threadneedle Street, was barred, at any rate for the time being, by the hallowed ground on which stood the church of St Christopher-le-Stocks and its graveyard. However, the church's glebe-lands, to its north, were taken over, and in 1766 further powers were obtained for the purchase of houses, surrounding the church, in St Christopher's Court and Three Nun's Court. On this site, in 1767, Taylor started the construction of a new Court Room and Committee Rooms, with Discount and Chancery Offices to their north. The Court Room was Sir Robert Taylor's finest achievement, and it is pleasant to record that in a sense it still exists, although translated. It survived one threat when Soane wished to rebuild it, but the Directors would not grant his wish; and it emerged from the gutting which overtook most of the 'old' Bank during Sir Herbert Baker's rebuilding between the two World Wars. Taylor's Room was reconstructed almost in its entirety on the first floor of the present building. Even the lovely wood columns, which originally supported the roof, are still in position, although, of course, their purpose is now aesthetic only, for there is the weight of six storeys above them.

Despite the great amount of work which Taylor must have had on his hands, he nevertheless still found time to practise sculpture, the art in which he had been originally trained. He embellished the Bank with a number of his own statues and carvings, and some of these survive, notably his statue of Britannia which for many years graced the pediment of Sampson's Pay Hall. It now looks down upon the Lothbury Court, though at the moment it is difficult to admire, since, from the ground, it is obscured by a defensive roofing placed over this Court in the Second World War and not yet removed. There are also two marble caryatids upholding the mantel of the central fireplace of three ranged along one of the Court Room walls, and although there is no actual record of who carved them, they are, according to the late Sir Albert Richardson, undoubtedly by Taylor and to be ranked among his finest work.

Thus, by 1770 this phase of the Bank's structural expansion was ended. Some small supplementary pieces of work were done between 1771 and 1775, but apart from these no more building was undertaken until 1782.

Enlargements of the Bank's capital and business, premises and staff having been recorded, one decrease, simultaneous and probably resultant, remains to be noted – the contraction of the Bank's power into fewer and fewer hands. When the alarms, the agitations, and the dust arising from the South Sea Bubble and the move to Threadneedle Street had died down, the government of the Bank settled into a somewhat static routine which remained undisturbed until the 1780s. A symptom of the changed state of affairs was the virtual 'standing down' of the General Court. Important, indeed essential, in the early years, it had frequently been called to give rulings on constitutional matters or to rally with the Directors against infringements of the Bank's privileges, whether by the Government or by other bodies. With the passage of time, however, the need for its help and support grew less and less, until, by the middle of the century, its functions had become more or less formal. Occasionally, as for instance was the case when, in 1750, there was a threat by the Government to lower the rate of interest on its debt to the Bank, the backing of 'the generality' of Proprietors would still be sought, but even then it was merely to fortify decisions already reached by the Directors. In the ordinary course the General Court held its statutory meetings only. These, according to the Charter, had to be called quarterly. Twice a year, usually in January and July, it met to declare or, in Clapham's nicer phrasing, to 'accept' the dividend, which, from 1722 to 1787, customarily fluctuated between 5 and 6 per cent per annum. In either March or April it met to elect Governors and Directors, while the remaining meeting must usually have been called simply because the Charter said so. Additional meetings were, then, always rare: the General Court would, however, meet when a renewal of the Charter was under consideration or when a vacancy had to be filled among the Directors. And for more than sixty years it accepted, without murmuring, the negligible role to which it had been assigned, until the closing years of the century, when, as will be shown in due course, it stirred in its sleep and asserted itself once more.

The Court of Directors held its regular weekly meetings. Each year, after the elections, it appointed the various Standing Committees, the Committee for the House and Servants and, what was to become the

59

principal directive body, the Committee of Treasury. Initially referred to as the 'Committee for yᵉ Trea'ry' and later, more precisely, as 'The Committee to attend the Lord Treasurer', it also took over the duties of the original Committee for the Accounts. With the Bank's books of account always under its eyes coupled with its direct *ex officio* contact with the Government, it became from its nature the normal source of policy.

The Committee of Treasury, the nucleus of the Bank's energy, consisted of the Governor, the Deputy Governor and the more senior of the Directors, most of whom had already 'passed the Chairs'. As we have seen, the General Court had ceased to matter and, from its contemporary records, it would seem that the Court of Directors itself did not matter very much either. One piece of evidence which strongly suggests that the real seats of authority lay in the Committee of Treasury is that it apparently kept no permanent records of its decisions and recommendations; supreme power keeps its own counsel. It is true that in May 1721 the Court of Directors, doubtless much perturbed by the rather narrow shave the Bank had had during the recent South Sea scandals, instructed the Committee to keep records of their transactions, but if this was done the records have been lost, and the earliest surviving Minute Book opens as late as 1779. Even this is a very rough record, kept by the then Deputy Governor. Clapham thinks it unlikely that it could form one of a series: 'if [he says] it had been the fifteenth or twentieth of a series extending over more than half a century, but since lost, it is a fair inference from the known history of records that something tidier and more formal would have evolved'.

The orders concerning the staff made by the Court and the Committees were copied into books kept by the Chief Cashier and the Chief Accountant, but it is questionable whether systematic steps were taken to keep the staff informed or reminded of their terms, and the general state of discipline was, in the perhaps too kindly words of Acres, 'somewhat lax'. This does not mean that all delinquents escaped with impunity: in 1736 a clerk was dismissed for frequenting a public house in which a gaming table was kept 'at which he used to play'; in 1738 one Peter Gregory was dismissed on his being declared a bankrupt; in 1747 Thomas Dowdeswell was first suspended, and, on a repetition of the offence, dismissed for coming to the Bank 'disordered with liquor'. In 1749 two clerks were dismissed for drunkenness and rioting outside the Bank. Insolent behaviour towards a customer caused the suspension of a clerk in 1778, but after being reprimanded he was reinstated. The dismissal of a clerk on account of his religious beliefs occurred once only and then at a time when there must have been considerable tension following the '45 Rebellion. This was in 1746, when the Directors discovered that they had been harbouring a 'Papist', one Thomas Macdonnell, who had been elected in 1743. Since all Roman Catholics were then suspected of favouring a Stuart restoration, Macdonnell was discharged. It was not until 1829, after the passing of the Catholic Emancipation Act, that Roman Catholics were deemed, a little grudgingly, to be 'not ineligible' for clerkships. During the First World War Sunday overtime was made obligatory because of the pressure of work; one clerk who would not 'break the Sabbath' was required to resign.

Throughout the century there was slight change in the conditions of employment. Salaries commenced at £50 a year and any clerk who, after long service, attained the maximum of £200 was fortunate. In 1745, the Chief Accountant and the Chief Cashier, the two most highly paid officials, received £250 a year each; the Secretary got rather less. There was money to be made, however, for extra duties, for extra work in times of pressure and for work in connection with lotteries. From 1761 annual gratuities were awarded to the particularly industrious – and, it may be, to the fortunate and the fawning as well – and in the case of the higher officials these *ex gratia* payments were often considerable, sometimes amounting to more than the annual salaries of the recipients. There was a steep rise in the cost of living between 1747 and 1767, so at the end of this period the clerk still on £50 a year must have been indigent indeed. Even so, compared with someone in a similar position outside the Bank, he would be relatively well off: the hours of work were lighter and salaries were paid during sickness. Furthermore, although there was then no regular pension system, retirement allowances were usually granted, if not always on a very generous scale. Each case seems to have been considered strictly on its merits, and in the case of Daniel Race, a Chief Cashier who had rendered exceptional service, the allowance was equal to his full salary of £250 a year. Race, however, had more than earned his pension – he had served the Bank for over fifty-six years. Entering in 1719, he was appointed, twenty years later, Joint Chief Cashier with James Collier on the retirement of Thomas Madockes in 1739. From 1759 Race was sole Chief Cashier until his retirement in 1775. He was so highly regarded by the Directors that they commissioned Thomas Hickey to paint his portrait, and ordered that it be hung in the Bank, which it does to this day. As so often happens, once the shafts were removed, so to speak, the old horse collapsed. Race died within a few months of his retirement, in his seventy-eighth year, and was buried in St Luke's Church, Old Street, where there is a tablet to his memory, on which a long inscription sets forth his merits. This was composed by a Director of the Bank,

Thomas Plumer, who had known him for upwards of twenty years.

Other eighteenth-century personalities whose memories are preserved by portraits are Bowler Miller and Abraham Vickery. Neither attained to anything like Race's distinction. Miller served from 1744 until his death in 1796. He was painted by Thomas Thompson in a full-length portrait which shows him in profile standing beside a large heating stove in one of Taylor's Transfer Offices. Vickery himself had his portrait painted by Zoffany, with whom he may have been personally acquainted, and the original, in this case, now hangs in the Bank Parlours. It has undoubtedly earned this place of honour from the distinction of the artist rather than that of the sitter. Vickery, in fact, made something of a nuisance of himself. In defiance of an order of the Directors in 1784, which prohibited clerks from acting as stockbrokers, he continued in partnership with one Salmon, a stockbroker, though he concealed the arrangement by withdrawing his own name from the partnership and substituting that of his daughter. The Directors did not look kindly upon this device and Vickery promised to arrange a dissolution. He apparently had no intention of keeping his promise, and in 1796, being at last suspended for breaking the rules, he submitted his resignation. He, too, served in the Three per cent Consolidated Office, for Zoffany portrays him as standing there, full length, holding a power of attorney in his right hand and with an unidentified colleague seated at a counter behind him.

For the rest, a number of clerks emerge from the mists of time in more melancholy guise, having fallen into fraudulent ways, while others are remembered simply for their association with characters more famous. Among the former must be singled out William Guest, who contrived for a while to set at naught the protection against the clipping of coin afforded by the milled edge. He did this by means of an ingenious machine of his own devising, which made a new edge after he had abstracted as much gold as he thought could be safely filed off. He used new guineas picked out by him from those he handled in the course of his duties as a teller. On his arrest, a bag containing gold filings, nearly five pounds in weight, was discovered in his house in Broad Street Buildings. Guest was found guilty of high treason, and on 14 October 1767 was drawn on a sledge to Tyburn and there hanged. Those interested in coins, and in criminology, have ever since tried to discover the nature of his machine, but as there was then no Scotland Yard 'Black Museum', no trace of it remains or, for that matter, any description. (For obvious reasons it would not have been described in public at the time.)

Charles Clutterbuck, whose duties included the completion of bank-notes by the writing-in of the amount and other details before they were passed to the cashiers for signature, abstracted a number of blank forms which he filled in for various sums, amounting in all to £5,930. Having forged the necessary signatures, he cashed some of the notes and fled to France. He was arrested at St Omer in August 1782, but extradition was refused by the French Government. He was, however, put on trial in France and in September 1785 the Governor was able to inform the Court that he had been 'transported from Arras . . . pursuant to the sentence of His Most Christian Majesty condemning him to the Gallies for life'.

Among those remembered for less distressing reasons is John Payne, Chief Accountant from 1780 to 1785, who was a friend of Dr Samuel Johnson and to whom there is a reference in Boswell's *Life of Johnson*. Mention should also be made of Robert Browning, grandfather of the poet, who entered the service in 1769. He was a man of irascible temper whose 'abusive language and ungentlemanly behaviour' was complained of by those working under him when he was Principal of the Bank Stock Office, a post he attained in 1784 and in which he remained until his retirement in 1821.

Meanwhile, especially from the middle of the century onwards, there had been wide developments throughout Great Britain in the field of banking generally. In London a group of stable houses with businesses nearly a century old were joined by a fluctuating collection of newcomers, some successful, some not. The established houses, many of them descendants of the goldsmith-bankers, had for the most part ceased, by this time, to issue their own notes, having found their needs better met by the Bank of England note and the cheque. In the country towns certain of the larger merchants had for many years performed, as an incidental part of their main business, a number of banking functions such as the acceptance of deposits and the negotiation of bills of exchange. They now extended their activities to the issuing of their own notes and in the course of time they were joined by smaller merchants and even shopkeepers who proudly set up the sign 'Bank' outside their premises. Many failed within a few years, but some became rich and respected country banking houses whose assets and goodwill still form part of the resources of one or another of the great monolithic banking corporations of today. Those who attained any measure of permanency are shown in the List of Amalgamations, etc., of Banks since 1700, given annually in *The Bankers' Almanac*.

In Scotland there was no legal restriction on the number of persons allowed to form a partnership, nor was a charter, or other special sanction, needed for the foundation of a company, however large. By habit and tradition, men of business were therefore accustomed to having a rather freer hand in the conduct of their affairs than did their brethren south of the border; in 1765, however, the Scottish bankers suffered an interference with this freedom when an Act of Parliament imposed a check on the issue of notes in Scotland for amounts smaller than £1 sterling. Ten years later this prohibition was extended to English country bankers. In 1777 the limit for both countries was raised to £5 and a highly desirable statutory regulation of note issue was thus brought into force.

In 1764, just after the end of the Seven Years War, a mania for speculation broke out such as had not been seen since the time of the South Sea Bubble; it involved not only London but Amsterdam as well. Lottery prizes, offered by the Government to tempt investors to accept the conversion of their 4 per cent annuities into the 'Reduced 3 per cents', gave the holders a taste for seeking money for nothing. There followed a frantic market activity, especially in the stock of the East India Company. In 1772 difficulties arose: the Company was embarrassed by the expense of its growing political and military commitments in India and the Bank was less ready than usual to grant credits to the Company. At the same time, for those who could read them, there were the customary signs that the long period of overspeculation would give way to a collapse. The Bank Directors therefore introduced limitation of the discounts.

Serious trouble began in June 1772, when Alexander Fordyce, an attractive and plausible Aberdonian, a partner in the banking house of Neale & Co. of Threadneedle Street, absconded. On 20 June his firm went bankrupt and two days later Glyn & Halifax of Birchin Lane stopped payment. Panic followed throughout England and Scotland and before the year closed there were 525 bankruptcies in all. Nor was the trouble confined to Great Britain. Speculation had been widespread on the Continent also, and credit, both private and public, threatened to be wrecked all over Europe.

One result of the panic reveals how much the Bank of England had become by now a recognized and trusted institution. Many traders, fearing that their cash was not secure in private hands, transferred it to the Bank, thereby occasioning, according to the *London Chronicle*, 'so much employment for the clerks, etc., in the offices there that several supernumerary hands were obliged to be called to their assistance'.

Wishing to ease the pressure on the private firms, the Bank reversed its policy of limiting the discount and throughout June 1772 it discounted liberally. Government aid was sought to overcome the difficulties into which the East India Company had fallen. In January 1773

64

it had been pressed by the Bank for the repayment of its debt of £600,000, but in the end it was the Bank rather than the Treasury which came to the rescue, by lending the Treasury £1,400,000 at 4 per cent 'for the relief of the East India Company', and by 1775 the relations between Bank and Company had returned to normal. There was sustained pressure, in many other respects, upon the Bank's resources during 1773, mainly arising from its Continental commitments. For example, in Amsterdam the great house of Clifford & Sons broke in October 1772, the Bank at the time being one of its larger creditors; this firm, older than the Bank itself and among the earliest of its correspondents, had speculated deeply in East India stock.

Another episode in this crisis of 1772 led to long-drawn-out negotiations which figure prominently in the Bank's records for that year and for twenty years after. William Alexander & Sons of Edinburgh had been allowed, by special arrangement, to discount bills for £160,000, having engaged to repay one-third of this amount before 11 April 1773. They also mortgaged to the Bank and to the two firms on whom the bills were drawn – Walpole & Ellison and Walpole, Clarke & Bourne – their estates in Grenada known as Rivière du Chemin and Bacolet. Alexanders failed to repay the agreed portion of the loan when it became due and were made bankrupt in 1775. Proceedings were then taken to obtain possession of the estates. Litigation was protracted, and while the mortgagees were awaiting a decision the War of American Independence broke out. France allied herself with the American Colonies and captured Grenada. The brothers Alexander fled to France in order to obtain French citizenship and, with it, the properties.

The ensuing negotiations between the Bank and the Walpole firms on the one side and the Commissioners appointed by the King of France on the other indicate that war was still very much regarded as an affair conducted between gentlemen, who were not released from their honourable obligations towards one another simply because they happened to be fighting. Although hostilities were still in progress, the French courts in 1781 decided in favour of the Bank. Peace was concluded in 1783 by the Treaty of Versailles, under which Grenada was restored to Great Britain. By 1789 the Bank had come to an arrangement with its fellow mortgagees whereby it agreed to take over their share in the Grenada estates in part settlement of its debt, and in February 1790 the Bank recovered £100,000 of the original £160,000 by selling the estates with 'all the negro and other slaves, men, women and children, and the issue, increase and progeny of such of the said slaves as are female'.

This episode is important in the history of banking policy in that, although there is no recorded view on the matter, it confirmed the Directors in their dislike of accepting real property on mortgage as a banker's security. Mortgages had been granted by the Bank in its early days, but the practice was not continued for very long. For a brief period after 1815, under State pressure to help landowners, mortgages were again accepted, but again, after a short experience, they were adjudged to be no proper part of the Bank's business.

The War of American Independence, as wars always have done, added greatly to the Bank's work of managing loans for the Government. When, on 3 September 1783, England recognized the independence of the United States by signing the Treaty of Versailles the National Debt had jumped from £128 million to nearly £250 million, and this led to the customary increase in the Bank's staff; in 1760 it was 264, in 1790 it was 375.

There also began, during this period, the next stage in the growth of the Threadneedle Street premises; this time, however, it was brought about not so much by hostilities abroad as by civil commotion at home. These new building extensions, which were started in 1782, were directly occasioned by the Gordon Riots of 1780, when the London mob spewed forth from its dens and warrens in fouler and more ferocious spate than at any time before during the eighteenth century. Once again a religious pretext was the excuse for an orgy of pillage and looting and once again matters were allowed to get out of hand largely because the City authorities had so rooted and, in the light of past history, so justifiable a suspicion of military interference. Alderman Brackley Kennet, the Lord Mayor, was secretly sympathetic towards the anti-Catholic rioters, and he and his fellow magistrates stood by, with only the mildest of protests, as for two days and nights the mob sacked, burned and looted the Irish-Catholic district of Moorfields. The Government, although it realized that it was touching a very tender spot, had brought in troops, but at the outset there was little that the soldiers could do. For a long time no magistrate could be found to read the Riot Act and for an officer to act against the rioters without civil sanction was unthinkable and, indeed, illegal.

So long as the rioting was mainly directed to the burning of Catholic chapels and schools and the houses of individual Catholics, Kennet forbore to call in military aid, but the burning down of Newgate Prison, on the night of 6 June, was another matter entirely – and when it became clear that the Bank, with its gold, was the mob's next objective, Kennet, albeit still with some reluctance, applied to the Government for a force of Horse and Foot Guards to assist in its defence.

Had the mob gone straight on from Newgate to the Bank, no one can say what might have happened. As it was, it was not until eleven o'clock in the evening of 7 June that the first assault was launched. The Bank had been surrounded, but by that time it had been garrisoned by the military: three cannons were drawn up in the courtyard and troops were manning not only the body of the adjacent church of St Christopher-le-Stocks but its tower as well – for the capture of these positions just outside the walls of the Bank would have greatly aided the rioters in their objective of raiding its vaults. The Guards were reinforced by detachments of militia and by a band of volunteers formed by the London citizens; John Wilkes, the famous and infamous champion of liberty, who had once commanded the Buckinghamshire militia, was one of the leaders of these volunteers.

The story of the assault, led by a brewery drayman riding a cart-horse 'caparisoned with chains filched from Newgate', is a familiar one. Wilkes recorded in his diary how his volunteers had 'fired six or seven times at the rioters at the end of the Bank. Killed two rioters directly opposite to the Great Gate of the Bank: several others in Pig Street and Cheapside.' As might be expected, the volunteers, under their civilian commanders, seemed far more ready to open fire than the troops were. At the height of the battle Lord George Gordon made a breathless and agitated appearance on the Bank steps. Distracted by the bloodshed, for which he felt guilty, he tried to persuade the rioters to go home, but they mistook his incoherence for encouragement. He was pushed aside and the battle went on with renewed fury. At last the mob was driven back and at midnight the Governors and Directors sent a note to the military authorities 'that they were at present safe and hope to continue so'. Another attack was made between 3 and 4 a.m. from Cheapside; the rioters were stopped near the Poultry by the fire of the military, eight of them being killed and a great number wounded.

On the following day most of the City shops were shut and barricaded, but the Bank remained open, though only to transact the most necessary business. Order was gradually restored and no further attack was made on the Bank. The military guard was, however, retained for some weeks and permission was also sought by the Directors for the retention of the troops occupying St Christopher's Church. On 17 August the Governors and Directors, following an example set by many other important City institutions, entertained all the officers who had been on duty in the City to a dinner at the Queen's Arms Tavern in St Paul's Churchyard. The dinner consisted of a turtle (which alone cost 23 guineas), a dozen haunches of venison and the first dainties in season, together with all sorts of wines, and the bill amounted to £200.

The Bank records are silent about the part played in its defence by its own staff, though Acres considers it possible that most of the porters and any of the clerks who could use fire-arms were pressed into service. In 1783, during the course of an inquiry by a Special Committee, it was reported that there were '31 musquets with bayonets and other accoutrements in the Porter's Lodge', and that these were taken down and loaded at the time of the Riots. John Francis, Chief Accountant from 1870 to 1875, in his history of the Bank, published in 1848, said that the 'old inkstands were cast into bullets'.

A direct outcome of the Riots was the installation of a permanent nightly guard for the Bank, drawn from the regiment of Foot Guards on duty. Barracks were eventually erected to accommodate the guard and were completed in 1788; they lay in a yard to the west of the Court Room. The number was agreed with the military authorities at thirty men. Greatcoats and blankets were provided by the Bank for the soldiers and an allowance of bread, cheese and beer was made to them; the officer was given a dinner and wine supplied by a neighbouring tavern. It need hardly be added that the whole arrangement was much resented by the City Corporation.

The Riots had made one thing plain – the Bank's premises were vulnerable to attack by reason of their being commanded by the church and tower of St Christopher's. The Directors immediately considered what must be done to reduce the danger, and a suggestion, already mooted in 1766, arose once more that they should acquire the church and demolish it. The parishioners objected, as well they might, but their numbers and power had been weakened over the years by the disappearance of various parishioners' residences into the Bank's swelling demesne. The Bishop of London, Robert Lowth, was approached; the Prime Minister, Lord North, promised his support, and so, following a Petition by the Bank to Parliament on 24 April 1781, an Act was passed later that year vesting the church and churchyard in the Bank. The parish of St Christopher was united with that of St Margaret Lothbury and to this day St Margaret's is the parish church of the Bank of England.

An agreed sum was paid in compensation to the incumbent, the Reverend Sherlock Willis; he lived only a short while to enjoy it, however, for he died on 21 April 1783: the tithes and other dues then went to the Rector of St Margaret's. Bodies in the church and church-yard could, if desired, be removed by relatives or friends for reinterment elsewhere; those in the church not so removed were to be placed in vaults under the northern side of the churchyard, and the churchyard itself was to remain an open space, unbuilt upon for ever. The price

Laus Deo. In London the 27 July 1694

Cash

To ... Cash ... subscription cash for £ of £30,0000 subscribed ... Bank of England		£ 30000
1 To S.r Edw.d Abney rec: the 28 instant		1000
2 To Thomas Dalton apothecary rec: the 18 Instant		300
3 To Obadiah Sedgwick rec: the 23 Instant		485 · 8 · 10
4 To Jn.o Smith Esq.r neat on y.e Exchequ.r y.e 24 instant B.B		520 · 16
5 To Peter Albert a bill of exc: is rec: 200: by ... 250:10:7 by D.H:		480 · 10 · 7
6 To John Smith Esq.r rec: the 28 instant B.B		2000
7 To Obadiah Sedgwick rec: the 28 instant		400
8 To Daniel Tanturier Esq.r a bill of Fonlis rec: y.e 31 ditto		450
9 To Eliz: dowag.r Countes of Carlisle rec: this 31 ditto		200
10 To Peter Albert a bill of exc: on Tho: & Tho: Dadre rec: y 31 ditto		74 · 14 · 0
11 To Abraham Houblon Esq.r rec: on.e exch: orders 159: 249		632 · 15 · 6
12 To Jn.o Smith Esq.r of Beaufort building rec: of Moore & Prime		1000
		31242 0 11 · 5

Wednesday the 1. of August: 1694

13 To S.r John Houblon rec: of him y.e following bills viz		
a bill on S.r Stephen Evans for	£ 500: —	
a bill on Joseph Henriques Medina	£ 280:12: —	
a bill on John Barnard	£ 95: —	875 · 12
14 To W.m Hudman a noat on M.r Johnson		150
15 To John Houblon jun.r Esq.r 3 bills viz		
2 bills on Jn.o Turner jun.r	£ 303:16:	
1 bill on W.m Rayske	£ 113: 5	417 · 1
16 To Theodore Janssen rec: y.e Hindley		339
17 To Henry Spencer a noat on Edw.d Lambert		400
18 To M.r Sam.ll Bulteel a bill on Minshell & Smith		260
19 To M.r Arn.d Phillips jun		4915 · 6
20 To M.r Thomas Vagan 4 bills viz		
1 bill on ... Henry for	£ 90: 8 4	
1 ditto on Tho: Powel &c	£ 113: 0 5	
1 ditto on Comp.a Rob.t Doughty	£ 59:15:	
1 ditto on ditto	£ 128: 2 6	
	£ 391 10: 3	
	£ 1:17:	389 · 9 · 3
allowing for discount		1 17
21 bills of exc: discounted for the discount abovesaid		100
22 To John Gandey rec: 560: & 740: by two noats of ... B.k		
24 To Abraham Houblon Esq.r for the following Exchequer orders & bills exc: &c		
1: 59: a tally & order on the exchequer for	£ 521: — 10	
60: ditto	£ 521: — 10	
a bill on John Lordell	£ 592: 3: 5	
a bill on W.m Clarke	£ 100: —	
a noate of M.r James Houblon	£ 102: 3 9	
a bill of exc: value of Edw.d Roth	£ 224: 4 4	
a bill of exc: value of W.m Gunn & Humphry Bernard £	£ 96: 5: 4	2156 18 2
this ... 24 bills ... in one noate for £2969:13:8		£ 317566 · 4 · 4

Carried over to next leafe

5139 · 12 · 11

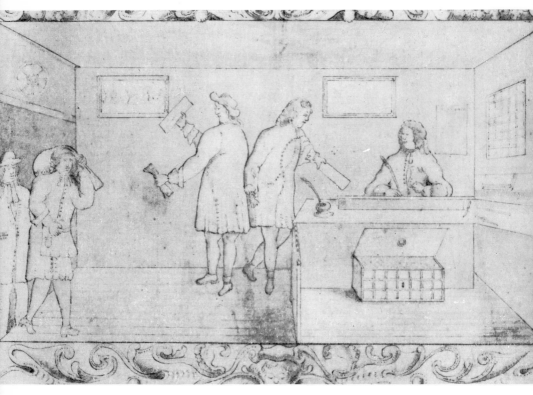

A room in the Bank. From a drawing of *circa* 1695, showing a clerk at a desk and two merchants depositing money

Sir John Houblon, First Governor of the Bank, 1694–7. In his robes as Lord Mayor of London (1695–6). From an oil painting by Isaac Whood

The Silver Tankard of 1697, presented by the Directors to Sir John Houblon 'in token of his great ability, . . . at a time of extreme difficulty'

Three types of Exchequer Bills, as originally introduced by Charles Montagu (bottom), in 1696, and as subsequently developed

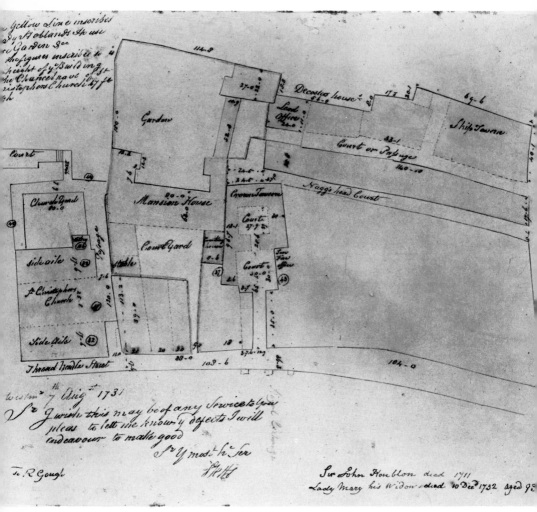

1731 A drawing prepared for the Bank showing the four houses in Threadneedle Street on the site of which the Gatehouse was erected; Sir John Houblon's mansion, the site of the Great Hall; and the garden behind, on which further offices were built. St. Christopher's Church is shown in some detail to the west. To the east is Nag's Head Court, through which access to the back of the Bank could be obtained from Bartholomew Lane. The Crown Tavern, which stood until further purchases of land were made in 1760, is also shown

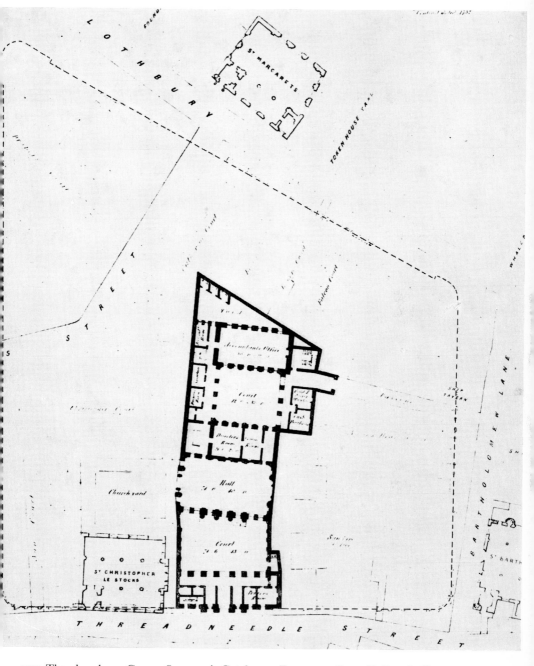

1735 The plan shows George Sampson's Gatehouse, Forecourt, Great Hall and offices behind, erected upon the sites in Threadneedle Street shown in the previous drawing. The dotted line indicates the perimeter of the present building

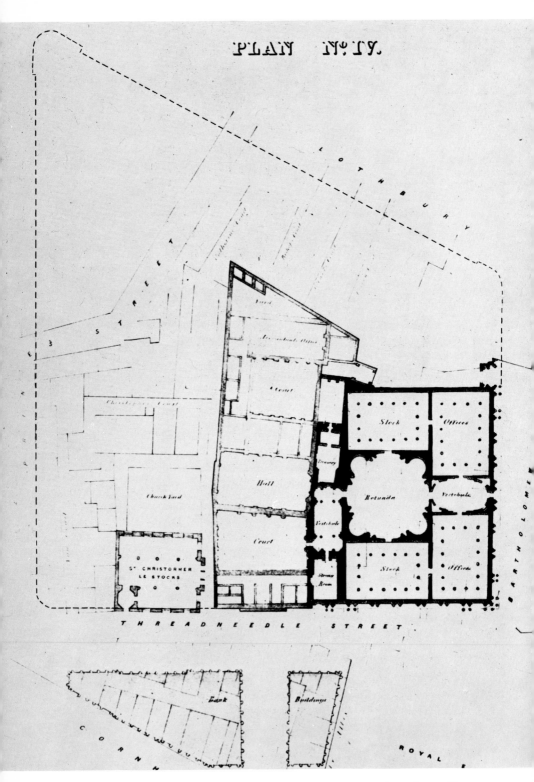

1770 Shows the addition of Sir Robert Taylor's Offices, on the site of the Crown Tavern, with his Rotunda and Stock Offices, behind his screen walls to the east of Sampson's original buildings. Taylor's Bank Buildings and Bank Street are shown on the south side of Threadneedle Street

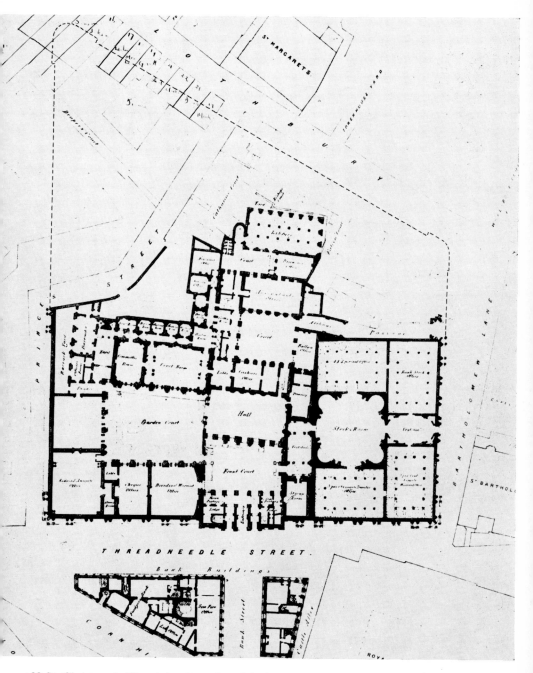

1788 St. Christoper's Church has been demolished and Sir Robert Taylor's Court and Committee Rooms, with offices surrounding the Garden Court have been erected and enclosed behind his extended screen walls to the west of the original buildings. Behind the Bank Princes Street, following the line of the Wallbrook, bears to the right across the present site

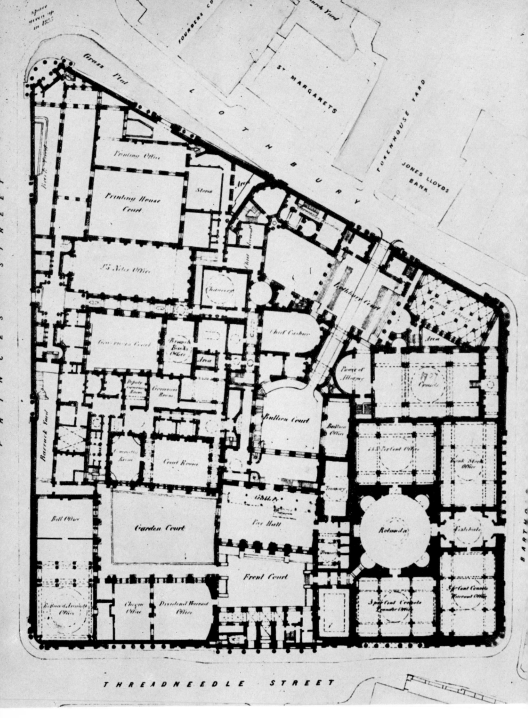

1833 Princes Street has been straightened and Sir John Soane's work completed. His new courts and offices, together with a new Rotunda and Stock Offices to replace Taylor's, which had fallen into decay, are enclosed behind new, and higher, screen walls which surround the Bank site. Today these walls, slightly modified in places, are all that remain of Soane's Bank. Except for relatively minor alterations Soane's Bank stood as shown for nearly a century. On the opposite side of Threadneedle Street Bank Buildings were demolished in 1844, in conjunction with the building of the present Royal Exchange

paid for the property was agreed by a jury at £4,462 4s. In 1782 the church was taken down, most of the fittings going to St Margaret Lothbury, but the seventeenth-century reredos was removed to Great Burstead in Essex, to form a screen beneath the tower arch of the parish Church.

The churchyard was duly laid out as an open space and the two lime trees which became so delightful a feature of the old Bank Garden were almost certainly planted at this time, a fact which was established by a count of rings of the one tree remaining when it was cut down in 1932 to make way for Sir Herbert Baker's rebuilding. The windows of Taylor's Court Room and Committee Rooms looked out on the Garden.

So, at the end of its first fifty years in Threadneedle Street, the Bank had grown mightily. Its premises were more extensive, its staff more numerous, its business thriving. This had been a phase of steady expansion and consolidation and yet, on the whole, apart from a few turbulent episodes, a strangely quiescent one. Some light on the general semi-somnolent air which reigned during this half-century is thrown, towards its close, by the records of a Special Committee of Inquiry set up by the Court of Directors. They had suspected and feared that the Bank's methods had failed to keep pace with the growing volume of business and that its practices were 'haphazard and antiquated'. So in March 1783 the Committee started its labours, and the need for reforms was quickly disclosed.

In many offices security arrangements were found to be lax and in some almost non-existent. Books were left overnight on the desks; on almost any pretext 'improper persons' could obtain admittance after business hours; the keys, left at the Gate Porter's lodge, were allowed to remain there overnight carelessly lying upon a table. Despite periodical orders by the Court of Directors forbidding them to do so, many clerks in the Stock Transfer Offices engaged in business as stockbrokers; at the close of the day the chiefs of the departments and the heads of offices were the first to quit, 'leaving the charge of everything to the vigilance and honesty of junior clerks'; and perhaps most serious of all, since it could so easily be conducive to fraud and forgery, the accounts of business done were, in many offices, written on loose sheets of paper only, no permanent records being kept.

Immediate steps were taken to rectify the worst of these abuses, but it was not until November 1790 that another Special Committee was appointed to consider the various problems of staff discipline which had been uncovered and to draw up a code of 'rules and orders' applicable to all members of the staff.

Chapter 5

'The Old Lady', William Pitt and the French Wars

If, during its first fifty years in Threadneedle Street, the Bank's policies had been stolid and unimaginative and if the office methods used in carrying them out had sometimes been archaic and lackadaisical, the era which followed was to see much change and innovation. The Bank, and the country, had many hard lessons to learn, for during a large part of this time Britain was in mortal peril, a peril from which she was not to emerge until the downfall of Napoleon, at Waterloo, in 1815.

It has often been remarked that at times like these, when she is fighting for her life, Britain has so far always managed to produce leaders of genius who have guided her out of danger – men of energy and courage, fortitude and cunning, who have never been afraid to apply desperate remedies to desperate situations and whose very mistakes bear some mark of magnificence about them. On this occasion the man was William Pitt the Younger.

All these great leaders have, of course, realized that if a war is to be won it must somehow be paid for, but Pitt seems to have been the only one who was interested in the actual techniques of finance and economics. His first ambition, before war loomed, was to make his country great by making it rich and, with this goal in view, he accepted office as Chancellor of the Exchequer at the early age of twenty-three. This was in July 1782 and when, a short while later, in April 1783, he was appointed Prime Minister, he revealed his abiding interest in finance, as such, by continuing to act as Chancellor. In these first few years of peace he showed himself to be a reformer of the best type, improving but not destroying, and when Britain entered into the last and most deadly of her many struggles with France it was he alone of the nation's great war Prime Ministers who consciously and deliberately used money as a weapon. This meant that his relationship with the Bank was far more direct and personal than that, say, of Lloyd George or Churchill. It was, to use the jargon current today, a 'love-hate' one. He often outraged the Directors by his proposals and demands: they as often made him angry and impatient by their caution.

When he died, on 23 January 1806, at the age of forty-six, he had been Prime Minister for nearly half his life. He left an example of bold and venturesome finance to his successors at the Treasury and he had drilled the Bank, despite its qualms, into an acceptance of his ideas. Yet, for all the tension between them, he and the Directors were never fundamentally at odds. They had sought common ends: their quarrels were about means. The Directors remembered that, a century before-hand, the Bank had been conceived as a measure of wartime finance, and the majority, if not all of them, were grateful in their inmost hearts for an opportunity of showing that they, too could rise to a great occasion.

With this wind of change about to blow through the Treasury, it was as well that the Bank, acting on the recommendations of its Special Committees of 1783 and 1790, had taken steps to put its house in order. Even before Pitt came to power, there had been faint stirrings in Whitehall. Edmund Burke, almost in a literal sense, had removed some dead wood, a measure which also affected the Bank's work in a minor way – he proposed to abolish the wooden tallies which had been issued by the Exchequer from time out of mind and to substitute indented cheque receipts. He was, however, extremely tender towards a certain vested interest – the tallies were not to disappear until the death of the tally-cutter. The cutter, as it happened, enjoyed very good health, so the tallies continued to be cut, notched and split for many years to come: when it was Pitt's turn to institute reforms he was far less concerned at hurting anyone's feelings.

The Bank's Charter, having been given another twenty-one years of life from 1 August 1765, had nevertheless been further renewed well before the expiration of that term. This took place in 1781 and the new term – of twenty-six years – was granted in consideration of a loan to the Government of £2 million at 3 per cent against Exchequer bills. It had been intended that the loan should be for three years only, but on assuming power Pitt found it necessary to insist on a postponement and it was not until 1786 that repayment could be arranged.

In 1786 Pitt secured a reduction in the charges made by the Bank for the management of the National Debt. After consulting the General Court, the Directors agreed that the Bank's fee, which had hitherto been £562 10s. per £1 million of capital managed, should in future be £450. The same year saw the bravest of Pitt's attempts, as a financial reformer, to lessen the nation's outgoings and, consequently, the amount it had to demand in taxation. He constituted a Sinking Fund and appointed Commissioners for the Reduction of the National Debt. The Debt was still not so large that a considerable reduction could not be visualized, and perhaps even its virtual extinction, but, as we need not be reminded, the harsh necessities of fate and economics decreed otherwise. His scheme was that £1 million a year should be placed in the hands of the Commissioners for the redemption of an equivalent amount of the Debt: to this was to be added the interest on the sums so redeemed and the operation of the Fund was to continue whatever the financial position of the country. By 1793 an amount of £10¼ million had been paid off. The existence of the Fund gave confidence at the inevitable periods of depression, but what Pitt had overlooked was a circumstance which became evident when war broke out later that year. Government expenses necessarily mounted, so it became, if not impossible, at least insane to carry on the Fund, for this would have meant borrowing at high rates of interest in order to pay off debts bearing a low rate.

Pitt's continual demands for money, his streak of high-handedness and his occasionally unbusinesslike methods started the first bout of friction between himself and the Bank; then, at the end of 1790, a full-scale tussle developed. Pitt had been inspecting the Exchequer and Audit Roll – the record of Government money passing through the Bank to be paid out in dividends – and he had noticed that the balances of dividends left unclaimed were constantly increasing. He proposed to raid these balances, suggesting that he should take all but £50,000 out of a total of £547,000. The Governors were firm in their opposition; they were supported by the Court of Directors and, shortly afterwards by the General Court as well, which had awoken to sudden life at this threat to its funds. The Bank's concern over the principle involved was genuine and honourable enough – the Directors regarded themselves as the trustees for the owners of these dividends, many of whom had simply left them in the hands of the Bank, since they felt that they were safer there than anywhere else. The views of the Directors were supported by a memorandum presented by a number of important financial houses, including some of great wealth and repute on the Continent, in both foreign and British ownership. A deputation from the Court of Directors waited upon the Chancellor, bearing with them the opinions of six eminent counsel, all opposing Pitt's proposals, and when his Bill was read for a second time, on 15 March 1791, a petition against it was presented to the House of Commons by Samuel Thornton, M.P., in which the Bank's concern was set out at great length. Despite these tactics, however, and a certain amount of the anti-Pitt opposition to be expected as a matter of course from Burke and Fox, Pitt was clearly bent on having his own way.

The Bank's next move was a simple and effective one. On 24 March the Directors decided to publish a list of all really old unclaimed dividends, that is, those up to September 1780. Four days later so great was the press of owners wishing to snatch their dividends out of Pitt's grasp that the staff had difficulty in dealing with them. Pitt, who would never have given in to direct opposition, was forced to yield to this oblique pressure. On 29 March the Directors, supported by the General Court, agreed to offer a 'perpetual loan', free of interest, if Pitt would drop his Bill, and after some bargaining, honour was satisfied on both sides upon these lines. The Bank lost nothing by this display of firmness: its credit and reputation were, indeed, augmented. It maintained its dividend of 7 per cent and in 1792 the maximum price of Bank stock was higher than it had been in any year since the days of the South Sea Bubble.

The sacrosanctity of private property, founded on a belief that the just man is usually rewarded in this world as well as the next, was a cornerstone of the 'Protestant Ethic' which still so strongly inspired the Bank, and the applause it received for making its stand was doubtless amplified because of what had been happening across the English Channel – in 1789 the Revolution had broken out in France and in the eyes of most Englishmen it seemed that that unhappy country had been overrun by a pack of godless thieves.

On 1 February 1793 France declared war on England, and a commercial crisis, which had begun in the previous autumn, was intensified. There was a run on the Bank which the Directors met in the now traditional way by restricting note issue and raising the discount rate. By March the country was in the throes of the worst commercial and financial crisis it had yet experienced, its severity being most acutely felt in Bristol, Liverpool and the City. Initially the collapse was in confidence and the circulation of currency: there was no collapse, to start with, in production. But as widespread runs brought down the weaker banking houses and their customers with them, as the number of resulting bankruptcies mounted higher, cash and notes in circulation became scarcer and scarcer. Then, as other banks, both in town and country, wishing to maintain a precarious solvency, clung to their cash by refusing to undertake discounting, the nation's industry was brought almost to a standstill, for it had relied upon the discounting of bills in order to procure the ready money it needed to carry on manufacture and even to pay wages. A change of tactics was therefore seen to be necessary and on 18 April, after giving notice in the *London Gazette* of the 16th, the Bank issued £5 notes, considering it expedient to do so 'in the present situation of Credit and the want of confidence in many of the Country Bank Notes'. Extensive advances were also made to bankers in Liverpool and in the City: even the Lord Mayor of London himself, Sir James Sanderson, M.P., a partner in a Southwark banking house, was helped by an advance of £6,000 to his firm 'because of the mischief that might ensue from the Bankruptcy of a Lord Mayor'.

On 22 April leaders of the City met Pitt in Downing Street to 'find out a Remedy' and on the following day a Committee of eleven met at the Mansion House to consider plans for State aid. The chair was taken by the Lord Mayor whose bankruptcy the Bank had averted: there were four Bank Directors on the Committee, Samuel Bosanquet, Samuel Thornton, Benjamin Winthrop and Thomas Boddington; of the other members, the most notable was Francis Baring, founder of the banking house bearing his family name. The plan recommended by the Committee, and adopted by Pitt, was an issue of Exchequer bills 'as a loan to the mercantile interest'. It was for an amount of £5 million, from which Commissioners appointed by the Government might make advances upon approved security or upon goods deposited to double the value of the sum advanced. It had been put forward, in discussion, that the administration of the Fund should be in the hands of the Bank Directors, but this suggestion had been rejected by Pitt, who pointed out that long advances were not the business of the Bank, its normal term being two months. A number of Bank Directors sat on the executive committee, however.

These 'commercial Exchequer bills', as they came to be called, eased the situation immediately; sound firms received something which they could discount at once and with the aid of the Bank's £5 notes the gap in the circulation was filled. An inevitable outcome of the means used to meet the crisis was an increase in the Bank's total issue: with the new £5 notes it stood by the middle of that year at £12,200,000, a higher total than had ever been reached before.

Confidence returned in 1794, and with the exchanges favourable the Bank was able to build up its bullion reserves once more. The respite was, however, a short-lived one. In 1795 there began an extensive drain of gold to the Continent, especially to France, where the revolutionary Government was restoring the currency to a metallic basis after a long and disastrous experiment with 'assignats'. Direct export of gold to France was, of course, forbidden. The Bank could not take part in it, nor would it have wished to do so, but less scrupulous dealers could make a large profit by 'working' the London-Hamburg, Hamburg-Paris exchanges; and there was, naturally, much direct smuggling of gold into France as well. Another reason for loss of coin was a loan – by no means favourably regarded by the Bank, but sanctioned by Parliament – which was made to the Hapsburg Emperor of Germany. The amount had been agreed at £4,600,000 and the Government had guaranteed the payment of their dividends to the subscribers. The sum raised was sent partly in bills and partly in foreign bullion, both gold and silver; subsidies to allies also had to be paid in the same way: and in addition, there was a heavy and continuous overseas expenditure on Britain's own armies and fleets campaigning abroad. Constantly driven by his awareness of the country's danger and prepared to go to any lengths in the financial efforts he considered essential for its survival, Pitt made repeated applications to the Bank for advances.

January 1797 saw a continuing drain of gold from the country and from the coffers of the Bank. On top of this, fears of a French invasion were beginning to lead to a hoarding of coin and heavy demands for cash were consequently being made on the country bankers by the more timid of their customers. Pitt, on asking the Bank to provide £200,000 in specie for Ireland, was told that 'any further drain of cash from the Bank would in these times be very dangerous, as the cash has been very materially lessened of late'. The Governor hoped, therefore, that half this amount would suffice. By 21 February the Bank's stock of coin stood at not much more than £1 million and a deputation went to the Prime Minister to call his attention to this grave state of affairs. Efforts were made to purchase guineas or gold bullion from Hamburg, but on 23 February £90,000 more in cash was withdrawn from the Bank and on the next day another £130,000. Once again a deputation waited on Pitt and this time put the ball firmly into his court by asking how much farther they might venture in the payment out of cash. Then, on 25 February a *London Gazette Extraordinary* was published reporting the landing of a force from a French frigate in Wales. In the already perturbed state of the public this news seemed likely to cause a violent run on the Bank. A meeting of the Privy Council was convened for the following day, Sunday, and when on the morning of Monday, 27 February, a crowd of persons gathered at the Bank to obtain cash for their notes, they were handed, instead, a circular which conveyed the terms of an Order in Council directing the Bank to forbear issuing any cash in payment 'until the sense of Parliament can be taken . . .' This copy of the Privy Council's Order was prefaced by a notice signed by the Secretary of the Bank, Francis Martin, assuring the public that the Bank's 'general concerns' were in the 'most affluent and prosperous situation'.

This was the greatest test that the Bank's credit had ever had to face. That cash could not be obtained there was more than a shock – it might have caused an uncontrollable panic, or even riots. But again the City leaders took a firm and calm hand. There was a meeting at the Mansion House later in the day, presided over by the Lord Mayor, Brook Watson, an MP for the City and a Bank Director. The leading merchants rallied to the support of the country and the Bank. Following the precedent set by themselves in the troubled times of 'the Forty-Five', they issued a declaration, displayed in all the coffee houses, stating that they would not refuse bank-notes offered in payment of any sums due to them and that they would use their 'utmost endeavours to make all their payments in the same manner'. More than 4,000 persons appended their signatures.

A secret Committee of the House of Commons, appointed on 28 March, confirmed the statement of the Directors that the Bank's general affairs were in 'an affluent and prosperous condition'. The Committee's report, presented to the House on 3 March, showed a surplus in the Bank of nearly £4 million, exclusive of the permanent debt of £11,686,800 owed by the Government.

To provide a means of making small payments, the Directors arranged to print notes for £1 and £2, but all this still left the public without 'small change', so as a further measure the Government authorized the circulation of Spanish dollars – 'pieces of eight' – the booty of war, of which a large number lay in the Bank's vaults. The Spanish dollars were put in circulation after they had received the minimum treatment considered necessary – the head of George III, in a small oval, was impressed on the neck of the Spanish monarch, the stamp being that used at Goldsmith's Hall for hall-marking silver. This gave rise to a couplet, composed, in the words of Acres, by 'some witty person who was no respecter of crowned heads', and which ran as follows –

> The Bank, to make their Spanish dollars pass,
> Stamped the head of a fool on the neck of an ass.

It was first proposed to issue these overstamped dollars at 4s. 6d. apiece, but it was immediately realized that, the bullion content of the coin being worth 4s. 8d., they would be quickly melted down. The issue was therefore delayed from 6 to 9 March, when the coins were put into circulation at 4s. 9d. – hence the further witticism 'two Kings' heads and not worth a crown'. They were in great demand to start with, a demand stimulated by the Whig opposition, who were ardent opponents of paper money and ceaselessly urged all and sundry to change their notes for cash. Applicants were at first entitled to £5 worth of dollars and for a few days the counters in the Bank's Pay Hall were crowded ten or twelve deep. The demand then subsided; nevertheless, considerably more than two million of these bastard but very useful coins are known to have gone into circulation. To this number must be added many more, imported from abroad and stamped in imitation, not to mention further copies in base metal uttered by industrious rogues. The Spanish dollars were withdrawn after 31 October. They had by then served their turn, but were to be used again to relieve a coin shortage some years later. According to accounts subsequently rendered, the exact number issued was 2,325,099 to a value of £552,211.

The public did not hesitate, as they might have done in earlier years, to accept the Bank's £1 and £2 notes. The gravest trouble about them was that they were extensively forged. The Directors therefore altered their form early in 1798 and withdrew the first issue. Cash reserves had considerably increased by then, so the Bank was able to offer holders of the old notes the alternatives of taking payment either in cash or in new notes, on or after 5 February 1798. The Directors evidently expected that the restriction would soon end, but the course of events quickly dashed their hopes.

Meanwhile, the Government's need for money to carry on the war was unabated. In May 1797 two Acts were passed, one for raising £14½ million against annuities, the other for an additional loan to the Hapsburg Emperor – this time for £1,620,000. Only those who sub-scribed to the first might do so to the second. The Hapsburg Loan was a bad mistake, at any rate if it is regarded simply as an investment. By the following October the young General Buonaparte had crowned his run of victorious campaigns by the Treaty of Campo Formio, under which the Emperor had surrendered his territories in the Netherlands, the Rhine Frontier and Lombardy in exchange for the Republic of Venice. One result was that no interest was ever paid on these 'Im-perial loans', which, it will be remembered, the Bank had disapproved of from the start. Twenty-six years later the Emperor's successor paid back 2s. 6d. in the pound. Pitt and his colleagues were to realize too late that, in a time of war to the death, it is wiser to give money to your allies than to lend it to them, a course which, as Mr (later Sir John) Clapham rightly pointed out in 1917, in an article in *The Economic Journal*, their remote successors of 1914–18 would also have done well to follow.

A brief period of peace followed the signing of the Treaty of Amiens on 27 March 1802, and in 1803 Addington changed the name of Pitt's Income Tax to 'Property Tax' and introduced a system of deduction at source; perhaps he thought a new description would sound less forbidding, but whatever he did, he could not lessen the tax's unpopularity. It was initially intended that the deduction at source should apply to dividends, but this notion was abandoned and the Court announced that it would pay the tax on its gains and profits from general funds 'without deducting the proportion from the dividend'. Dividends on Bank stock were therefore always paid free of this tax, until its abolition after Waterloo.

The currency problem was endemic and there was a second issue of Spanish dollars in 1804, the impression of the King's head being this time a somewhat larger one in an octagon: it was, in fact, the head used by the Mint on the silver Maundy penny, without the surrounding inscription. This issue was withdrawn on 2 June 1804, the Bank having discovered a more satisfactory way of transforming the dollar into a different coin. They had called upon the resources of the industrial revolution by arranging with Messrs Boulton & Watt, of the Soho Works in Birmingham, that their powerful steam presses should obliterate the Spanish markings and should superimpose an entirely new design, English in character. By arrangement with the Privy Council the Bank of England dollar was first issued on 21 May. Its appearance called forth some comment, for it was a hybrid coin, bearing the King's head with a Latin inscription on one side, and on the other a seated figure of Britannia and the inscription 'Bank of England Five Shillings Dollar'. Boulton's work was most efficient and only very rarely are specimens found which bear any trace of the original design.

A rise in the price of silver had made these coins worth the five shillings at which they were issued, but some years later a further rise made them worth more than their nominal value. To stop them from being melted down, the Privy Council, in 1811, authorized the Bank to receive and issue them at 5s. 6d. each. Later in the year these dollars were supplemented by Bank tokens of 3s. and 1s. 6d. made from smaller Spanish coins; in the following year a fresh issue of the smaller tokens appeared, bearing a revised design. The general shortage of silver coin was also alleviated to some extent by tradesmen and others who had shilling and sixpenny tokens struck for them, and these enjoyed a considerable local circulation. From its nature – for it was an invasion of the State's privilege of being the sole coiner – this expedient was never liked by the Government and in July 1812 the use of such local tokens was prohibited. Persons having them in their possession or attempting to circulate them after 25 March 1813 became liable to a fine of £5.

Concern at the high price of gold bullion and the unfavourable state of the exchanges led to the appointment, in February 1810, of a Select Committee of the House of Commons which became known as the

Bullion Committee. Its Report, in June of that year, adversely criticized the Bank's policy, attributing the country's currency difficulties mainly to an excessive issue of paper: it maintained that a paper currency which had ceased to be convertible into gold or silver coin could not be kept up to its proper value except by a limitation of its quantity. The only remedy, the Committee considered, was the speedy repeal of the law suspending cash payments and it suggested that this should be done in two years' time. The Bank, as such, had not been consulted, though the Governor, John Whitmore, and his Deputy, John Pearse, had given evidence, in the course of which they had argued that, with the exchanges as they were, repeal of the Suspension Act would drain the Bank dry. It would be best to wait for peace and then consider the position.

The findings of the Committee were largely based upon the views of David Ricardo, a shrewd enough man of business, but, as a theoretical economist, apt to be blind to what was happening under his nose – for example, the fact that the country was at war. The Bank's opposition to the Report's proposals was backed by the Chancellor, Spencer Perceval, who informed the Governor in December 1810 that he and his colleagues entirely dissented from the Committee's recommendations. The Report was debated in the House of Commons in May 1811, when Perceval had his way. Sixteen resolutions embodying the findings of the Report were rejected and the House then approved a further series of resolutions which refuted the findings. These resolutions declared that the high price of bullion and the unfavourable exchanges were due not to an excessive issue of bank-notes, but were, rather, the result of Napoleon's Berlin Decrees, excluding British trade on the Continent, the interruption of trade with the United States, poor harvests and great expenditure on the war. The House agreed that the restriction should be removed when 'compatible with the public interest', but not, in effect, while hostilities continued.

The Government never ceased calling for heavy advances during the war's later stages and these went on even after the abdication of Napoleon on 3 April 1814. The resumption of cash payments was therefore still deferred, and even after Waterloo resumption was postponed for another two years to give the Directors time in which to make such preparations 'as to their discretion and experience may appear most expedient'.

The final seal was placed on victory by the repeal of the tax which had been equally obnoxious whether called Income Tax or Property Tax. It had proved so unpopular that its records were ordered to be destroyed. The consequent loss of revenue meant that the Bank had to afford further help to the Government. A loan of £3 million at 3 per cent was agreed and the Bank's capital was increased to £14,553,000 by adding 25 per cent to the holding of each proprietor of Bank stock. In addition, the Directors were required to pay quarterly into the Exchequer all sums in excess of £100,000 held by them on account of unclaimed dividends.

By 1816 the Mint, in its new premises on Tower Hill, and equipped with up-to-date machinery, was at last able to resume the coining of silver. When the new coins were ready in February 1817 the Bank set about calling in its tokens for 3s. and 1s. 6d. The issue of the new coinage caused difficulties closely resembling those which had attended the recoinage of 1696. Tradesmen would not accept thin and worn silver for fear that they would be unable to recover its face value. This made for stagnation in all trades and in September 1816 there was rioting in Hull and Sunderland. As in 1696, the Bank could do nothing about accelerating the actual manufacture of the new coinage, and since in those days it had no provincial branches, much as it would have liked to help, especially in those parts of the country where severe unrest and distress had developed, its hands were tied. However, it did what little it could: notice was given that 'plain' coins, provided they were English, would be accepted at Threadneedle Street, and crowds thereupon flocked to exchange their smooth shillings and sixpences for what they regarded as the more satisfactory bank-notes and tokens.

In 1817 the Mint started coining gold, making sovereigns of the one pound silver value which the old guineas had been meant to have but had failed to keep. Half-sovereigns were also minted. Henceforward the silver standard was abandoned and the gold standard took its place. Bi-metallism continued to be debated, but the difficulty of adjusting the relative values of gold and silver coins was no longer anything but a matter of academic interest. In 1817 £4,275,000 of the new gold was coined and in 1818 £2,862,000.

It had been hoped that these supplies of new coinage would be sufficient to make the resumption of cash payments possible, but it was not until 1821 that this was ultimately achieved. An unfavourable turn in the exchanges, drains of gold abroad and the need for heavy imports of wheat in 1817 and 1818 were all factors contributing to the delay. At long last by an Act of 1819 the Directors were given power to resume cash payments on 1 March 1822, but since the situation permitted it, a further Act was passed, at their request, giving them this power earlier, that is, on 1 May 1821. Bank of England notes for £1 and £2 were discontinued and were not issued thereafter except during a short period of crisis in 1825.

If at the start of the restriction in 1797 the Bank's Directors had been told that it would continue for so prolonged a time, they would have found it almost incredible. It was the negation of all they meant by 'credit'. But they came gradually to learn that credit did not rest on an entirely material basis. They conducted their business throughout the war and its aftermath on a foundation of inconvertible paper, with the aid of regular notes of small denominations, and found at the end that their credit was still unimpaired.

The Napoleonic Wars occasioned an interlude in the Bank's domestic history which was colourful in both senses of the word. This was the formation of the Corps of Bank Volunteers. War had been going on for five years and expectations of a French attempt at invasion were general when, in April 1798, the Governor, Thomas Raikes, suggested to the Court of Directors that it would be 'expedient to arm the Servants of this House to be employed for the immediate defence of the bank'. The Directors agreed and a 'Military Committee' was formed to wait upon the Secretary for War, Henry Dundas, later Viscount Melville. Royal approval was forthcoming and by 28 May the Committee was able to report that 503 of the clerks had signed a declaration of willingness to serve, that the regiment had been formed on 10 May and that the men were to be clothed in scarlet coats with green facings (one of which is on display in the Bank Museum) and white Kerseymere waistcoats and breeches. This uniform, together with an undress one, was supplied at the Bank's expense. The commanding officer, second in command, and eight captains of companies were commissioned from among the Directors. The junior officers were members of the clerical staff, and John Soane, the Bank Architect, was appointed quartermaster.

The formation of these Volunteer units, of which the Bank's was only one among many in the City, caught the interest of the public, and it was not long before the print-shops, those popular galleries of the time, were displaying etchings of Bank Volunteers and others among the reproductions of cartoons and caricatures, by such artists as Gillray and Rowlandson, which made up their regular stock in trade. The first recorded coloured etching of a Bank Volunteer was published on 31 October 1798 by H. Middleton. It was followed by three further such etchings, published by the artist, P. Whitehead, on 1 January 1799. On 15 February 1799 Rowlandson himself included the figure of a Bank of England Light Infantryman in his series of 'Loyal Volunteers of London and Environs' published at Ackermann's Gallery.

By 21 June 1799 the Corps must have been considered fit to attend a ceremonial parade, for with other Volunteer Companies it was inspected by the King, and on 2 September following, at a special parade at

Lord's Cricket Ground, the Regiment was presented with Colours by Mrs Thornton, wife of Samuel Thornton, MP, the Governor. The Colours were consecrated by the Reverend Richard Lloyd, Rector of Midhurst, and due respect is still paid them, for, after a thorough restoration in the 1930s, they now hang in the Bank. They display no false shame regarding the more permanent occupation of those who bore them, for a pair of bankers' scales feature prominently in the design, which, as might be expected, gives Britannia the place of honour as the central figure. Thomas Stothard, RA, was privately commissioned to paint the presentation ceremony in oils. The choice was not a completely happy one, for Stothard's gifts lay in the delineation of the delicate and graceful rather than the heroic: his painting is therefore a charming one, but not really suited in style and manner to a martial occasion. The subscription was inadequate, so the Bank bought the painting, which still hangs in its Parlours.

The Regiment was disbanded in May 1802 after the abortive Treaty of Amiens. Twelve months later war broke out again. Napoleon threatened invasion, which he commemorated in advance by a medal, and the Corps was immediately reconstituted on lines similar to the previous ones. No less than 430 clerks at once volunteered and 120 more were recruited in the following August. A number of porters were enrolled as pike men at the same time. A recruitment of 550 from a staff then numbering between seven and eight hundred seems to indicate that every clerk who was not incapacited by age or infirmity gladly came forward, and there is certainly no suggestion in the records that any form of compulsion was exercised. The sceptical may murmur that such suggestions are not in the habit of appearing in official records and may prefer to point to the diary of Samuel Harrison, a clerk elected to the service in 1806, who somewhat ambiguously says: 'I had to join the Bank Volunteers.' He also describes how the Regiment paraded at 6 a.m. in the Royal Exchange, then marched, sometimes to Moorfields, sometimes to the Shepherdess Fields, Hoxton, where they exercised. The members returned, left their arms in the Bank Armoury and then breakfasted in a coffee-house.

The main function of the Regiment during the years when invasion was likely was to cover the removal, should it prove necessary, of the Bank's gold and silver, books, printing presses and other paraphernalia, from Threadneedle Street to a destination in the country. Wagons were supplied by the Government through Sir Brook Watson, the Commissary-General. In January 1804 it was estimated that fifty-five covered wagons, capable of carrying three tons each, would be needed. The plans for the operation provided for a clerk to be in charge of each wagon, with four members of the Bank Corps as escort. Various tests and other 'evacuation' exercises were carried out during the years when the threat was at its height. After Trafalgar, in 1805, the danger passed, but the Corps was maintained in a state of efficiency until 1 July 1814, when the arms were returned to the Tower Ordnance, except for 100 muskets which were retained in the armoury of the Bank in case they should be required for its defence. The Regiment was then disbanded, though the Directors made arrangements for the porters and messengers to continue being trained in the use of arms.

Once again, a great war had led to a great expansion of the Bank's work and a corresponding growth of the staff. The extra work arising from the issue of notes for £1 and £2 and the increasing number of Government stocks registered at the Bank were the main causes of the urgent need for more clerks. Suitable applicants were not coming forward in the required numbers, so in 1799 the Court of Directors ordered that at each election not more than one-sixth of the vacancies should be reserved for the sons of clerks with a service of fifteen years and over – the limit was fixed in order that the privilege of nomination held by the Directors should not be invaded. The introduction of this practice, which was, of course, greatly appreciated by the family men among the staff, led in time to a number of cases in which several generations of the same family served the Bank. The longest record is held by the Maclaines, whose service has been continuous since 1804, except for a short break from 1839 to 1842. A representative of the sixth generation is at present working in the Bank. Other families can show a continuity of service over five, four and three generations.

Accompanying the various increases in the clerical staff since the days at Grocers' Hall there had been corresponding though smaller increases in the number of porters and watchmen. During the first fifty years or so in Threadneedle Street there was a slow growth in the numbers of both porters and watchmen and by 1790 there was a total of twenty-six. Then, in the list for 1791, there is a reference to an entirely new category, viz. 'Day Porters, 11'.

The day porters, to whom the term 'Office Messengers' was later applied, were to be in attendance from eight o'clock in the morning until five o'clock in the afternoon and part of the order appointing them provides that 'the said day porters be furnished with coats and badges'. Apart from the seventeenth-century orders regarding the dress of the Gate Porter this is the first reference to any form of livery for the non-clerical staff, and in the opinion of the present writer the distinctive and unusual dress of pink coat and scarlet waistcoat, remarked upon by almost every visitor to the Bank, dates from this time.

Various theories have been advanced to account for so striking a combination of colours. The most popular has always been that they were derived from the livery of some early Governor, Sir John Houblon's name being frequently mentioned. This seems no more than a romantic fancy. How Sir John clad his manservants is unknown; moreover, there is no record anywhere that the Bank porters and watchmen of the eighteenth century ever wore a livery, but with the appearance of messengers in public offices during business hours a distinguishing uniform would become necessary.

Early in the nineteenth century the Bank's system of 'dual control' was introduced; under it no single official or clerk has sole control over any item of monetary value. The immediate cause of the system's introduction was the discovery, in 1801, of extensive frauds by Robert Aslett. Aslett, a protégé of the famous Chief Cashier, Abraham Newland, had himself become prominent in the Bank's service. He had been a competent and energetic Secretary to the Special Committee of 1783, had been appointed Assistant to the Chief Cashier in 1793 and in 1799 had succeeded to the post of Second Cashier. It was the general belief that he was Newland's all but inevitable successor.

Aslett's mode of life was simple and inexpensive, but obsessed by a desire to amass money in emulation of his chief, who had built up a large personal fortune over many years, Aslett began speculating in the funds. He was either inapt or unlucky and in order to make good his losses he stole from the Bank. Under the system then obtaining, he had no difficulty in abstracting Exchequer Bills amounting to some £200,000, and he lodged a number of these as security for an advance with a Mr Bish, a Lottery Office Keeper of Cornhill. Unfortunately for Aslett, Mr Bish was an observant man who noticed that the same bills had already passed through his hands and had been lodged at the Bank. He informed the Directors and Aslett was questioned by the Deputy Governor, after which he was arrested and imprisoned in the Poultry Compter. Bills for £16,000 were found in his desk, but others which he had used as security for advances cost the Bank £78,000 to redeem. Nor was this all, for other Receipts to a value of £224,000 had also been stolen by him.

When Aslett appeared for trial in May 1803 – 'plainly dressed in a bottle green coat, white waistcoat and black silk breeches' as *The Times* reports – he was fortunate in that the prosecution had some doubts as to whether a conviction could be obtained because of certain technical points of law: there had been various irregularities in the original issue of the misappropriated bills and the defence might have been able to turn this fact to advantage. The trial was therefore postponed. There was an immediate outcry in the Press, which declared that it would be scandalous if a Deputy Chief Cashier in the Bank's own service and a confessed thief of half a million sterling should escape the penalty of his crimes 'while a poor culprit purloining a Bank Bill of £1 value must inevitably expiate his offence on a gibbet'. Later he was put on trial for embezzling the effects of the Bank and was found guilty, but the sentence of death was never carried out and he remained a prisoner in Newgate. The reason for the delay cannot now be discovered, though the Bank had the ear of the authorities and with very rare exceptions, according to its lights, it has always tried to be generous, this side of profligacy, to all its sons, even its prodigals. In 1810, and again in 1814, Aslett petitioned for his release to the Directors and the Government, but without success. In 1820, however, he was pardoned on condition that he quitted the country, after which no more is heard of him.

Because of the ease with which Aslett had stolen so large a sum, it was ordered that in future all documents of value should be accounted for by at least two persons, each holding different keys, one of which would be ineffective without the other.

The concluding chapters may now be written of a long story that has been appearing intermittently in these pages – that of the acquisition of the present island-site and the building of the 'Old Bank' raised upon it by Sampson, Taylor and Soane successively.

In September 1788, Sir Robert Taylor had died and John Soane was appointed Architect in his place. The first work he undertook was the completion of the offices which were being built where St Christopher's Church had once stood. Meanwhile, always with an eye to the future, the Directors continued to buy up property in the still unacquired north-eastern angle between Lothbury and Bartholomew Lane, and in 1793 they secured an Act which enabled them to purchase all the premises in that area which still remained in other hands. For the protection of the whole area enclosed within Threadneedle Street, Bartholomew Lane, Lothbury and the old Princes Street, Soane constructed the first of his famous screenwalls, work on which began in 1795 and ended in 1797.

While this work was going on the Directors knew that, when complete, it would still be insufficient to solve their problem of accommodating a much-expanded staff, and that they must therefore look even farther outwards. In February 1799 they decided to acquire a large estate in Tokenhouse Yard, north of the Bank and on the opposite side of Lothbury, but this project never got beyond being discussed, for a more ingenious plan was adopted. This was to obtain Parliamentary sanction for the acquisition of properties adjoining the Bank to its north-west and to have Princes Street straightened and widened, when the new plot of land could be included within a rebuilt wall. The Bank would then, given proper alertness, enjoy physical security of a very high order indeed: all its offices would be protected from rioters and other marauders by a strong, high, blank wall, while the danger of fire would be greatly lessened, for the existing Princes Street was so narrow that should fire break out on its western side the flames might all too easily leap across to the Bank.

The desired Act was obtained, being passed on 30 June 1800, though the inevitable delays at the hands of legitimately aggrieved or ransom-seeking leaseholders had still to be overcome. It was not until 1805, therefore, that the Lothbury wall was extended to the present north-west corner, there to be lovingly knotted, as it were, to a similarly extended Princes Street wall by means of Soane's justly famous Tivoli Corner.

In 1814, Soane drew the attention of the Directors to the dilapidated condition of the stonework of Taylor's south front, but he had to wait until 1823 before it was agreed that the whole of this front be rebuilt 'from beyond the gate in Bartholomew Lane, and nearly to the gate in Princes Street'. This work, which included some alteration to Sampson's centre, was completed by 1828, and the exterior of the Bank acquired the uniform appearance and familiar aspect which it was to wear for the next hundred years.

Soane's name will always be connected with the 'Old Bank', which contained so many of his masterpieces of architecture. It is sad that when the Bank, no longer able to grow laterally, had perforce to expand in the only directions possible, upwards and downwards, much of his work and of his predecessors' should have been either destroyed or embedded, and so to some degree lost, in a much larger and differently conceived structure. But he himself never hesitated to remove or adapt the work of former architects, so perhaps his shade, though grieved, did not complain too violently when circumstances demanded that a similar fate should overtake his own. His was a unique and mysterious genius: without descending to mere trickery he was a master of illusion. In some strange way any space which he enclosed became fluid, the same hall or chamber seeming to become two or three different ones according to the angles from which it was viewed. Like all 'originals', he made his own rules.

Sir Herbert Baker, who designed the present building, says in his autobiography *Architecture and Personalities* that it was 'in the ingenuity of his designs of domical vaulting and domed sky-lights that Soane excelled', and in many of the existing banking halls the domes and

86

skylights call up, for those who once worked in it, the elegant and gracious atmosphere of the old Soane Bank.

After his retirement and death minor changes made over the years by succeeding architects rarely, if ever, improved what he had done. He was knighted in 1831 and resigned his Bank appointment, at the age of eighty, in 1833. He died four years later, leaving his patrons a magnificent treasure-house, almost formidably plain outside save for one exquisite decoration, Tivoli Corner, while inside there was an intricate and beautiful Daedalian labyrinth of halls, courtyards and corridors.

The Bank now stood on the threshold of its golden age, when for nearly a hundred years it was to be a world-wide symbol of wealth and safety, literally able to honour its promises to pay with gold itself. The country, too, was about to enter an era when, relative to the rest of the world, it was to wield its greatest power and majesty. Through its Navy it was to impose the long *pax Britannica* that would endure, with only minor disturbances, until 1914, when the world burst into flame, to burn or smoulder ever since. Britain's first Empire, in America, had dropped off from its own weight, but she was to build another and a greater, which was not to go through a parallel process until our own times. The island's population was to grow enormously and new markets were to open for British goods and money both at home and abroad.

The great transport engineers of the eighteenth century – Brindley, Metcalfe, Telford and Macadam – had covered the land with a system of roads, bridges and canals as fine as any in Europe, and the short-lived age of the stage-coach had already begun. Rich City men, even then, were able to 'commute' between London and Brighton, and the coach routes also awakened many sleepy towns in the Home Counties, where a new kind of inhabitant settled whose labours lay outside their confines. Soon, however, the Stephensons, Brunel and others were to harness steam, giving mankind a greater mobility and a greater restlessness. Fast freight trains were to bring about a relative stagnation on the canals, while the new steamships were to open up prospects of an overseas commerce undreamed of in earlier days, when even the proposal to dispatch a single trader under sail to the South Seas could help to bring about a great financial crisis. South America, for example, had thrown off the yoke of Spain and offered vast though speculative fields for investment.

The Bank was ready for the new age. Now more than a hundred years old, it confidently looked forward to the next hundred. It had withstood many buffetings and had come through them sturdier than ever. It had earned the grudging respect of its enemies and critics and the staunch admiration of its friends and supporters. And this was not only among those directly engaged in finance and commerce: the public at large now regarded it as a great and permanent institution, one sign of which was that it had been given a familiar nickname – the Old Lady of Threadneedle Street.

On 22 May 1797 a cartoon by James Gillray had been published which showed Pitt attempting to gain possession of the Bank's gold from an indignant dame seated upon a strongbox labelled 'Bank of England'. It was entitled 'Political Ravishment: or, The Old Lady of Threadneedle Street in danger'. Any earlier use of the nickname cannot be traced; the credit for its invention possibly belongs, therefore, to Gillray himself, though he may have taken the idea for the cartoon from Sheridan, who, in a speech in the House of Commons, had referred to 'an elderly lady in the City, of great credit and long standing who had . . . unfortunately fallen into bad company'.

The name would not have become so universally used and recognized if it had not summarized with a sort of affectionate cruelty, as most nicknames do, certain outstanding characteristics. Like many a well-to-do old lady, the Bank seemed proud but not arrogant, self-assured but not stubborn, shrewd but not grasping. If she was rarely ungenerous with her help, she was perhaps on occasions considered a little too generous with her good advice when giving that help.

Chapter 6

The Nineteenth Century I

Of the many generalizations that have been made about nineteenth-century Britain, a few may be accepted with reasonable safety. As a pioneer of the Industrial Revolution, the country reaped all the advantages, enjoyed all the benefits, made all the mistakes and suffered all the miseries inherent in that historic role. The mistakes and miseries were chiefly caused by the ever-swelling population's too rapid change from being a mainly rural to a mainly urban one. The immense overall growth in prosperity was neither steady nor evenly distributed; it was therefore accomplished at a cost of great social unrest, nearly reaching the flash-point of revolution at home and actually reaching it abroad: at the same time, the strain of financing the roaring expansion of trade and industry led to many commercial and financial crises, all to a greater or lesser degree involving the Bank and modifying its policies. Nevertheless, the nineteenth century was above all an age of hope. One bright strand always gleamed amid its predominantly drab fabric – a belief in the ultimate perfectibility of man by this or that 'reform' of his institutions.

One institution certainly in need of reform at the opening of the period was the criminal law. It was Draconian in severity and the Bank became intimately and unhappily caught up in one aspect of its workings. A convicted forger of a bank-note was hanged, while anyone found guilty of possessing a forged note was sentenced to transportation. The smaller £1 and £2 notes had not only been easier to imitate than those of higher denominations but easier to pass into circulation as well. As a result, the gallows claimed a host of victims. The Directors were in a distressing position: in their fiduciary capacity they could not fail to prosecute a detected forger and, if the prosecution succeeded, they could only stand by and watch a law they had not made take its horrible course, yet there is evidence to suggest that, as humane and sensitive men, they were on occasion as sickened by the whole disgusting business as anyone else.

Their position would have made them appear hypocritical and absurd had they publicly ranged themselves beside such reformers as Sir Samuel Romilly who were advocating the abolition of capital punishment for minor felonies. They therefore had to bear in silence tirades of abuse in the Press and elsewhere, being stigmatized in a contemporary periodical, *The Black Dwarf*, as 'grand purveyors to the gibbet' and 'priests of Moloch's blood-stained altar'. In January 1819 George Cruikshank's macabre and horrifying 'Bank Restriction Note' was published; at first glance a replica of a bank-note, it displayed with savage realism a string of bodies, both male and female, hanging from a gibbet, felons in chains or behind bars and the Bank's Britannia devouring a live infant. Cruikshank was to claim later that his 'Note' had led to the abolition of the death penalty for forgery – with the forgivable vanity of most successful propagandists he probably claimed too much, but he had undoubtedly helped to whip up public indignation to a ferocity which enabled the active reformers, such as Romilly, to force through the necessary Parliamentary measures.

The Directors did all they could to alleviate the sufferings of offenders and, from a legalistic viewpoint, even more than they should. Whenever possible, on the excuse that the evidence might be too weak to support a charge of actual forgery, they would acquiesce in the accused's pleading guilty on the 'lesser count' of possessing, until it was conveyed to them by the authorities that by doing so they were compromising the Royal Prerogative of mercy and interfering with the course of justice. They also made application to the Secretary of State that men sentenced to transportation should be allowed to take their families with them to Botany Bay, and frequently made grants of money to convicted women so that they might not be penniless on the voyage or suffer unduly while in gaol awaiting transportation.

The fact remains, however, that between 1797 and 1829 an estimated total of 618 persons were capitally convicted of forging bank-notes and that the large majority of these unfortunates were hanged. The death penalty for this offence was abolished in 1832 and transportation for life substituted.

Therefore, for reasons both financial and humane, the Directors ceased issuing the smaller notes as soon as they could, that is, when sufficient supplies of the new sovereigns had become available. There was no great display of public satisfaction at the decision; many now preferred notes to sovereigns, being less worried by the theoretical 'unsoundness' of the one than by the real inconvenience of the other – more easily lost, in many ways more difficult to handle and liable to be mistaken for shillings in the dark.

So far as any one point of time can be regarded as marking an important historical change, it was in the early 1820s that the general structure of banking in this country began assuming its modern form. The Bank of England was about to enter into a century-long debate, not only with others but with itself, as to whether it was a State bank or a private institution making as much profit as it decently could while enjoying at the same time certain advantages over its competitors because some of its functions and privileges were those of a State bank proper. With its exact nature undefined, its position often illogical and its interests sometimes divided, all that can be said of it – though that perhaps is enough – is that usually it worked very well. Its fear and jealousy had always been most sharply aroused by any threat that a banking house of comparable magnitude might be established, but the age of joint-stock banking was about to begin, with results familar to all of us today, while the Bank itself was to go through the first stages of its long and sometimes painful metamorphosis into a nationally owned central bank.

In 1825 there was another financial crisis. It arose chiefly from a wave of speculation during the preceding eighteen months or so – over 600 joint-stock companies had been formed, many of them being wildcat South American mining schemes. A great many country bankers, caught up by this wave, had grossly overissued their notes, and there were consequent large withdrawals of gold from the Bank. In the summer of 1825 the prices of commodities began to fall. At the end of November the failure of a number of large cotton firms caused at first alarm and then panic. The London Bank stopped payment, bringing down sixty other financial companies with it. Sir Peter Pole & Co. (Pole, Thornton, Free, Down & Scott) were in difficulties on 5 December. They approached the Bank for help and although some was given it was insufficient to prevent the firm's failure on 17 December. They were agents for a large number of country banks – forty-four in all. In addition to Poles, five other London banks stopped payment. By then the Bank of England's reserve of gold had been reduced to about £1¼ million, but it continued to grant what accommodation it could by increasing the note issue, and in the last week of the crisis, as a further measure to relieve the drain on coin, it put back into circulation a number of the withdrawn £1 notes: most of these went to country bankers. The Bank was almost forced to suspend cash payments again, the worst strain coming during the week from Monday the 12th to

Saturday the 17th, when the Court of Directors sat on five days out of six, but at last, through the good offices of Rothschilds, they began obtaining some much-needed gold from Paris and the danger passed.

By the end of the year seventy-three of the principal banks in England and Wales had ceased payment. Some recovered later, but thirty-seven issuing banks went bankrupt, together with a number of those not issuing notes. Immediately the panic had subsided Lord Liverpool and his Chancellor, F. J. Robinson ('Prosperity Robinson', later Viscount Goderich), held an inquest on the crisis. They considered the advantages of permitting the foundation of large joint-stock banks: this would mean withdrawing the Bank's privileges granted by the Act of 1708, under which it was the only banking company with more than six partners, but finally they recommended the opening of branches by the Bank itself in different parts of the country.

The Directors had simultaneously referred the question of opening branch banks to a Special Committee, which within a week had reported that this course was highly expedient. It would greatly increase the Bank's own note circulation, would give it much greater control over paper money of all kinds, would probably lead to a large increase in deposits, and would help to protect the Bank against the competition of 'large banking companies' should the Government encourage their formation – which it was obviously thinking about doing. So far as the public was concerned, there would result a better circulation and an easier transmission of money, and it would have at its disposal a number of widespread, perfectly secure places of safe deposit.

In the end the Government decided to have the best of both worlds. The ensuing Act of 1826 made a major breach in the privileges which the Bank had worked so hard to acquire, and had always fought strenuously to protect, by limiting the Bank's monopoly in the future to within sixty-five miles of London and making possible the foundation of joint-stock banks with more than six partners outside that limit, such banks having the power to issue their own notes. At the same time the Act authorized the Governor and Company of the Bank of England to 'empower agents to carry on banking business anywhere in England'.

Whether or not the Act, in its entirety, was to the satisfaction of the Bank, it had at any rate settled the question of branch banks and the Directors at once set about establishing them. The first branch to be opened was in Gloucester, from which city an assurance had been received, in April 1826, that one would be welcomed, as there had been 'considerable inconvenience and distress from the failure of banks in the surrounding districts'. This branch started business on 19 July 1826, and was followed by branches at Manchester and Swansea, which were opened on 21 September and 23 October, respectively. In 1827 the Birmingham, Liverpool, Bristol and Leeds branches were opened, as well as one at Exeter, though here the Bank's arrival was much resented and in 1834 its business was transferred to Plymouth. A branch at Portsmouth was also opened in 1834.

Meanwhile joint-stock banks were also coming into existence, though rather more slowly; as yet they were, in law, large partnerships only, the liability of every partner being unlimited. Four were started in 1827, at Huddersfield, Lancaster, Bradford and Norwich, none in 1828 and seven in 1829, of which two were in Manchester and one in Birmingham. The most interesting development was in Somerset, where a private banker of Langport, Vincent Stuckey, gradually built up a large banking firm not only by opening branches but by absorbing four or five other banks in which he was a partner, thus showing how banking might evolve from the private into the joint-stock phase.

The large number of failures among small banking concerns, many of them badly managed, which had occurred during the war and the ten years following it had undoubtedly contributed to the large increase in the number of accounts kept at the Bank of England: in 1823 they numbered just over 850, a figure which had grown to nearly 4,000 ten years later. In 1825 customers were given improved facilities, a further cause of the Bank's increasing popularity. Those cashing cheques, for example, now received any notes they might require directly across the Drawing Office counter instead of being given a ticket which had to be taken to another office where it could be exchanged for the notes. Another concession was the reduction of the minimum amount – from £10 to £5 – for which cheques might be drawn. In 1830 cheque books were introduced; they contained 50, 100 or 200 forms, replacing the single pieces of 'cheque paper' which had hitherto been considered sufficient to meet the needs of the customers.

Around the year 1830 there took place one of those great upheavals which have altered the course of our constitutional history – the country-wide agitations, ugly enough for a while to look like the opening stages of a civil war, which were the prelude to the passing of the great Reform Bill of 1832. The storm raged at its fiercest in the capital and some of its blows were inevitably felt by the Bank. In 1830 labourers in the southern counties were marching through the countryside demanding a living wage. In October 1831 riots broke out in London and other large towns, with great damage to property and, in Bristol, even with loss of life. In November troops stood by at the Bank and arrangements were made for fifty clerks and some of the porters to supplement the usual military guard. The particular meeting of reformers which, it was feared, would lead to dangerous rioting was, as it happened, called off and no collision occurred. The Duke of Wellington was universally regarded as the arch-enemy of reform and when in May 1832 he had again come into office the reformers pursued other and less violent tactics: they issued a poster reading 'To stop the Duke, go for gold', and this led to a heavy run on the Bank, so severe that £1¼ million in gold was paid out in a few days. Wellington abandoned his attempt to form a Government; Earl Grey was returned to power and the Reform Bill became law on 7 June.

One of the first acts of Lord Althorp, Chancellor of the Exchequer in Grey's ministry, was the appointment of a Committee of Secrecy to inquire into the question of the renewal of the Bank's Charter, together with a grand inquiry into the 'existing system of banking by Banks of Issue in England and Wales'. The evidence given in this inquiry throws much light on banking history and the policy of the Bank of England: there was a general demand for more public information about the Bank's affairs. Against all precedent, the Report and the evidence leading to it were ordered to be printed; this caused a rapid fall in the price of Bank stock. On 16 August 1832 a specially convened General Court was held, when the accounts which had been rendered to the Secret Committee were submitted to the Proprietors. At a further Court, held on 20 September, the Proprietors expressed their complete confidence in the Directors.

In 1833 the Bank Charter was extended to 1855, but one clause of the Act extending its Charter was very strongly contested by the Bank. This permitted the establishment of joint-stock banks in London 'and within 65 miles thereof', provided that they were banks of deposit only and did not issue their own notes. The Bank and its legal advisers contended that the clause infringed its existing privilege of exclusive banking, which should, they urged, be interpreted as a prohibition of all joint-stock banks in London and its environs, whether they issued notes or not. Althorp and his advisers were convinced, however, that under existing statutes such non-issuing joint-stock banks were legal and refused to give way. When the Bill passed into law, the prospectus of a London joint-stock bank had already been prepared and was thereupon published: it was that of the London and Westminster Bank.

A further clause was, however, highly satisfactory to the Bank – that which exempted from the usury laws all bills and notes with less than three months to run. Since it enabled the rate of discount on bills of this kind to be raised, in case of necessity, above the 5 per cent which had been its legal limit since the days of Queen Anne, it made the rate an altogether more effective instrument for currency stabilization: a

Minute of the Committee of Treasury records, in 1841, 'that the modification of the Usury Laws has contributed greatly to the security of the Bank, and is essential for the proper management of the circulation'. The Act of 1833 thus prepared the ground for the radical reshaping of the banking world of England and Wales which took place in the eleven years between the passing of that Act and of the next Charter Act in 1844. By that year the Bank of England stood at the centre of the system. (It is of interest to note that the term 'central bank' seems to have first appeared in a work published in 1830, where it was used to designate a bank which would be the 'depository of all wealth' in a socialist community.) Around the Bank of England were the London private banking firms, some sixty in number, and to these must be added the new non-issuing joint-stock banks, the first of which, the London and Westminster, has already been mentioned. Among others which opened offices in the City during the period under review were the London Joint Stock Bank and the National Provincial, together with joint-stock banks having Imperial connections, such as the Bank of Australasia, the Royal Bank of Australia and the Bank of British North America.

Though it had thus come to stand in a special relationship with all other banks and bankers, it would nevertheless be far from correct to regard the Bank of England of those times as a central bank in the modern sense of the term. In the previous century it had attained special prominence by becoming Banker to the Government and Registrar of Government Stocks; with the reform of the old Exchequer it was now to all intents and purposes the Exchequer itself, from a technical as opposed to a political viewpoint, and it was also to an ever-increasing extent the bankers' bank, gradually coming to be regarded as the lender of last resort. It was still, however, an open and acknowledged competitor in the banking field, and whether it was to prove a help or a hindrance in the building up of a really stable country-wide banking system was yet to be determined.

As for the old Exchequer, with its roots in the days of the Norman kings, its last remnants were swept away by the reforms of 1834. The Auditor, the four Tellers, the Clerk of the Pells and a host of picturesquely named but now useless subordinates were thrust into oblivion and all moneys hitherto paid into the Exchequer were paid into the Bank and credited to the 'Account of His Majesty's Exchequer'.

During this period also the essential importance of a sound note issue, as an element of monetary stability, was increasingly recognized. Behind all the arguments for and against the continuation of local note issues, the fact was clearly emerging that their usefulness was passing, if not over. With better communications, trade was no longer confined within

95

narrow bounds. Goods could now be sent to all parts of the country and of the world. Trading would therefore best be served by there being only one note-issuing body, whose notes would be legal tender throughout the country – and Bank of England notes, it will be remembered, were already legal tender under the Act of 1833.

Horsley Palmer, Governor from 1830 to 1833, and one of the more outstanding holders of that office, made no secret of his opinion that mastery of the circulation should be vested in the Bank. In 1831 he told the Governor of the Bank of Ireland that it was his wish to get the law altered so as to concentrate issue for England and Wales in the Bank of England and for Ireland in the Bank of Ireland: he would also have liked to see Scotland giving up its multifarious issues for one central one.

The years between 1833 and 1836 were prosperous: harvests were abundant, commerce and manufacture expanding. In 1836, a peak year, there was the first real railway boom. It was also an outstanding year for Anglo-American trade, but at its end a fresh crop of difficulties was to arise from this. The United States was buying and borrowing to excess and its banking system was at the same time being vigorously reformed – not before this was due – by President Andrew Jackson. His reforms necessitated the laying down of a strong basis of gold. Much of this was obtained by the sale of American securities in England, while many of the new joint-stock banks had found an outlet for their resources by purchasing American bills in large amounts with the intention of rediscounting them. The Bank Directors, wishing to check the resulting drain of gold and any further extension of credit, especially to America, announced in September that they would not discount any bills bearing the endorsement of a joint-stock bank of issue.

One of the first houses in difficulties as a result of the Bank's decision was the Northern and Central Bank of England, a mushroom growth of considerable size, only three years old, deeply involved in American investment. Its headquarters were in Manchester and it had thirty-nine branches and agencies. In November it applied to the Bank for a loan, which was granted, probably because the Directors recognized that the failure of so large a bank might cause a general panic: they therefore advanced £500,000 on condition that the Northern and Central closed all its branches and agencies forthwith, except those in London and Liverpool. As this help proved insufficient, a further advance of £870,000 was agreed, on terms that were even stiffer. The Directors of the Northern and Central were to assign all their securities to the Bank and permit an inspection of their accounts. The inspection, carried out by two Bank of England Directors, revealed that the business had been conducted recklessly and that misrepresentations had been made when application had first been made for an advance. The Bank had to take entire control and with much difficulty collected a committee of shareholders to help in a liquidation. It had safeguarded its own position and, in the end, saw that the depositors were paid in full. The shareholders of the Northern and Central were the only losers: its Directors and their friends owed the company large sums, but they could safely ignore their obligations, for, as the law then stood, shareholders and Directors were partners alike, and on the plea that one partner could not sue another for debt, they escaped.

Those in the greatest trouble, however, were the 'American Houses', a group of firms, English or Anglo-American, which were all closely concerned with the flotation of American loans or the financing of American trade. Their difficulties became so pressing that in March 1837 the Bank agreed to advance them £6 million against bills drawn on American firms. This was to lead to its sending an agent, J. W. Cowell, at that time agent of the Bristol and Gloucester branches, to the United States to inquire into the debts due from there. He and an assistant, M. B. Sampson, later to become City Editor of *The Times*, remained in Philadelphia during 1838 and the spring of 1839, collecting the debts and negotiating with American banks. The liquidation of the advance to the 'American Houses' was therefore a long and complicated process, but in the end the Bank recovered all but about £200,000 of the large sums it had originally advanced.

It was generally recognized, as an earlier historian of the Bank, A. Andreades, has put it, that 'unlimited freedom of issue was a danger to a country exposed, by its exceptional position as the commercial centre of the world, to the effect of crises occurring in all the other markets of production and consumption'. For the first time the suggestion was made that the Banking and Issue Departments of the Bank should be separated, so that the Bank's function as 'manager of the circulation' should be distinct from its ordinary banking business. It was also proposed that the Bank's note issue should be regulated by the principle that a suitable and defined ratio should be maintained between the amount of bullion held and the value of the notes in circulation.

The subject was discussed at great length and with the aid of multitudinous evidence by Committees appointed by the House of Commons. It was not, however, until after Sir Robert Peel had become Prime Minister that the talking stopped and some real moves were made. It had been a great Tory Prime Minister, William Pitt, who had spurred the Bank on into playing its part in the overthrow of Napoleon, and it was Peel, another great Tory Prime Minister, who was to open up for it the stimulating prospect of new, great responsibilities.

When Peel came into power in 1841 the first task he had to undertake, before he could turn his hand to anything else, was to remedy the acutely unsatisfactory state of the public finances. His expedient, the temporary reimposition of the hated Income Tax for three years, has remained with us from that day to this, though not at the 7d. in the £ then deemed extortionate.

It was, therefore, not until January 1844 that Peel could direct his attention to the Bank and to the question of the country's whole banking system. By a clause in the 1833 Charter Act the Government were empowered to suspend the Bank Charter on giving one year's notice within six months after 1 August 1844. Peel was in communication with William Cotton, the Governor, and J.B. Heath, the Deputy Governor, and he and the Chancellor of the Exchequer, Henry Goulburn, discussed with them, between January and April, questions relating to the Charter generally and, in particular, the possibility of a 'single issue' and the suggested setting up of separate departments for issue and for ordinary banking. Some correspondence followed, but on 3 May the Court consented to the conditions imposed in consideration of the Charter's renewal up to 1 August 1855. The previous pattern, set by the 1833 Act, was followed in that, thereafter, the Charter might be terminated at any time, on twelve months' notice, if the debt owing to the Bank by the public were repaid. There was little opposition in Parliament and the new Charter Act received the Royal Assent on 19 July 1844.

The Act embodied the principal reforms which had been suggested: issue was to be kept 'wholly distinct from the general banking business' in a separate department to be called 'The Issue Department'; the Bank would issue notes against securities appropriated to this department to a maximum value of £14 million, of which the Government debt of £11 million was to form the main part. Beyond the £14 million, notes might be issued only against gold coin or gold and silver bullion transferred from the Banking Department, and the silver could not exceed in value one-fourth of the gold.

Regarding other banks, none was to issue its own notes unless that had been its previous practice: banks in England and Wales retaining the privilege could issue only up to fixed limits, calculated on the average issue of the twelve weeks preceding 27 April 1844; a lapsed issue might not be resumed and a partnership, should its numbers rise above six, would forfeit its right to issue. Under the Act, seventy-two joint-stock banks and 207 private banks retained the privilege of issuing notes, to a total of some £8½ million. The intention of the Act was, however, gradually to eliminate from circulation in England all notes except those of the Bank of England, an aim that was at last, though slowly, achieved.

Provision was made for compensating those country bankers who had previously arranged with the Bank to discontinue their own issue: other bankers who surrendered their right to issue were to be compensated also. On the cessation of issue by any bank the Bank of England might, under an Order in Council, increase its own issue, against securities, up to two-thirds of the amount of the notes so abandoned. Under these arrangements, the final figure at which the authorized issue of the Bank stood was £19¾ million, the rights of issue of all other banks in England and Wales having been surrendered. This was not to be for a long time, however – it was not, in fact, until October 1921 that the last country bank to issue notes lost its right to do so.

A few provisions of the 1844 Act, regulating English banking, remain to be mentioned. The Bank of England was required to publish a weekly summary of accounts. It was released from the payment of stamp duty on its notes, in consideration of an addition of £60,000 to the £120,000 it already paid the Government annually in this connection. All persons would be entitled to demand notes at the Bank in exchange for gold bullion at the rate of £3 17s. 6d. per ounce of standard gold. All joint-stock banks, though carrying on business in London or within sixty-five miles thereof, might draw, accept and endorse bills of exchange except those payable on demand.

Despite the small opposition to the Bill in Parliament, doubts had been expressed as to whether it was elastic enough – the rigidity to which issue was confined might, it was suggested, actually lead to anxiety and perhaps even panic in difficult times. Nothing in the Act itself would check a drain of gold should there be a bad harvest causing the import of grain, yet it would prohibit the Bank from repeating the openhanded issue of notes and granting of loans by which it had overcome the crisis of 1825. In three years' time the validity of these objections was to be tested.

When, save for some small embellishments and alterations, Soane had completed his work, the men conducting the Bank's business behind his great screen-walls faced the tasks which lay before them in the nineteenth century in convenient, spacious and beautiful surroundings. The nominal owners, the Proprietors, were almost entirely English; the Dutch, who during the eighteenth century had found the Bank a good investment, had practically disappeared from the registers of Bank stock. With other Europeans they had, up to as late as 1811, made up one-tenth of all the holders, but in the twenty years following Waterloo they had sold out, and by 1835 there were no more than sixty-three foreigners among the 2,846 Proprietors. The Directors continued to be recruited from traditional sources, the great London merchant firms which had been the strength behind the Bank from its beginnings. The staff had declined in numbers. From the 1,000-odd it had reached in 1820 it fell to 870 or so in 1830, around which figure it remained for ten years, and even after that rose very gradually: it reached 900 in 1860. The chief reason for the reduction was the abolition of the £1 and £2 notes. The clerks whose services were no longer required when the small notes were abolished were given generous pensions.

After the reduction of staff there was a revision downwards in the salary scales. Maximum salaries for the various posts were cut and so were the annual increments by which these maxima were gradually attained, but perhaps as a reward for the prolonged patience these revisions demanded a special allowance of £30 a year was introduced, payable to those of thirty years' service and upwards. Payments for certain special duties were retained, but in 1823 these were also reduced: such reductions were, however, usually imposed only when an existing recipient died or resigned or was promoted to a better-paid position. Overtime payments earned during the war had, of course, ceased and this, with the other cuts, soon placed a number of clerks in financial difficulties: at first, these cases were treated leniently and loans, repayable by small instalments, were granted free of interest.

Clerks were expected to stay as long as the business of their offices required, but the normal hours were by no means long. Attendance was from 9 a.m. to 3.30 p.m., or to 5 p.m. should an optional one and a half hours be taken 'for dinner'.

In 1830 the Directors decided to reduce the large number of 'holydays' observed by the Bank, for long complained of by customers and others having dealings there. 'To prevent the interruption of business' it was ordered that the Bank should in future be closed on eighteen days only during the year instead of the forty-two days then customary. The loss of twenty-four holidays was serious enough, but in December 1834 matters became far worse, not to say intolerable, when the staff lost practically all that remained. It was then announced that the Stock Offices would be open to the public for the transfer of stock and the receipt of dividends on every weekday except Good Friday, Christmas Day, 1 May and 1 November. Bad as this was on the face of things, it was even meaner in practice. The clerks could not be denied spending Christmas Day in the bosom of their families, or Good Friday, for these were 'holy days' by Act of Parliament, but on 1 May and 1 November

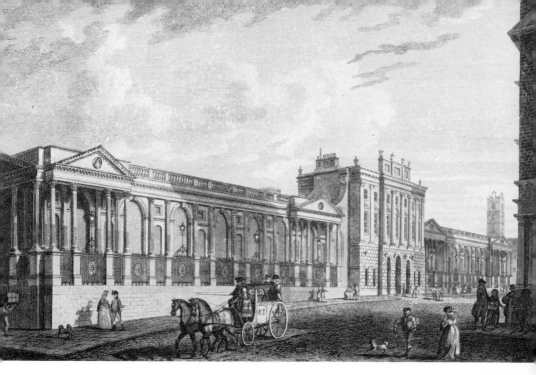

The Threadneedle Street front of the Bank in 1797, with George Sampson's gateway and Sir Robert Taylor's screen walls

Sir Robert Taylor's Statue of Britannia, originally on the pediment of the Pay Hall

Bowler Miller, a Clerk in the Bank from 1744 to 1796. After a painting by Thomas Thompson

The Pay Hall, or Great
Hall. From the drawing
by A. Pugin and
T. Rowlandson, 1808

Daniel Race, Chief
Cashier 1739–75. From
a painting by
Thomas Hickey

the offices were closed to the public merely to enable the staff to strike a half-yearly balance in the ledgers without interruption. This ill wind did blow some good, however, for the closing of the Stock Offices on these two days led to their being observed as genuine holidays on the Stock Exchange.

For ten years no compensatory 'leave of absence' was granted in any form, so it is perhaps hardly surprising that the records show the period as one in which careless work, insubordination, quarrelling and fighting were rife. Opportunities for relaxation were few and, had they existed, luxuries of any kind could scarcely have been afforded by those whose only incomes were their salaries. *Punch* in 1842 described bank clerks as 'the hardest worked, the worst paid and the most polite body of men in the metropolis'.

On top of all this, the leniency shown to clerks in financial difficulty was withdrawn in 1836 when the Court of Directors ordered that bankruptcy would occasion dismissal: this must have had its effect on some of the clerks who had been given leave to carry on their own business. The frequenting of public houses, smoking and singing were offences which might lead to dismissal: a clerk whose principal reported, in 1842, that he was 'a smoking, singing, public house man' and another, in the same year, reported on as one whose 'habits are evidently those of a smoker and drinker', were both required to resign, even though, in the second of these cases, it was admitted that the offender had 'not been seen in a state of intoxication'. In the circumstances it seems as creditable to the staff as it was undeserved by the Directors that in the course of these long and dismal years cases of actual dishonesty were few.

A new and better spirit blossomed at the time of the Bank Act of 1844, although no connection can be traced between the Act itself and the reforms instituted soon after its passing. It seems that the Directors had at last realized that the best work is obtained from a contented staff, and although the regulations were made somewhat more rigid, with a view to excluding all but those of a high character, the conditions of service were made more attractive. A revised scale of salaries came into being in 1844, which considerably improved the pay of new entrants, the salary at the age of twenty-one being doubled, from £50 a year to £100: the maximum attainable was, however, left unaltered. But the greatest amelioration came in 1845, with the introduction of a scheme for leave of absence for periods varying from six to eighteen days each year according to length of service. These absences were granted at the discretion of the Governors, so a clerk on holiday since that time has always been recorded as being on 'Governors' Leave', not 'on holiday'.

In 1852 the allowances were increased, clerks with over twenty-five years' service getting eighteen days annually, and those with less, twelve: cashiers and principals of offices were allowed one month.

There was an improvement in the hours of work after 1848, in which year the City bankers came to a general agreement that public business should cease at 4 p.m. This time applied to Saturday as well as the other days of the week and it was not until 1860 that a further agreement was reached to close early, at 3 p.m., on that day: this was altered to 2 p.m. in 1886 and to 1 p.m. in 1902, when the modern 'weekend' of at least a day and a half free from business can be said to have been established. The Stock Exchange had started early closing on Saturdays in 1843, but in the Bank only the clerks in the Stock Offices felt the benefit of this.

The improvements in pay and leisure made in 1844 and the following years were accompanied by new and stricter regulations. In 1847 clerks were forbidden, on pain of immediate dismissal, from entering into bill transactions: this veto was fully justified, for judging by many incidents in the tales of Thackeray, Trollope, Surtees and other contemporary novelists, the guaranteeing of a bill could often be a highly dangerous form of friendly gesture, leading the innocent into entanglement with the bailiffs, if not worse.

The strong Victorian reaction against the feverish gaming which had disfigured the eighteenth century and the Regency was reflected in another order, made in 1850, forbidding betting, subscribing to sweepstakes or gambling transactions of any kind, even the inoffensive raffle being prohibited, and the penalty for infringement was liability to instant dismissal. These regulations were properly designed to suppress serious irregularities, though they may sometimes have tended towards an undue severity, but others betray, at least to modern eyes, rather too keen an inclination to interfere with private behaviour, although the penalties here were not so drastic. In 1846 clerks who smoked cigars during the hours of business, or lighted them before quitting the Bank's precincts, were warned that they would 'incur the displeasure of the Court', while in a memorandum book of the period there appears an order to which justice can be done only by quoting it in full:

Officially announced that the Authorities have seen a disposition upon the part of certain Bank clerks to wear moustaches; that they strongly disapprove of the practice, and that if this hint be not attended to, measures will be resorted to which may prove of a painful nature.

History is silent, however, on the question of whether the upper lip of any clerk was ever forcibly deflowered.

Considering that one of the charges most frequently made against the Bank is that it has always been too bound by tradition, it is interesting to find how often it has been a pioneer – to take one example, it is to be found early in the field of activities commonly known today as 'welfare organization', through which every business of any size encourages voluntary societies and associations, both provident and recreational, for the benefit of its staff. In many quarters, up to the end of the nineteenth century and beyond, it was regarded as the sole duty of an employer to pay his employees regularly, in exchange for their faithful and diligent services. What they did with their leisure (provided it did not meet with his disapproval) or what provision they made for themselves and their families against sickness, age, misfortune and death was held to be no concern of his and certainly called for no expenditure by him of his time or money. Yet the first of the Bank's staff associations were founded, with the full support and approval of the Directors, well over a hundred years ago. These were the Library and Literary Association and the Bank Provident Society.

The Library was established in 1850 and is therefore the doyen of the numerous clubs and societies, providing exercise, entertainment or relaxation, indoors and out, which now flourish within the Bank. Acting upon a suggestion made by William Smee, the Chief Accountant, to the then Deputy Governor, Thomson Hankey, the Court of Directors approved its formation on 15 February and made a grant of £500 for the purchase of books, besides authorizing the use of rooms over the Gold Weighing Room, overlooking the Bullion Yard, and the cost of fitting and furnishing them in a suitable manner. The Association's first President was Matthew Marshall, the Chief Cashier, and Mr Smee was appointed Treasurer. The annual subscription was fixed at 10s. and this remained the basic subscription, for two books at a time, for over a century. At the present time the Library contains 26,000 volumes, of which 8,659 are works of fiction. It has 1,865 members, including 787 women.

In 1850 free public libraries, as understood today, were practically unknown, and the establishment of a lending library within the Bank met a pressing need. By a coincidence, it was in 1850 that Parliament first gave local authorities the power to levy a rate for the establishment and maintenance of public libraries.

The Bank Provident Society was founded in 1854. As long as ninety years before that, in 1764, a Fund for the maintenance and relief of the clerks' widows and orphans had been established, but this had been done purely on the initiative of the clerks themselves. Subscriptions had been received by four of the Bank's principal officers, chosen as trustees, and had been invested in the public funds, to provide an income for the payment of annuities of £20 a year. The qualification was that the deceased husband should have been a subscriber for 'ten years and one day' from 10 October 1764. Later, the Directors had supplemented this arrangement: in 1791 they had instituted a fund of their own, the Directors' Charitable Fund, to which certain grants were made and to which the payment of an annual donation of £500 had been ordered. The funds thus accumulated had afforded pensions, ranging from 7 to 12 guineas a year, according to the length of the husband's service. In 1801, and again in 1807, the subscription rates to the Clerks' Widows Fund were revised, though the £20 pensions were not raised. The allowances from the Directors' Fund were, however, increased from time to time, and in 1807 they varied between £27 and £45 a year. In 1831 the Clerks' Fund was reconstituted, under new rules, as the Bank Annuity Society.

Upon its foundation in 1854 the Bank Provident Society took over the funds of the old Annuity Society. The new Society was a savings association, paying interest on deposits, and it also undertook Life Assurance business. Interest at 4 per cent per annum on the amounts of the premiums paid was guaranteed by the Directors, and in 1857 clerks, immediately upon election, were required to take out an assurance for £200 on their lives. This made necessary the appointment of a medical officer, and it so happened that a man well fitted for that position was already residing within the Bank's walls. This was Alfred Smee, who lived with his father, William Smee, the Chief Accountant, an occupant of official quarters. Since 1840, Dr Smee had been paid for occasional medical services. After the establishment of the Bank Provident Society he conducted medical examinations of candidates for life assurance. In 1857 he was appointed permanent Medical Officer to the Bank and thereafter received an annual salary until his death in 1877. He was a remarkable man, of a lively and inquiring mind, whose memory lingered in Threadneedle Street long after he had died. He was elected F.R.S. in 1841 at the early age of twenty-three, and was a pioneer of electro-metallurgy: most of the work which made him famous in this field was done while he resided at the Bank. He was remembered among the staff for his 'Cholera Mixture', made up to his prescription as a specific against this foul and dangerous disease which so often ravaged a then insanitary London: bottles of the mixture were kept in the Gate Porter's Lodge where, during an epidemic, doses could be obtained on application. A more lasting memorial was the 'Bank Ink', compounded according to a formula of his. Officially its use was obligatory, but with the entry of the fountain pen the more fluent proprietary inks were used, and this was tacitly allowed. Nevertheless, it was a magnificent, solid ink and it was used for the Court Minute Books until comparatively recent years. Records made with it remain jet black to this day. It was almost as thick as soup, smelled of vinegar, and using it was rather like writing with mud. Beside the inkwells small vessels were placed, containing a heap of lead shot immersed in water. Stirred in these, the clogged pens were cleared.

The Threadneedle Street premises remained largely unaltered during the whole of Queen Victoria's reign and for thirty years afterwards, apart from adjustments in the use of space already available. One such adjustment concerned that noble feature of the old Bank, the Rotunda. Since its erection in 1765 it had been allowed to serve as a market for buying and selling stocks, and even after 1801, when the members of the Stock Exchange had opened a building for themselves in Capel Court, this use, or misuse, of the Rotunda continued, being mainly confined then to jobbers and to those brokers who had not obtained membership of the Stock Exchange Association. The bustle and confusion of this market is admirably depicted in a water-colour drawing by Thomas Rowlandson now in the Bank's collection. The dealers made themselves very much at home, not hesitating to go behind the counters in the Stock Transfer Offices in order to consult the ledgers, or even to enter transfers of stock for themselves: a succession of orders in 1788, 1801 and 1806, forbidding them to do so, were ignored. In 1806 it was reported that these denizens of the Rotunda were 'by no means of a reputable description, consisting in general of persons who will not subscribe to the Stock Exchange or have been excluded, female jobbers and idle persons'.

In 1825 this unruly throng began invading the Bank Stock Office; here they were repelled, to some extent, in the following year, but they were not dislodged from the Rotunda itself for twelve years after that. At last, in April 1838, its floor had to be relaid, and the opportunity was seized to exclude the dealers while this work was being done. The desks and tables they used were removed and T. A. Curtis, the Governor, instructed the Head Gate Porter that they were not to be readmitted. Acres states that the Governor's decision was probably not unconnected with the burning down of the Royal Exchange a few months earlier; some brokers had lost their offices because of this, and had then made the confusion in the Rotunda worse confounded by using it for meeting with their clients.

The Governor's decision was much resented, but as the dealers could not get at him they vented their ill-feeling on the unfortunate Bank porters. In November one Matthew Costan created a scene by refusing to leave when requested and assaulting one of the porters who had been ordered to eject him. He was prosecuted and fined £5, after which there was no further trouble, but Mr Curtis remained very unpopular and when, in 1841, he was declared bankrupt, three cheers were called for on the Stock Exchange.

The exodus of the dealers resulted in some much-needed space becoming available for use by the actual owners of the premises, and in 1840 the Rotunda was converted to the use of a Dividend Pay Office. This enabled the work of the Private Drawing Office to be transferred from the Great Hall, where it was very limited for space, to the office, erected by Soane from Taylor's plans, which stood on the former site of St Christopher's Church, at the junction of Threadneedle Street and Princes Street, and hitherto used as the Dividend Warrant Office.

Though the Bank was little changed during this period, there was some change among the streets and buildings around it. On the night of 10 January 1838 the Royal Exchange was destroyed by fire, as its predecessor, Sir Thomas Gresham's original Exchange, had been in the Great Fire of 1666. Old Bank Buildings on the angle of Threadneedle Street and Cornhill were saved at the time, largely by the exertions of Bank officials and porters, but the City Corporation was subsequently empowered by an Act of Parliament to improve the approaches to the new Exchange, and as one of the means of doing so it was given authority to purchase Old Bank Buildings and demolish them, which would leave the triangular plot of ground to the west of the new Exchange as an open space. The present Royal Exchange was opened by Queen Victoria on 28 October 1844, when the Transfer Offices were shut for the day and other business at the Bank ceased at noon. In the same year, when the triangular space to the west had been cleared and looked very much as it does today, the statue of the Duke of Wellington was set up; the Bank had contributed 100 guineas towards its cost in 1838.

While Charles Robert Cockerell was Architect to the Bank there occurred the curious episode of the man who got into the gold vault by way of the sewers. There seems little reason to doubt that something of the kind actually happened, though official records, if not entirely silent, are understandably discreet. The story has enjoyed many versions in print and a highly imaginative one was given, some few years ago, in a film, *The Day They Robbed the Bank of England*. The incident was probably rather more humdrum than some of the stories built around it. The most widely accepted one goes that a sewerman discovered an old drain which ran immediately under the bullion room. He had a highly developed sense of honesty and a highly developed sense of drama, too. He therefore sent an anonymous letter to the Directors offering to meet them in the bullion room at any hour they pleased to name, and the rendezvous was duly arranged for some 'dark and midnight hour'. At the appointed time a noise was heard from beneath the floor, some boards were displaced and the man emerged to confront the astonished Directors. Nothing had been taken and the honesty of the discoverer of the 'secret passage' was rewarded with a substantial sum, most accounts agreeing that this was £800.

Whatever the truth may be, the records show that in February 1839 Cockerell wrote to the Building Committee that: 'In May 1836, having had reason to apprehend danger from our sewers, it was discovered that an open and unobstructed sewer leads directly from the gold vaults down to Dowgate', and that in April 1836 the Secretary of the Bank applied to the Commissioners of Sewers asking for plans of the sewers and drains under and around the Bank premises. Application was also made, in 1837 and 1838, to George Baily, Curator of the Soane Museum in Lincoln's Inn Fields, to return the plans of the drains beneath the Bank which had been retained by Sir John Soane. After this, nothing more is mentioned about the matter, so it would seem that no further weakness was discovered.

The year which saw the passing of the 1844 Bank Act was a prosperous one for England, but the Act's power to check too violent a boom or too profound a depression was shortly to be tested. Three abundant harvests had resulted in money being plentiful and available on good terms. Railway investment in particular attracted a large amount of capital from seekers of easy fortunes and many became the victims of unscrupulous promoters. An Act of Sir Robert Peel's had, by the strictness of its terms, discouraged these pirates from roving what would have been, save for his foresight, the lucrative seas of joint-stock bank promotion, so when the 'railway mania' was at its height in 1845 the country's banking system was happily spared any corresponding forays.

Shortly after the Bank Act had become law the Court of Directors decided that the discount rate – soon to be generally referred to as 'the Bank Rate' – should be fixed weekly. It has been seen how, in 1841, the Committee of Treasury had recorded its view that the modification of the Usury Laws, by the Act of 1833, was essential for the proper management of the currency, and it was hoped that by fixing a weekly rate with no upper limit dangerous fluctuations in the amount of discounts held would be eliminated. A weekly review would also permit the Directors to exercise a greater influence on the flow of gold in and out of the country.

To stem a current loss of gold by the Bank, caused in this instance largely by the 'railway mania', the rate was raised in November 1845 from 2½ to 3½ per cent. This had the desired effect and in August 1846 the rate was lowered to 3 per cent. But in the meantime the failure of the Irish potato crops in 1845 and 1846 had made necessary the import of large quantities of corn, which had to be paid for in gold, and from September the Bank's reserves suffered a steady drain. In January 1847, somewhat belatedly, Bank Rate was raised to 4 per cent and on 10 April to 5 per cent, by which date there was less than £10 million of bullion in the Bank and the reserve in the Banking Department had sunk to £2½ million. To prevent a possible panic and check the demand for notes, it was decided to discount short-dated bills only, to limit the amount of bills accepted and to refuse the renewal of advances. This 'squeeze', as it would now be called, staunched the outward flow of gold and in early May the pressure was relieved, at any rate for the time being.

Soon, however, the persistent heavy fall in the price of wheat, owing to excessive imports on the one hand and the prospect of a good harvest on the other, led to several bankruptcies in the corn trade, including those of some firms in which Bank Directors were partners. William R. Robinson, who had been elected Governor the previous April, the senior partner of Robinson & Co., Sir John Reid, a partner in Reid, Irving & Co., and Abel Lewes Gower, a partner in a firm of Mauritius merchants, all had to leave the Court when their firms failed, and elections were held to fill their places – James Morris, the Deputy Governor, was elected Governor in Mr Robinson's place. There had never before been, in Clapham's words, such commercial slaughter among the Directors, though Sir John Reid was not the first ex-Governor to go through the Bankruptcy Court – it will be remembered that T. A. Curtis had once suffered that fate. For the honour of Mr Robinson's firm it must not go unrecorded that it eventually paid 20s. in the £.

These failures in the corn trade began in early August 1847. On the 5th, Bank Rate was raised to 5½ per cent. Between August and October further failures involved some £15 million. On 1 October the Bank announced that the 5½ per cent rate would apply only to bills due within the month; others would be discounted at 6 per cent or more. It was also decided that, for the time being, no further advances would be made on the security of Government stocks or Exchequer bills. Holders of Government securities, unable to borrow on them and in urgent need of cash, were forced to sell at the best prices they could get. A general panic ensued, manifesting itself at its worst on the Stock Exchange, where the price of Consols plunged and Exchequer bills were at a heavy discount: no possessor of hard cash would part with it. The failures spread from the commercial houses to the banks, both private and joint stock, principally in the north and west of England. Eleven in all went down, the most serious failure being that of the Royal Bank of Liverpool, which had a paid-up capital of £800,000. The worst-hit places were Liverpool and London, though the London banks did manage to stand firm.

The merchants, bankers and traders of London and deputations from Liverpool and the industrial towns made repeated requests to the Government to suspend the Bank Charter Act, but the Chancellor of the Exchequer, Sir Charles Wood, refused to do so. The Prime Minister, Lord John Russell, considered that Government interference in the form of permitting the issue of more notes might postpone distress, but would only aggravate it in the long run. The week from 16 to 23 October saw the crisis at its height. On the 23rd, when the banking reserve was down to £1,194,000, the Government could no longer refrain from acting, and it told the Bank that if the amounts of its discounts and advances could be increased, at a rate, it was suggested, of not less than 8 per cent, a Bill of Indemnity would be forthcoming if the Bank issued notes beyond the statutory limit.

With this announcement the panic subsided. Once money was available the former hoarding of it ceased and the banking reserves swelled rapidly until they reached safe amounts. Bank Rate, which, according to the Government's suggestion, had been raised to 8 per cent on 23 October, went down to 7 per cent on 22 November, to 6 per cent on 2 December and to 5 per cent on the 23rd. The letter authorizing the issue of notes above the statutory limit had meanwhile been withdrawn, on 23 November. £400,000 worth of additional notes had been prepared against the emergency, but it had not been necessary to use them.

Subsequent investigations into the causes of the crisis were made, at first in the House of Commons and later by Committees of both Houses. The Chancellor of the Exchequer declared that the panic in the spring had resulted from the failure of the Bank Directors to raise the discount rate and from the subsequent decision to limit the scale of discounting at a time when there was already uneasiness at the low state of their reserves. Sir Robert Peel also blamed the Bank. Speaking in defence of his 1844 Act, he said that the Government might never have had to authorize its violation 'if the Bank had possessed the resolution to meet the coming danger by a contraction of its issues, by raising the rate of discount, and by refusing much of the accommodation which they granted between the years 1844 and 1846'. Giving evidence before the Committees, the Governor and Deputy Governor admitted that the

Bank had acted mistakenly in the spring of 1847 in not raising the rate of discount sooner; they, too, were against any alteration of the 1844 Act. The Committee of the House of Commons also came to the conclusion that no alteration was necessary, and although the Lords' Committee disagreed and recommended changes to provide specifically for such emergencies as the recent one, attempts to persuade Parliament to alter the Act were unsuccessful.

Danger of another kind next threatened the Bank. The violent stresses set up by the Industrial Revolution in the fabric of nearly all European societies made 1848 a classic year of revolt by the workers, whose miseries formed the darker side of the rapid growth in wealth and industry. In England this movement took the form of Chartism. A civil war, establishing a new Commonwealth, was widely feared – or hoped for – when, at their convention in London on 3 April, the Chartists decided to present a monster petition to Parliament on the 10th of that month. Supporters were to assemble on Kennington Common and to march in procession to Westminster. Recollections of the outcome of a similar march, some sixty-eight years earlier, could not fail to arouse great uneasiness in the City.

The years which had elapsed since the Gordon Riots had, however, seen many changes. On this occasion the Government saw to it that adequate precautions were taken in advance and, with the Duke of Wellington in charge, their measures were effective ones. Troops were stationed at strategic points to defend the bridges, and the police force, which Peel some ten years earlier had so efficiently reformed, was strengthened by the enrolment of about 200,000 special constables, whose numbers included, incidentally, all able-bodied members of the Bank staff. Public buildings were put into a state of defence, particular attention being given to the Bank. The island site made this far easier than on the earlier occasion. The Company of Royal Sappers and Miners, with four officers of Royal Engineers, took up their quarters at the Bank on the morning of Sunday, 9 April. On the entablature of the outer walls they speedily erected, by means of sandbags, a system of loop-holed parapets, with wooden projections to give direct and flanking fire. At selected positions on the roof massive wooden constructions were built, with embrasures for cannon. The sand had been carted into the courtyards on the previous day, but as there was not enough to fill all the bags, the gravel of the paths in the garden was dug up and used. Special precautions were taken with the gateways, the one in Princes Street being permanently bricked up, in which condition it remained until 1882.

Fortunately all this trouble was for nothing. As it has done before and since, the English weather took a hand in the shaping of history. The 10th April was a very wet day and the Chartist ardour was damped from the outset. When those who did turn out found their way barred at the foot of the bridges they quietly dispersed and the monster petition tamely ended its journey to the Houses of Parliament in three 'four-wheeler' cabs. This was the end of Chartism – though not of the anger and resentment which provoked it. The temporary defences at the Bank were dismantled two days later, to be replaced in due course by Cockerell's permanent ones.

Competition from the joint-stock banks after their establishment in London, in 1833, spurred the Bank into making many improvements in the conduct of its day-to-day business. The restriction on the drawing of cheques for under £5 had been abolished in 1838, and in 1841, when the Drawing Office could take advantage of the increased space made available by its move from the Pay Hall to the reconstructed Dividend Warrant Office, customers were permitted to pay direct into their accounts instead of having first to go to the Teller and obtain a 'ticket' from him in exchange for the amount being deposited and then proceed to the Drawing Office counter to pay in the ticket. In 1846 the introduction of printed credit slips, filled in by the customers and enabling them to pay in several items in one lump, must have saved much tedium and irritation both for the counter clerks and for the customers waiting to be attended to.

The work of weighing all gold coins received and separating the light ones from those of proper weight was laborious, and the introduction of a machine which performed the two operations in one, with speed and accuracy, was of great help to the Bank. It was invented by William Cotton, a Director, and Governor for the three years 1842, 1843 and 1844. A number of his machines were installed in 1843 after a working model had proved satisfactory: this model was made by D. Napier & Son, a firm famous for its precision machinery. The sorting-out of light gold coins is a process seldom called for in the Bank today, but one at least of William Cotton's machines still stands ready to perform its ancient task, whenever required to do so, with all its accustomed efficiency.

The machine enabled the Directors to notify the public in 1843, in accordance with a Royal Proclamation dated 1 October, that all gold coins tendered at the Bank on and after 1 January 1844 would be cut, broken and defaced should they fall below the legal weight. Some time before, in June 1842, the Government had arranged with the Bank that light gold should be received there at £3 17s. 10½d. per ounce, and that gold coins below a certain weight must be withdrawn from circulation. Bankers at that time therefore gave credit for gold paid into them according to its weight alone, with the result that many people carried pocket scales or balances; it also became common practice for shop-keepers to deduct twopence for every grain they found short in the gold coins tendered them.

Improvements in bank-note printing continued to receive considera-tion and one of these was the printing of notes from electrotype in relief instead of plate printing from plates engraved in recess. The idea was originated by the Bank's versatile medical man, Alfred Smee. His experiments in electro-metallurgy had produced what he called his 'chemico-mechanical battery', more commonly referred to as the 'Smee cell', and the steadiness of its current made it particularly suitable for electrotyping work. Investigations on these lines went on for a number of years until, round about 1850, the introduction of a newly designed note was once more considered. Daniel Maclise, RA, was commissioned to submit a new vignette of Britannia. Maclise was a much-admired producer of immense overcrowded canvases of historic, dramatic and biblical subjects, but he was a superb draughtsman. In his vignette he adhered to the general tradition of the Bank's Britannia; he delineated her as bareheaded, seated full-face and armed with a spear. His vignette remained a distinguishing feature of the old black-and-white bank-notes during the hundred years or more which were to pass before their withdrawal. The first notes of the new design were issued in 1855.

Among other changes was the disappearance of the name of the Chief Cashier as payee, the notes now being made payable to 'the Bearer on Demand'. The signature was still that of one of the Bank's cashiers, but it was now printed, not handwritten. This, however, was not exactly an innovation, since the printing of the signature had been introduced a few years earlier. The new note also embodied improvements in the paper and the watermark.

Gold in ever-increasing quantities was being called for in order to finance the immense increase in world trade. The strides which had been made by scientists and inventors were immense, but they were not alchemists, and it was only the opportune discovery of the rich new goldfields of America and Australia that made possible the continuation of the currency on a gold basis: had the currency been dependent upon the chance finding of occasional nuggets and gold dust in scattered gulches and river beds, stability would have been lost and a painful deflation inevitable. It is some indication of the sudden growth in the world's supplies of gold that in this country alone, between the years 1851 and 1857, the quantity of gold coin in circulation increased by

30 per cent, reaching nearly £50 million at the close of that period.

The forty-year-long reign of peace was broken between 1854 and 1856 by the Crimean War and this was followed in 1857 by the Indian Mutiny. The first cost the country £70 million in money and 20,000 lives: the second ended the rule of the East India Company, when in 1858 its rights were transferred to the Crown. A drain of gold abroad began in June 1855, brought about by the needs of war and by the renewed importation of corn caused by bad harvests. The discount rate went up to 5 per cent on 27 September, to 6 per cent in October and remained high for the next two years, owing to a sustained and growing uncertainty which burst into a climax with the great crisis of 1857.

This commercial crisis had certain characteristics hitherto unexperienced. It has been recognized as the first really world-wide one in history, when the dangers rather than the advantages of a global network of transport and communication had to be faced. It broke out almost at the same moment in the United States, England and Central Europe, and its effects were felt in South America, South Africa and the Far East. It was sparked off in the United States in September 1857 when the Ohio Life Insurance and Trust Company failed, causing a panic in New York which quickly spread throughout the States. Between a quarter and a fifth of all British exports had been sent to the United States in 1856; in consequence there were many large open credits for American firms here and the effects of the American panic were soon felt. The bank failures in the United States were numerous – in October 1,415 stopped payment – and business there came to a virtual standstill. In this country Liverpool, then as now the main terminal of the north transatlantic trade routes, took the shock first with the failure, on 27 October, of the Liverpool Borough Bank. The Bank of England had foreseen its difficulties and had offered help to the extent of £1½ million on condition that the Borough Bank cease to transact new business and liquidate its affairs. The offer was, however, unavailing. In Glasgow, too, the collapse of a number of important firms created a panic and a run on the banks for gold: rioting was feared and the magistrates sent for troops. Large supplies of gold were sent to both Scotland and Ireland to forestall bank runs. On 12 October, Bank Rate went up to 7 per cent, on the 19th to 8 per cent and on 5 November to 9 per cent. On 9 November it went to 10 per cent; it had never previously reached this high point.

This almost savage policy certainly stopped the drain of gold abroad, but it put the London bill-brokers into serious difficulties and demands for advances were large both in number and amount. On the evening of 12 November the Government – Palmerston was then Prime Minister and Sir George Cornewall Lewis Chancellor of the Exchequer – advised the Governors that a Bill of Indemnity, on the lines previously adumbrated during the 1847 crisis, would be forthcoming should the Bank issue notes above the legal limits set up by the Act of 1844, always provided that the Bank Rate was not reduced below the 10 per cent at which it was then standing. The announcement calmed public excitement, but the demand for advances continued for a much longer time than it had in 1847. There were further failures in Birmingham and Leeds, and in Ireland there was a persistent run on gold. On Tyneside and in Teesdale, in Wolverhampton and Newcastle, cash for the payment of wages was found wanting: in Newcastle, indeed, the stringency was so severe that the Bank authorized its Agent there to make advances upon security 'not of a strictly banking character'.

Notes for £2 million in excess of the statutory limits were issued in the ensuing weeks, though the maximum value of additional notes in actual circulation was never more than £928,000: this figure was recorded on 20 November, but by the end of that month there was no excess at all. So far as money was concerned, therefore, the crisis had passed, but its adverse effects on commerce were felt considerably longer, while industry did not properly recover for an even longer time. Officially, the emergency ended on Christmas Eve, when Bank Rate was brought down to 8 per cent. By the following 11 February it was at 3 per cent, having descended by varying stages. As the country and the City licked their wounds they must have reflected that a world slump was a very different affair from one confined to Britain or Europe.

In December the House of Commons appointed a Select Committee to inquire into the operation of the 1844 Act and the 1845 Acts for Scotland and Ireland, an instruction being added to the terms of reference that inquiry should also be made into the causes of the recent financial and commercial distress and how far it had been affected by the laws regulating the issue of bank-notes. More than 5,800 questions were put to witnesses, but the study of world economics and finance was not at that time sufficiently far advanced for the Committee to reach any really sound or useful conclusions regarding the nature of the crisis they were examining. It reported that it was not considered necessary to unsettle the 'great principles' regulating the monetary system merely because the pecuniary relations between the Treasury and the Bank might require reconsideration, nor would any 'mischief' result from the Bank's retaining, at least for the time being, its powers under the 1844 Act.

In an appendix to its report the Select Committee considered the question of establishing a National or State Bank of Issue according to a proposal by David Ricardo, published after his death, and an examination of this plan by George Arbuthnot of the Treasury. The question had been referred to Lord Monteagle, who was against the proposal, his view being that a National Bank of Issue, charged also with banking functions on Government account, 'would rest on no defensible principle whatsoever'. He went further: he considered that 'the honour and independence of the Bank of England and the sense of duty invariably manifested by that great corporation . . . furnishes a security which may not always be found in a mere executive department of the State, bound to obey the commands of a superior authority'.

Monteagle's views carried great weight with the Committee and also had their influence on future Governments in their dealings with the Bank. So a nationalized Bank was still a long way off, but arguments in its favour were even then being heard and were serious enough to demand serious refutation.

Chapter 7

The Nineteenth Century II

In 1854 yet another great Chancellor of the Exchequer – William Ewart Gladstone – began his first term of office at the Treasury. On his entry into political life he had been a protégé of Peel's and, like his master, he took an interest not only in the broad principles of finance and commerce but in their smallest details as well. The son of a Manchester merchant of Scottish descent, he was a fervid preacher of the great Victorian gospel of thrift, and it was almost inevitable, therefore, that a Chancellor such as he should have a number of brushes with the Bank. The first was over the method of paying the dividends on the various securities inscribed at the Bank which formed the funded part of the National Debt.

The custom had been for the Treasury to credit the Bank with the whole amount of a dividend on the first day of the quarter in which it would fall due. If, for example, a dividend was payable in April, a Treasury Warrant for the total amount would be delivered to the Bank on the day following Lady Day – the relative traditional quarter-day – that is, on 26 March. The Chancellor's current funds would, in consequence, be severely depleted and, to carry him over, he would be obliged to borrow by issuing interest-bearing deficiency bills for the full amount involved. The Bank, of course, paid out in small sums to the various stockholders over a more or less prolonged period and the proportion of the total which at any time remained in its hands had always been reckoned as part of the moneys at its general disposal. Gladstone maintained that it was public money until actually disbursed. In April 1854 he therefore decided that dividend moneys would be provided only as and when they were needed, with the result that in the following October the Bank received a Treasury Warrant for an initial instalment of £4,718,000 instead of one for over £6½ million as previously.

Sir Robert Taylor's Rotunda,
when used as a Stock
Exchange. From a
drawing by Thomas
Rowlandson

Lothbury in 1797. Showing
Sir John Soane's North Front,
as completed prior to the
straightening of Princes Street.
From a drawing by
Thomas Malton

'The Old Lady of Threadneedle Street in Danger.' From a drawing by James Gillray, 1797

A Bank Volunteer of 1804. From a drawing by P. W. Tomkins

In the Bank's view the Chancellor was bound by statute to pay the whole amount on a prescribed date. Gladstone, however, regarded the Bank, in this matter, as a mere agent of the State and much resented that it should, as a servant, question the legality of its employer's decision. Nevertheless, after a long and contentious correspondence he agreed to take the opinion of the Law Officers of the Crown. They decided in his favour. An appeal by the Bank, which only increased Gladstone's fury, resulted in his views being again upheld, and the Bank at last surrendered. In the following year Gladstone left the Exchequer, and the Bank, still smarting under what it regarded as probably an illegality and, if not that, rather sharp practice, immediately approached his successor, Cornewall Lewis, on the point of law, but Lewis not unnaturally was loath to sacrifice the principle established by his predecessor and forgo the savings, small though they were, resulting from it.

In 1859 Gladstone returned to the Exchequer and once more busied himself with effecting all possible economies. In December 1860 he suggested a large reduction in the allowance which the Bank received for managing the National Debt. This had not been reviewed since 1808, when it had been fixed at £340 per million for the first £600 million and at £300 per million for anything beyond that amount. Gladstone suggested that these rates should be cut to £300 and £150 respectively. He also proposed the abolition of the yearly payment of £4,000 'House Money' which the Bank had enjoyed since its very first foundation in 1694, and of a similar yearly payment of £1,898 which it had inherited from the South Sea Company when it took over the management of South Sea annuities. In all these matters Gladstone had his way: the General Court acquiesced in his proposals on 7 February 1861 and the new arrangement became law in the same year. On his suggestion the Directors also agreed to shorten the periods of the quarterly 'shuttings', during which the ledgers were closed to transfers while the dividend warrants were being prepared, and to pay out dividends at the branches as well as Threadneedle Street.

This second spell of Gladstone's at the Exchequer, which lasted until 1866, was indeed marked throughout by a progressive strengthening of the Treasury's hands at the expense of the Bank. For one example, he set up the Post Office Savings Bank in 1861: his primary purpose was to provide places of deposit for the small savings of those members of the community who did not normally use the services of bankers, and by doing so he met a long-felt want, but by 1870 the Post Office deposits had reached £15 million and the ready accessibility of these funds to the Treasury also relieved him of the distasteful necessity of continually having to go to Threadneedle Street 'to beg'.

In 1863, as a result of the American Civil War, cotton had to be sought outside the United States – principally from India, China, Egypt and Brazil. World prices soared and a large drain of bullion to the East resulted. Bank Rate now rose swiftly from the low levels at which it had been standing for nearly two years. It was raised to 5 per cent on 2 November, to 6 per cent on the 5th, to 7 per cent on 2 December and to 8 per cent on the 3rd. It remained high during 1864. This particular upward movement of Bank Rate displayed an unusual feature. The rises were by 1 per cent at a time instead of the $\frac{1}{2}$ per cent which had previously obtained. This would seem to show that the Court had been influenced by the views of a young Director, George Joachim Goschen, who had been elected in 1858, at the age of twenty-six, and served until 1865. Goschen published in 1861, at first anonymously, his *Theory of the Foreign Exchanges*, advocating that when the Bank wished to affect the exchanges in order to attract gold an upward step of 1 per cent would work to cover the cost of transmitting bullion and that, once it was on the move, a further double step of 1 per cent would keep it moving. This change of policy was far from popular when introduced, but it certainly proved efficacious on this occasion, with the result that Britain escaped a collapse which occurred on the Continent. Goschen was to become Chancellor of the Exchequer from 1887 to 1892.

By 1864 the cotton famine was at its height and for two periods in that year – a fortnight in May and the two months from 8 September to 10 November – Bank Rate was at 9 per cent. The Bank's action in keeping the rate at so high a point during the latter of these periods won the approval of the foremost economic writer of the day, Walter Bagehot, who was editor of *The Economist* from 1860 to 1877. In his *Lombard Street* (published in 1873) Bagehot said that the high rate at that time had 'preserved the country from calamities which, if we had looked only to precedent, would have seemed inevitable. All the causes which produced the panic of 1857 were in action'.

Nevertheless panic came at last, though not until 1866. Even then it was due in the main not to any general deterioration in the financial situation but to the unexpected failure, on a large scale, of a single famous and long-established City house, a failure brought about by the folly and greed of men who, when they were brought to trial three years later, were solemnly admonished by the Lord Chief Justice, Sir Alexander Cockburn, for 'turning aside from the safe and settled path of business and going astray after vain phantoms and illusive dreams, embarking their capital in the wildest speculations and the rashest enterprises'.

These men – who, however much they may have deserved the strictures thus eloquently delivered, were found not guilty of fraud – had been the directors of Overend, Gurney & Co. Ltd, a firm which, during a large part of its existence as a private company, had worked in the closest association with the Bank, had stood next to it in the eyes of the City and, abroad, had been more highly esteemed than any similar company. On 1 August 1865 it had become a limited liability company. This step, though welcomed by *The Economist*, since it meant that the directors would in future have 'to publish an account of the nature of their business', was almost certainly ill judged; the obligation to publish accounts, if it did not actually occasion the firm's downfall, must have hastened it and, as Bagehot pointed out later, had Overends continued as a private partnership they need not have disclosed their losses, and if they had weathered their difficulties they could have quietly written these losses off against the eventual huge profits they might well have accumulated. As it was, the firm failed on 10 May 1866, with liabilities approaching £10 million.

The earliest record of Overends' association with the Bank dates from December 1829, since when they had been ranked among its most important customers. They had always styled themselves bill-brokers, but they were, in fact, much more than that – they were money-dealers on a large scale. The relationship had been constant, and side by side with the Bank they had come through the two great crises of 1847 and 1857. Afterwards, however, there had been some falling off in cordiality, the coolness arising from reasons connected with the second crisis. From certain lessons the Bank had learned during its course it had, in 1858, thought it advisable to withdraw some of the facilities previously enjoyed by bill-brokers in general. The brokers resented this, but though they had at first expostulated, they had all tacitly accepted the new position, save for Overends. At the time the firm was passing into the control of the men who eventually wrecked it – they determined upon a show of strength to 'punish' the Bank. In concert with the banking firms of Barclay, Bevan & Co. and Barnett, Hoares & Co., and with the assistance of their stockbrokers, Messrs Shepherd Bros, Overends effected the withdrawal from the Bank, on 9, 10 and 11 April 1860, of £1,545,000 in £1,000 notes. This came to public notice when the Bank return of 12 April disclosed that notes in the hands of the public had risen abruptly by £1,622,000 in the course of the previous week. The only immediate effect was the raising of Bank Rate from $4\frac{1}{2}$ to 5 per cent. Rumour went round the City, however, that Overends intended to embarrass the Bank by disturbing the currency. Alderman David Salomons, M.P., of the London and Westminster Bank and a proprietor of Bank stock, approached the Governor and, having learned from him that the Bank would not object, put down a question for answer in the House of Commons. It asked whether the Chancellor of the Exchequer could throw light on what appeared to be a concerted attack on the currency, and was down for reply on 19 April. On the 16th, Overends, through Barings, intimated that the notes would be returned that evening if the Bank would modify the discount rule it had introduced in 1858. These overtures were met by an uncompromising refusal.

On 18 April, at the Exchequer, Gladstone was in consultation with the Governor, Bonamy Dobree, and the Deputy Governor: he also saw representatives of Overends. Dobree tells in his diary that on returning to the Bank he found that the notes had been returned by Overends 'within the last half-hour': they had all been cut in two, probably in order that the separate halves might be deposited in different places of security. The reason for their return at this particular moment remains a mystery.

Gladstone informed the House that Overends had been most frank and had argued that their action had been by way of a public protest against a public evil; as for himself, 'he gave no opinion on the existence of any such public evil'. He considered that the Bank had acted with propriety and prudence. In private he expressed his satisfaction that the Governor had not yielded to Overends' pressure.

Whom the gods wish to destroy they first make mad. It was in the six years following this ill-advised action that, as Bagehot puts it, the immensely rich partners of Overends 'lost all their own wealth, sold their business to the company, and then lost a large part of the company's capital', and although informed opinion in the City can hardly have been surprised by their failure, the shock to the general public was profound. The day following the announcement of the failure (11 May 1866) was long remembered as 'Black Friday'; during that day the Bank made advances, to bankers, bill-brokers and merchants, to the 'unprecedented sum' of nearly £4 million. Bank Rate was already high – it had been 6 per cent since March – and on 3 May, as a presage of the coming thunderbolt, it had been increased to 7 per cent and then on the 8th to 8 per cent. On Black Friday it was put up to 9 per cent and on the next day to 10 per cent. The reserve was halved, falling from nearly £6 million to £3 million.

The Directors did not consider that the circumstances involved any real necessity for the issue of a Chancellor's letter such as had been issued during the crises of 1847 and 1857, but Gladstone thought that it would have a steadying effect. It was therefore agreed that the Bank would make no discounts or advances below 10 per cent, and that if proceeding upon the prudent rules of action by which their administration is normally governed' the Directors then saw fit to issue notes beyond the limits set by the Bank Charter Act of 1844, the Government would at once make application to Parliament for this course to be sanctioned. No necessity for this in fact arose, though the demand for advances remained considerable. Bagehot approved the Bank's conduct – 'the latest panic', he said, was 'the one in which on the whole the Bank acted the best'. Bank Rate remained at 10 per cent until 16 August, though this long spell of three months would doubtless have been shorter but for the outbreak of the 'Seven Weeks War' in which Prussia conquered Hanover and drove Austria out of Germany.

Then, for the next half-century, the history of the Bank, financially, is to all intents and purposes nothing more than a history of Bank Rate. There were no panics on anything like the same scale and no fresh need arose to consider the suspension of the 1844 Act until 1914. Nor, until the fateful August of that year, did Bank Rate ever again touch 10 per cent. It rose to 7 per cent in June 1873, and after dropping to 3 per cent in August went up again to 9 per cent on 7 November. These fluctuations reflected financial crises on the Continent and in America respectively. Thereafter, for forty years, the course of the rate indicates the nature of the period, the deep though tense peace of the later nineteenth century. As Sir Gordon Nairne, Chief Cashier from 1902 to 1918, and his successor, Sir Ernest Harvey, told Sir John Clapham, this was a time when 'the Bank was amazingly detached from international affairs; heard from no one; saw no one, only watched the gold and took the necessary steps automatically'. In other words, the Bank pursued a safe and formal course, declaring steady dividends. The 'amateurs', as Bagehot called them, the discreet merchants whose counsels had guided the Bank since its inception, were in unquestioned control, and should trouble occasionally threaten there were always men strong enough among them to see it safely overcome.

In an article in *The Economist* of 22 September 1866, dealing with the crisis of that year and the part played in it by the Bank, Bagehot drew attention to what was coming to be regarded as the Bank's central duty. His view was that the Bank held, should hold and should be responsible for holding 'the sole banking reserve of the country'. This doctrine was gathering a growing number of supporters, including several members of the Bank's own Court of Directors, though it was one which could not fail, in that age, to provoke powerful opposition as well.

Despite the fact that this conception of its central banking function was now finding authoritative and well-argued expression, the Bank at that time was still very much a commercial bank, in competition for everyday business both with the old private banks and with the joint-stock banks which were constantly expanding their functions and activities. In deposits alone the joint-stock banks had acquired enormous resources; they allowed interest on these deposits, unlike the Bank of England and other banks conducted 'on the old system'. They had also built up a more elaborate conception of banking until it had become what Bagehot described as being 'almost a new business'. They relieved their customers of much of the responsibility of looking after their own incomes in such ways, for example, as cutting off the dividend-coupons on their bonds and transmitting them for payment when due, along with a number of similar services. All this needed special organisation of a kind which a large joint-stock bank could naturally evolve, but one which would have to be initiated *ab ovo* by the Bank of England if it was to undertake similar tasks for its customers and obtain a larger share in the now greatly extended fields of banking and money-dealing.

Nevertheless, the Bank had not entirely failed to keep abreast of changing times and changing methods. In 1855 it had opened its Western branch in the West End of London in order to retain customers of a kind it had greatly valued from its earliest days, the wealthier merchants who no longer resided in or near the City. The building acquired for this new branch was Uxbridge House, in Burlington Street. The alterations necessary to adapt the house to banking purposes were made by Philip Hardwick, who had recently succeeded Cockerell as Architect to the Bank, and the branch was opened on 1 October. The business done there was mainly an extension of the ordinary banking business in Threadneedle Street; there was little discounting, though large advances were frequently arranged. In addition to the accounts of private customers and firms it was found convenient for a few of the Government accounts to operate there also.

In May 1864 the Bank joined the Clearing House. The private banks, whose preserve it was, had not allowed the joint-stock banks to become members. In 1848, Alderman Salomons of the London and Westminster Bank had proposed that the joint-stock banks, the Bank of England and any private banks which cared to join in should set up a daily clearing system between themselves. The Chief Cashier, Matthew Marshall, had, however, reported against the suggestion and the Directors had thought that complete agreement should be established between the private and the joint-stock banks before the Bank of England could 'entertain the question of its own co-operation'.

Thus matters remained until 1854, when the joint-stock banks ran out of patience and threatened to set up a system of their own. The private banks at last gave way and six joint-stock banks were grudgingly admitted to the Clearing House. Under the agreement then arrived at, clearing by transfer of bank-notes was abandoned in favour of cheques drawn on the bankers' accounts at the Bank of England. This much reduced the demand for bank-notes, since they had ceased to serve as the instrument for the settlement of these large and important financial transfers. The demand was further reduced by the institution, in 1858, of the 'country clearing' of cheques from country banks, which more than anything else brought about the use of cheques in England, to the exclusion of notes and coin, for most major transactions.

In 1869 there was a change in the method of paying out dividend warrants which had far-reaching effects; it eliminated a familiar and long-standing City event, a vivid illustration of which was provided by one of the most popular paintings in the Royal Academy Exhibition of 1859. This picture, 'Dividend Day at the Bank of England', was by G. E. Hicks and shows forty or more stockholders and others gathered in one of Soane's vaulted halls to receive their dividends. The suggestion that the dividend warrants should be dispatched by post came from the Chancellor of the Exchequer, Robert Lowe, later Viscount Sherbrooke. The Directors doubted whether the advantages would outweigh the delay and risk involved, but acceded to his wishes, on condition that Parliamentary sanction be obtained and the Bank compensated for any additional risk or expense.

'Dividend Day' was dead and its passing was mourned only by a few ageing clerks who missed the opportunities, formerly offered, of helping a favoured customer, in the lively hope of later obtaining a *quid pro quo* in some such form as a gift of game in season, a practice which the authorities had long frowned upon.

As for the staff, the middle years of the century were almost completely static. Numbers and duties remained much the same. The Crimean War and the Indian Mutiny had led, as wars always do, to a rather large increase in the cost of living about which nothing was done so long as no complaints were made and there had been no change in the scale of salaries since the revision of 1844. In 1854, however, because of the high prices of provisions and the burden of the Income Tax – it had been 7d. in the £ in 1850, although by 1864 it was reduced to 4d. – the staff petitioned the Bank to pay this tax for them. Their request was refused, but the Directors granted instead a gratuity of 10 per cent on salaries. Similar gratuities were paid in 1856, 1857, 1860 and 1864. One was also paid in 1865, but the percentage was then reduced to 5.

In that year, however, there was strong pressure from the clerks for a permanent increase. Comparative statements were prepared showing how various items of expenditure had risen since 1850, and 550 members of the staff signed a petition representing that they had 'much difficulty in meeting their unavoidable expenses and maintaining their social respectability'. As a result of the petition a new scale of salaries was introduced. The annual increments were increased and a clerk could therefore enjoy a better salary at an earlier age. The higher salaries, those of the chief officers and the principals of offices, were not altered, and such men had, in fact, to wait for another thirty years before receiving any increase.

In 1866 the annual allowance of leave of absence was increased, three additional days being granted to each clerk. This meant that, for the first twenty-five years of his service he would receive fifteen days instead of the twelve granted under the 1852 arrangement, and after that twenty-one days instead of eighteen. The 'one month' allowed to cashiers and principals of offices became 'one calendar month'. No further amendments to the scale were made until the century was drawing towards its close – in 1894, clerks of under fifteen years' service were granted twenty-one days and those of over fifteen years' service twenty-seven days. Principals were allowed thirty days.

In 1870 a retiring age limit was imposed. The Court ordered that retirement was to be compulsory at sixty-five. A clerk could, however, apply for a pension in accordance with the scale at sixty. No pensions would be granted to clerks below that age except for illness or incapacity. A full pension equal to two-thirds of the salary could be attained after forty-five years' service, and as eighteen was the usual age at entry, most clerks could therefore take a full pension, if they wished, at the age of sixty-three. The new arrangement called for the retirement of twenty-one well-seasoned servants of the Bank, though some of these were given an option to stay on. Among those who now retired was the Senior Cashier, David Hyett. He was seventy-nine years of age and had served for some sixty-one of them. George Earle Grey, the Chief Accountant, also retired – he had held this post for the last twelve years of a service of sixty-two years. These are impressive, not to say daunting, statistics. They can, however, be beaten – after a most thorough search Acres concluded that the longest service of all time, now unlikely to be eclipsed, was that of James Richards, who was elected in 1758 and then worked for the Bank for more than sixty-six years, dying in March 1825.

The profits from the branches opened by the Bank in country towns had in many cases been disappointing and round the middle of the century some which had been working at a loss for years were closed. When the country branches had been established in the earlier years of the century one of the first considerations moving the Bank had been its desire to increase the circulation of its notes and thus to obtain a greater control over the circulation of the paper currency as a whole. In 1844 the Charter Act gave the Bank a virtual monopoly of note issue in England and Wales and thereafter private issue steadily declined, but in the field of commercial business the agents could not, as the joint-stock banks did, offer interest to depositors; as a result, they did not gain a share proportionate to their branches' importance in the vast expansion of general banking business. Even so, at most branches commercial business was reasonably active and profitable and the agents had at least one advantage – they could offer finer rates for discounts than the other banks could and, on occasion, this was particularly effective in getting new business. Only towards the end of the century, when the Bank assumed even more responsibility in the country's financial system, did it begin to be realized on all sides that it was no longer appropriate for it to compete for ordinary banking business. The policy of commercial competition therefore began to be gradually abandoned, with a resultant general decline in the business of advances and discounts at the branches.

The only new branches to be set up while so many were closing were the Western branch, already referred to, and one at the Law Courts. The latter was needed in order that the large volume of work which almost from its inception the Bank had undertaken on behalf of the Law and lawyers might be carried out more easily; that is to say, business arising from trusts, estates in Chancery, sums paid into court and similar matters. An Act of 1725 had ordered the Masters in Chancery to use the Bank, and since the passing of that Act the Bank had maintained a 'Chancery Office'. In 1858 a suggestion was made by the Incorporated Law Society that the Bank should open a branch near the Law Courts, but it was not until ten years later, when the new Courts of Justice in the Strand were in course of erection, that it was definitely agreed that a branch be established 'in Chancery Lane or its neighbourhood'. Anything connected with the Law, however, seems to become infected with its proverbial delays, but eventually the present branch, at the corner of Bell Yard and Fleet Street, was erected to the designs of Sir Arthur Blomfield, who was at that time Architect to the Bank. It was occupied on 15 December 1888.

Only one Director of the Bank has become Chancellor of the Exchequer – George Joachim Goschen, the man whom Lord Randolph Churchill 'forgot' when, to his surprise and chagrin, Lord Salisbury accepted his offer to resign the Chancellorship in 1887. In 1888 Goschen triumphantly managed the largest Government debt conversion scheme of the nineteenth century. It became law on 27 March and dealt with approximately £600 million of debt, of which nearly 96 per cent was ultimately converted to the new stock on his terms, i.e. 3 per cent per annum to be the interest, as before, until April 1889, then $2\frac{3}{4}$ per cent for fourteen years and thereafter $2\frac{1}{2}$ per cent in perpetuity. Much of this huge sum forms the '$2\frac{1}{2}$ Consols' quoted on the Stock Exchange today.

The reduction of interest on 'gilt-edged' stock led, as it had on former occasions, to a period of speculation by those seeking investments which promised a greater, if less sure, return. Large sums were again invested in South American ventures, and this eventually had repercussions in the shape of the 'Baring crisis' of 1890. This crisis, which at first seemed likely to send the great house of Baring Bros & Co. the same way that Overend, Gurney had gone some twenty-five years earlier, owed its satisfactory solution mainly to the happy chance that there was at the time a strong Governor at the Bank, William Lidderdale, and a bold and able Chancellor, Goschen, whose joint efforts were backed by those of the Baring partners themselves.

Barings' difficulties had arisen because of their extensive commitments in South America, where political unrest, commercial instability and the often irresponsible financial policies of the various republics had made any form of investment highly speculative. The firm was solvent, as events showed, but was not in possession of sufficient liquid assets to meet its current liabilities. South American politics feature largely in the story – Barings' dealings were with the foreign governments, with the National Bank of Uruguay, the Buenos Aires Railways, the Buenos Aires Water and Drainage Company and many other such enterprises – and very early on, when the storm was brewing and it was known to the innermost City circles that Barings' position was insecure, the Governor had inquired of the Chancellor whether the Argentine Government might not be persuaded to deal in some way or other with the enormous bulk of discredited South American securities then weighing down the London stock market.

Bank Rate, which had been at 5 per cent since 25 September 1890, was raised by the Governor to 6 per cent on Friday, 7 November. On Saturday the 8th he met Lord Revelstoke (E. C. Baring) and Francis Baring; the meeting took place outside the Bank in the office of Everard Hambro, a Director of Hambros and of the Bank. The Barings placed before the Governor a statement of their firm's affairs which he found grave enough, but even so, insufficiently clear or exact. Revelstoke said that he should know by Monday whether or not Barings would be able to continue in business, and the Governor, who had asked the Chancellor to come to the City on the Monday, spent the Sunday wondering what Revelstoke's news would be. Clapham records that he passed part of what must have been for him a long and anxious day at the Zoological Gardens, in the company of a small son, 'a non-conductor of financial worries'.

Over the weekend Goschen also was not without his worries; if, he thought, the trouble involved Barings, 1866 would be a trifle in comparison. He made it clear, on the Monday, that should the firm be actually insolvent no governmental help could be expected. He suggested that the great City houses must get together and give the necessary guarantee. If the Governor so desired, he was prepared to let him have a Chancellor's letter of indemnity, but this offer was declined by Lidderdale, despite the fact that the Bank's reserve, then standing at £10,815,000, would have been inadequate should really serious doubts arise as to Barings' solvency. Instead, Lidderdale asked the Chancellor for his aid in obtaining several millions of gold from the Bank of France. Goschen was ready to help and by Wednesday, 12 November, £3 million in gold had been borrowed from the Bank of France. Another £1½ million was bought outright from Russia, being paid for in Exchequer Bonds. The necessary negotiations were carried through by Lidderdale, Goschen recording in a note to Lord Salisbury how very 'cleverly and energetically' he had done so. An Argentine Committee had also been set up to consider the 'discredited securities', though quick results were not, of course, expected from this quarter.

The more exact statement of affairs which Lidderdale had been waiting for from Barings was in his hands on the Wednesday morning. It showed the ultimate solvency for which Goschen had stipulated, but also showed that Barings might need as much as £8 million or £9 million to meet its immediately maturing liabilities. The figures were verified by B. B. Greene, a Director of the Bank, and by Bertram Currie, of Glyn, Mills, Currie & Co, a friend of the Barings. Lidderdale went to Whitehall to convey the information to the Prime Minister, Lord Salisbury, and secured an agreement of Government help regarding half of any loss which the Bank might sustain from taking in Barings' bills over a limited period. He then returned to the Bank to raise the guarantee fund that would make it unnecessary for the Government to implement its offer of assistance.

Within a few hours he had obtained promises of £3,250,000. The Bank led off with one million; the rest came from the private houses the Governor first approached. He then invited representatives of the five principal joint-stock banks to meet him and his Deputy, David Powell, at the Bank. Their replies were provisional, for the approval of their respective boards had to be obtained. Nevertheless, these replies furnish evidence of the immense power the joint-stock banks had by now attained, for the suggested joint contribution was as large as that of the

Bank and the private houses combined. The London and Westminster, the London and County and the National Provincial suggested £750,000 each; the Union of London and the Union Joint Stock £500,000 each. *The Times* of Saturday, 15 November, was able to announce that 'the worst was over', thanks to the 'prompt and courageous action of the Bank'. Bank Rate was back at 5 per cent by 4 December. At the end of January 1891 it was down to 3 per cent.

When the guarantee fund was complete it amounted to £17,105,000. In consideration of advances which the Bank had agreed to make to Barings in order to enable them to discharge, as they fell due, their liabilities existing on the night of 15 November 1890, the participating firms undertook to make good any loss which might appear at the final liquidation, their contributions to be proportionate to the amounts of their individual guarantees. Barings was reconstructed as a joint-stock company and by the end of 1894 the advances from the guarantee fund were repaid and the guarantors released from all future liability. Tributes to William Lidderdale were paid by the Chancellor of the Exchequer on behalf of the Government, by the Stock Exchange and, it need hardly be said, by the Court of Directors. In the spring of 1891 he was given a City banquet and the Freedom of the City and he was sworn of the Privy Council. He was also elected, by the General Court, to serve a third year as Governor.

The directors of the new Barings made it their first and main business to make reparation for the faults of the old. In this they were most successful, retaining nearly all the commercial credit business of the old firm and the accounts of the chief foreign governments which had been its customers. In the end not a single bill failed to be paid and no guarantor lost a penny.

The two hundredth anniversary of the Bank was now approaching, but a shadow was cast over the coming celebration in the year which immediately preceded it. In November 1893 a series of irregularities came to light which must have shocked the Court of Directors in a way it had not felt since the discovery, nearly two centuries before, of the frauds of Humphry Morice. This time, it is true, the offender was not a Director, nor in the opinion of counsel were his offences actionable ones, but he stood next to the Directors in the Bank's hierarchy and his offences, though not strictly fraudulent, involved the Bank in serious loss.

Frank May, who had entered the service in 1852, and whose father had served before him, had for twenty years been the Chief Cashier. To put his misdemeanours in the kindest light possible, he had totally misconceived the nature of his trust. He had shown favour to a number of customers, most of them with finance company or Stock Exchange connections, without first consulting the Governor as he should. He had allowed one firm an unauthorized overdraft in addition to its authorized advance against securities, another had been allowed to pay no interest on its authorized advance over a full year and a third advance, for which the Chief Cashier himself had provided the securities, had been continued for three years without any authority. These and various other irregularities were revealed in the report of a Committee of Directors which had been set up to investigate May's misconduct and the deficiencies in the Bank's system which had permitted it.

That it could take place showed a breakdown in ordinary security precautions and a grave weakness in the transmission of internal intelligence. May's unconditional resignation was required and on 17 November his post was filled by H. G. Bowen, who since 1888 had been Chief Accountant. The dirty linen was not washed in public, but it was noisome enough to be perceived beyond the Bank's walls, with the perhaps natural result that rumour in the City and, later, in the country at large made out that things were very much worse than they really had been, while the Directors individually and collectively, were accused of mismanagement. However, an article in *The Economist* soon showed matters in their proper perspective – there had been no corporate mismanagement and the scandal had arisen because of the faulty judgement of one man. A proposal that there should be a Parliamentary inquiry into the Bank's affairs was rejected by Sir William Harcourt, who had succeeded Goschen at the Exchequer. Today the episode is largely forgotten, its main surviving memory being embodied in a *Punch* cartoon by Tenniel, in the issue of 13 January 1894, which shows the 'Old Lady' holding up her skirts on a very dirty street-crossing marked 'Mismanagement'.

Investigations having once been started, they were continued by an enlarged Committee of Directors, whose terms of reference included examination of the 'Officers' Emoluments' as well as safeguards for the future control of advances, overdrafts and accounts generally. The raising of the salaries of the chief officials and the heads of offices was long overdue and the necessity for this was at last recognized – thirty years after the award of increases to the staff in their charge. The Chief Cashier was acknowledged to be the Bank's senior official in the most tangible way possible, his new salary being fixed as the highest of all those paid.

The Bank's internal system of 'checks and balances' had plainly been found wanting and the Committee recommended the setting up of an Audit Department, to operate under the control of a new standing committee of the Court to be styled the Audit Committee.

The creation of the Audit Department was not the only change in the Bank's organization to be made during the two hundredth year of its existence. The year 1894 saw a further innovation which drew much comment – some of it ribald – at the time, though its significance was not to be fully realized until two more decades had passed.

The Bank of England was the first house of importance in the City to employ women clerks. Their employment had first been suggested in a report by the three chief officers early in 1893 and had been recommended as a means of effecting administrative economies. The work suggested for them was the sorting and counting of bank-notes returned from circulation. The monotony of this work was relieved, for some of them, when a few years later a typing department was set up. It was not, however, until the war of 1914–18 had drained away most of the younger male staff that the women found their way at all extensively into the general offices and demonstrated that they could perfectly well undertake work hitherto sacred to men. It was this emergence of the women, twenty years after their first appearance within the Bank, which from then onwards gradually brought about a change in the whole nature and constitution of the bank staff.

For twenty years more, until the bomb at Sarajevo turned the world upside down, the Bank's course was steady and unexciting. Its policies and methods were in essentials those which it had pursued during the previous hundred years. In the City its place was virtually unchallenged. Honoured like royalty, and like royalty remote, it represented, in the financial world, Britain's power and splendour in the world at large. For most of the time this king of the City remained in his counting-house counting out his money, 'watching the gold'. The London money market continued to expand, the joint-stock banks opened more and more new branches on a country-wide scale, while in London itself there was a great incursion of foreign banks, representatives and agents of money centres abroad.

In 1899 the South African War broke out and lasted until 1902, a much longer time than anyone had foreseen, but the Boer farmers had disobligingly refused to take the short, sharp lesson prescribed for them. Throughout the world, except in Britain and her Dominions, their courage, tenacity and skill in warfare had earned for them the admiration always bestowed upon the underdog who puts up a good fight. As the struggle lengthened, to the country's surprise and growing dismay, more and more men and money were required. This inevitably laid extra work upon the Bank, though at no time did it entail any increase in the numbers of those dealing with it. Since 1888 the National Debt had been steadily reduced and in 1900 the total, funded and unfunded, had been £568,700,000. By 1903 it had risen to £715,200,000.

'Watching the gold and taking the necessary steps automatically' was now the Bank's main preoccupation, the maintenance of a sufficient, or more than sufficient, gold reserve having become an end in itself. In 1907 there was a crisis in America which shook the world's financial markets and there were widespread failures in New York, Amsterdam and Hamburg. In New York a run on the Knickerbocker Trust Company led to a call for gold from London. But in London itself there was no panic. In September 1907 Bank Rate had been at 4½ per cent, the gold reserve standing at £28 million – the highest it had been for several years at that particular season. On 31 October the rate was put up by one full point to 5½ per cent, the reserve having by then declined to £21 million. Four days later Bank Rate was raised by the Governor, W. M. Campbell, to 6 per cent and on 7 November to 7 per cent, where it stayed until the end of the year. On 6 November the banking reserve had gone down to £17,700,000: the City had criticized the high rate, but Goschen's theory was justified when the 7 per cent offered duly drew the gold in. £7,000,000 came from Germany, £3½ million from France, £2½ million from India and some £6½ million from the principal mining countries. By 1 January 1908 the reserve once more stood at around £21 million, in consequence of which Bank Rate was reduced to 6 per cent the following day. On 16 January it was lowered to 5 per cent and on the 23rd to 4 per cent. By 19 March it was down to 3 per cent. Goschen's mechanism had worked. During the critical period the number of bankruptcies in this country was in no way abnormal: there were, indeed, fewer in 1907 and 1908 than in the two years preceding the start of the American troubles. In 1908, however, the number of companies in voluntary liquidation was somewhat larger than in 1907, probably as the result of delayed action from the high interest rates prevailing in the earlier of these two years.

The effect of the South African War upon the Bank and its staff was not very great, but, in the light of events a dozen years later, what effect there was turned out to be of prophetic significance. This was the first overseas conflict in which any appeal was made for the services of Volunteers. That appeal and the formation of the CIV – the City of London Imperial Volunteers – indicated a new conception of the citizen's place in warfare. The Government's call for Volunteers, after the disaster of Colenso in December 1899, was enthusiastically answered, and the Bank, along with other employers, was ready to do what it could in the way of sparing men for military duty. In order to 'volunteer for the Cape' a clerk had to be already a member of a Volunteer unit, unmarried, and fit for foreign service. The Bank gave such a man leave of absence, on full pay, for six months; this period was subsequently extended for two further terms of three months each.

Nineteen clerks volunteered, and when fresh drafts were raised in January 1901 twelve more clerks were allowed to join, as was a clerk at the Manchester branch. Altogether, therefore, there were thirty-two who served.

The formation of the Bank's Sports Club was effected by the purchase, in 1908, of a site of some eighteen acres, in Priory Lane, Roehampton, near Richmond Park. A club house was constructed in the grounds, which in those days were surrounded by open country and the Bank used a corner of the ground for the building of a Record Office, since its archives were rapidly outgrowing the accommodation for them in the vaults at Threadneedle Street.

The Sports Club was the second of the Bank's recreational associations to be founded, providing healthy bodies for the presumably healthy minds nourished by the first of such associations, the Library. In the same year that saw the opening of the Roehampton playing fields the Library happened to be looking for a new President. This office had always been held by one of the Bank's chief officials, Matthew Marshall, Chief Cashier from 1835 to 1864, had been the first, as already recorded, and in 1908 the most recent holder of the office had been Kenneth Grahame, Secretary of the Bank since 1898, who had just retired from the service and, in consequence, from the Presidency. He was then at the height of his powers as an author and was, as he probably will remain, the Bank's most outstanding literary figure. Most fittingly, he had been President of the Library since 1905.

On his departure the members may well have felt, 'After this man, who is there?' but for whatever reason, it was decided to break with tradition and Grahame thus became the last President to be chosen from among the staff itself. For the first time the office was offered to a Director. He was by no means a senior one, having joined the Court as recently as October 1907. It is not certain who was responsible for suggesting that he should be approached, but the approach was made and was welcomed and he was elected as the new President. He was Montagu Collet Norman.

He remained President for more than thirty-six years. For the Library he always seemed to have a special affection and to take more than a merely formal interest in its fortunes. Unless prevented by illness, absence abroad or the most urgent business, he never failed to take the chair at the Annual General Meeting. These meetings grew to be quite important occasions in the Bank's domestic calendar, for at them he

Sir John Soane's Lothbury Court, looking south to the Bullion Yard. From a drawing by Thomas Malton, 1801

Soane's Tivoli Corner, erected in 1806–7 at the junction of Lothbury and Princes Street. From a photograph

Transfer Day at the Bank. View of one of the Transfer Offices, showing pickpockets and police officer. From a drawing by George Cruikshank, 1836

Five Pound Note of an early issue, dated 15th April 1793

took the opportunity of establishing some sort of personal contact with members of the staff to whom he would otherwise have been only the bearer of a name and a reputation. After the formal business was over he would give an address, completely 'off the record', on whatever aspect of finance, central banking, politics or the world situation in general happened to be uppermost in his mind at the time. Often he took his hearers, with great frankness and clarity, as near to the heart of affairs as he safely could. Those who heard him speak at the meeting in April 1939 will not forget how, on a sombre and prophetic note, he spoke of Europe's approaching doom. For some, at least, the second of this century's great wars became a reality on that spring evening, rather than in the following September, as he ended with Newman's prayer, 'Lead, Kindly Light, amid the encircling gloom'.

When he retired from the Bank, and the Presidency, in 1944 he gave the Library, as a parting memento, one of his most cherished possessions, a copy of William Morris's Kelmscott Chaucer.

The main thread of this story has not, however, reached the second of the great world conflicts, though it now reaches the first of them. The summer of 1914 opened much as had any other in the long years of peace. There were troubles enough, it is true; at home the suffragettes and the unemployed were on the march; in Ireland it seemed that an ugly civil war was brewing. But the man in the street went about his work and play in the sure knowledge that no one in his senses would dare, even if he wished, to attack his country. Unfortunately, on the Continent, men *were* beginning to lose their senses, the rattle of sabres grew more and more strident and on 28 June the Archduke Franz Ferdinand, heir to the Austrian throne, was assassinated by a young Bosnian fanatic. Assassination led to mobilization, mobilization to invasion, invasion to counter-mobilization, until, amid a flurry of ultimatums, the nations plunged to disaster.

During the fateful eleven days which followed the Austrian ultimatum to Serbia, Britain had striven for peace. The mood of the Liberal Government reflected that of most of the country: with Asquith as Prime Minister and Lloyd George at the Treasury, they were almost solidly against intervention. 'Up to luncheon time on the Sunday (2nd August) it looked', Winston Churchill wrote, in *The World Crisis*, 'as if the majority of the Cabinet would resign rather than accept' the necessity of going to war. Churchill himself, however, as First Lord of the Admiralty, had seen to it that 'the King's ships were at sea'. A 'deplorable measure', *The Economist* of 1 August called this, typifying the business world's horror and dismay at the prospect of a rupture of that rarely disturbed peace it had known so long. Lloyd George recalled later that the Governor of the Bank, Walter Cunliffe, told him on Saturday, 1 August, that 'the financial and trading interests in the City were totally opposed to our intervening in the war'.

The Bank, though a child of Mars, though its work during the hard wars of the later eighteenth and early nineteenth centuries had not only helped to save the country but had, as a sort of by-product, permanently enlarged its place in the nation, was certainly not at this point ready for war in the sense that it had any scheme of special financial measures prepared against a possible outbreak of hostilities. These had to be painfully thrashed out during the first week of war. Nevertheless, the Bank was 'in good condition' and had been about to raise its dividend from 9 per cent to the former 10 per cent. On 27 July the gold in the reserve was some £38 million and Bank Rate was at 3 per cent. On Thursday, 20 July, the rate was put up to 4 per cent, fear of war among businessmen, both at home and abroad, having resulted, *The Times* reported, in 'enormous sales of securities' in the London market and a rush for gold in Paris. A huge financial crisis was looming and this must have occurred whether the country kept out of war or not. There had already been a number of commercial failures and on 31 July, when £1½ million of gold was taken for export, *The Times* reported that 'other business was at a standstill'. On that day the Governor raised Bank Rate from 4 to 8 per cent, and on the next day, Saturday, after an informal meeting of Directors, to 10 per cent. That Saturday was a dark day for the City, for it was the one before Bank Holiday, so in addition to everything else there was the seasonal big demand for cash. The Stock Exchange was shut. Some of the London banks had called in short money from bill-brokers on the Friday and this had led to a rush of discounting of £3 million at the Bank, notwithstanding the imposition of the crisis rate of 10 per cent. Within the Bank itself queues of people were waiting to cash £5 notes for the gold sovereigns they then represented. Most of these people, if not all of them, could normally have obtained the sovereigns they wanted from their own banks, but some London bankers were cannily holding on to their gold stocks and referring applicants to the Bank of England. It was not that the notes were mistrusted, except perhaps by the foreigners who were observed to form rather a large proportion of those queuing, but people wanted cash for the holiday. On the Friday and Saturday over 5,000 asked for gold across the counters.

On the Saturday morning the Governor reported to the Chancellor that in five days the Bank had advanced over £27 million; the reserve by nightfall would not be more than £11 million, if that, and there was a risk of either having to refuse well-founded demands upon it or of

breaching the Act of 1844. The necessary letter of indemnity, signed by
Asquith and Lloyd George, was immediately forthcoming from Downing
Street, the Bank being promised indemnity with the customary proviso
that it must not grant advances at less than the crisis rate of 10 per cent.

Over the weekend there were a number of hastily called conferences
to devise expedients to ease the situation. The Chancellor and Treasury
officials met the Bank – in effect the Governor – the other bankers and
the more important City leaders. The Bank Holiday was prolonged; a
moratorium (though it was not called that) was declared in the form
of a Proclamation, issued on the Sunday, for 'Postponing the Payment
of Certain Bills of Exchange': postal orders were made into legal tender
and a promise was given that Government notes for £1 and 10s. would
be issued as swiftly as possible.

The country went to war before midnight on the Monday. The
threatened divisions that might have sundered Cabinet, Parliament and
country were extinguished at one blow by the German invasion of
Belgium. The violation of the frontiers of a country whose neutrality
had been solemnly guaranteed by Prussia itself settled the mind of the
Cabinet once and for all, dispersed the doubts of the Labour Party in
Parliament, and satisfied the people that the war was a just one.

August Bank Holiday – 'St Lubbock's Day' – the day which Sir John
Lubbock's stout humanity had wrenched from employers as a brief
summer respite for a hard-working and sometimes overworked populace,
had had the most sombre of shadows cast over it, but it now served the
country in a manner far different from any Sir John could have contemplated. It gave the Treasury and the City some breathing-space
and its extension gave them more. The Stock Exchange remained closed.
International remittance had ceased, so Tuesday would have brought
a full-scale crisis in the bill market; the proclamation of the moratorium
of a month for bills of exchange was therefore an essential and timely
measure. Postal orders filled the temporary gap in the currency and
filled it well. They were, if anything, rather more widely used then than
they are today, when increased poundage and the more general use of
cheques has to a large extent relegated them to service as vehicles for
'pools' subscriptions and avuncular gifts. The Government £1 and 10s.
notes were eventually to make the use of postal orders unnecessary, but
any idea that the orders or the notes were to do more than act as an
expedient to meet a temporary withdrawal of gold was in the minds of
very few.

The plan for the Treasury notes, as they came to be called, was
forthwith embodied in an Act passed on 6 August. The Bank was to
distribute them and to do this free of charge. They were, under this

135

original plan, to be issued to the banks in the form of a loan, interest on which would be payable to the Treasury, and banks might take them 'as and when required' up to 20 per cent of their liabilities on current and deposit accounts. Thus began the first chapter of the long, long tale of currency inflation which this century has seen. Why the notes were to be a Treasury and not a Bank issue is even now a matter for discussion, but the prime consideration was speed, and the Treasury may well have doubted whether the Bank, with its then limited printing equipment, could do the job fast enough. The Governor thought it could and a Bank £1 note, a miniature version of the £5 note, had, in fact, been devised, but when this was shown to the Treasury the Bank was told that a contract had already been entered into with Waterlow Brothers & Layton Ltd for the supply of currency notes.

The first issue of £1 notes under the Treasury contract with Waterlows was produced within three days, so the work could hardly have been done more quickly. The quality, however, was another matter. The note was a rather smudgy affair, surface-printed in black on the paper used for postage stamps. It bore the King's head in a panel on the right-hand side. The feature most seized upon for public comment was the bold and legible signature of Sir John Bradbury, the Permanent Secretary to the Treasury. Hence they soon became known as 'Bradburys', which they continued to be called even after 1919, when Sir John was succeeded at the Treasury by Sir Warren Fisher.

With the reopening of the banks much of the gold paid out by the Bank of England in the previous week was paid in again. The Governor could therefore report to the Chancellor that, except in Manchester, there was a complete absence of pressure, and the clearing banks confirmed this. So ended the first phase of adjustment to the conditions of war, unexpected and unprepared for. In the nine days during which Bank Rate had gone from 4 per cent to 10 per cent and down again to 5 per cent the Governor had played a vital part in overcoming the hesitancies of some of the bankers and in untangling the troubles of the money market. Appreciation of his 'courage and resource' at a time of great emergency was shown by the Prime Minister when three months later, on his advice, the King raised the Governor to the peerage as Baron Cunliffe.

It was soon realized that the new £1 and 10s. notes had come to stay. Their early character of being issued to the banks as a loan at interest was quickly modified. By a Treasury Minute of 20 August, currency notes might be drawn from the Bank of England by the other banks in the ordinary way as a cash withdrawal, no interest being payable. Perceiving that a permanent addition to the currency had almost certainly been made, the Court of Directors, by a vote, laid down its opinion that should the new notes continue to be used their issue should be in the hands of the Bank, but it was not until some fourteen years later, in 1928, that this wish of theirs was met.

Regarding the reserve, it soon became evident that there was, for the time being at any rate, no reason to fear that the country would be drained of its gold. War risks made shipment over long distances expensive, both in freight and insurance. This told both ways, of course – if it was costly to get gold out, it was equally costly to get it in. This difficulty was, however, overcome. Some £3·4 million of the Indian Government's holding of gold stored at the Bank was temporarily released to the Bank. Gold bought in Canada and the United States was stored at Ottawa on its behalf. South Africa had been somewhat concerned when a gold shipment, which should have been dispatched during the week following the declaration of war, was held up on information from the Admiralty, but arrangements were soon made for the Bank to make its purchases and for the gold to be deposited with the Treasury of the Union or with certain specified South African banks. Before the end of August the Bank of England could report a gold reserve of £43½ million, though, because of these special arrangements, not all of it was physically in its own vaults.

The Bank had at once assumed its historic obligation of finding day-to-day funds for the financing of a war. The Governor undertook to provide £6 million of 'Ways and Means Advances', to be paid in two instalments whenever the Chancellor called for them, and the Governor's action was approved by the Directors at the meeting of the Court on 13 August. £6,000,000, in 1914, would carry on the fighting for some while, but more would quite certainly be needed soon. The Court therefore gave general authority, in the following week, for advances to be made as required at rates to be agreed between the Treasury and the Governor, such rates not to exceed the Bank Rate of 5 per cent. Before the end of the year particularly heavy advances were agreed on at 2½ per cent.

Throughout all these operations the Stock Exchange remained shut. It had first been forced to close because of a never-ceasing flood of selling orders from the Continent. Such a thing had never been known before – but circumstances leading to such a situation had never arisen before. What is more, the New York Exchange had had to close also, though the entry of the United States into the war was then an idea too absurd for most people even to conceive.

When a leading economic journalist, Hartley Withers, later summed up the activities of the Bank during the first weeks of the conflict, in his book *War and Lombard Street*, he paid it a handsome tribute – 'If capacity for variation be the secret of strength and progress', he wrote, 'the Bank of England, for all its weight of years, can still claim to be young and lusty as an eagle when proved by the stress of crisis.' After mentioning the Bank's various successes – the new departure it had made in setting up offices for the receipt of gold in Canada, South Africa and India, the bills it had dealt with, the advances it had made and was prepared to make to holders of the new War Loan – he concluded by saying: 'And it was ready with a supply of tea and buns for Belgian refugees who brought Belgian money to be turned into sterling.' The Bank's position as the country's central bank was emerging more and more during these days of stress. Its status among the banks at home was already clear enough, but now another important sphere of activity was developing. On 13 August an account was opened in the Private Drawing Office for the Bank of France and one for the Banca d'Italia on the 20th. In September the National Bank of Switzerland followed suit and by November the Court of Directors was informed that the Governor had also permitted accounts to be opened for the National Bank of Belgium and for those of Serbia, Chile, Norway and the Netherlands. It was now dealing, therefore, as the central bank of this country with a large number of foreign central banks.

The Government's long-dated borrowings for the war, the great War Loans, form part of Bank history only in so far as it was the Bank which, in accordance with its established function, conducted the operations and kept the registers for the Government. The first, for a fixed sum of £350 million, issued in November 1914 at $3\frac{1}{2}$ per cent, was rather unsuccessful, and the Bank took up for the Government the £153 million unsubscribed for. The second, for an unspecified amount, at $4\frac{1}{2}$ per cent, was issued in June 1915 and brought in £592,479,544. The third, the great loan open for subscription from January to May 1917, at 5 per cent (or 4 per cent free of Income Tax), totalled just under £950 million, of which £22 million was of the tax-free category. This was the last actually issued in wartime, but in 1919 came the 4 per cent Victory Bonds and the Funding Loan, at 4 per cent, of that year.

There was a series of comparatively short-dated National War Bonds and various other borrowings from the public; among these, special mention must be made of the War Savings Certificates of 1916. These were an entirely new form of investment, devised by the Treasury to attract the smallest saving and nicknamed there 'the Baby Bond'. The original certificates were for five years – 15s. 6d. became £1 on maturity and there was no question of Income Tax. A nation-wide campaign to popularize them was undertaken, with a recently elected Bank Director,

138

R. M. Kindersley, later Lord Kindersley, at its head, and Savings Certificates have, of course, remained a familiar and well-supported form of investment ever since, not only with the less opulent, for whom they were chiefly designed, but also with those of the wealthy not averse from rescuing a pound or two from the grasp of the Income Tax collector.

Cunliffe's normal two-year term as Governor would have ended in the spring of 1915. He was re-elected in 1915, 1916 and again in 1917. No previous Governor had ever served so long. His handling of the crisis at the outbreak of war had been masterly and the Committee of Treasury was content to leave him free to act as he saw fit so long as prompt decision and strong action were essential. Even when the acute crisis was over his colleagues left him to run the Bank, advise the Treasury and maintain relationships with the City, offering very little interference. Not without good reason he became known as 'the Tyrant of the City'.

As time went on his abrupt manner and overbearing methods led to a strain between himself and his fellow members of the Court, especially those senior Directors forming the Committee of Treasury, to whom he did not always consider it necessary to mention what he was doing. His interest, however, in the details of the day-to-day working of the Bank led to many beneficial changes: for example, just before the war he had an extensive internal telephone system installed where previously there had been nine instruments and a small switchboard. And although he may have been brusque and domineering he had a magnanimity of his own, consigning certain petty distinctions to the oblivion of the dead age to which they belonged.

It was not only inside the Bank that Cunliffe was arousing strong feelings, but outside, too. In July 1917 he clashed with the Chancellor, a clash which might have had far-reaching effects on the course of the Bank's history had not good sense and restraint ultimately prevailed. None the less, in the first stages of the episode Cunliffe's behaviour put the Bank in one of the most awkward and delicate situations it had ever known. The full story has been told more than once, most recently in Sir Henry Clay's life of Lord Norman and Mr Robert Blake's life of Bonar Law, *The Unknown Prime Minister*. It indicates the dangers always inherent in and now brought to explosion point by Cunliffe's dictatorial ways. Andrew Bonar Law was Chancellor at the time. The original wartime Chancellor, Lloyd George, had succeeded Asquith as Prime Minister, then Reginald McKenna had served from May 1915 to December 1916, and he had been followed by Bonar Law. At this time the Treasury was faced with the possibility of having to cut expenditure drastically, so hard was it to finance the import of food and war materials, a strain which was no more than partly relieved in February 1917, when the United States became an 'associated power'.

In America, Bank and Treasury affairs were curiously intertwined. In Ottawa, where the gold was stored, some belonged to the Bank and some to the Treasury. Part of the Treasury's gold was security for advances made by the Government to Russia and part had been bought by the Government from the Bank. In New York, the Government owed a large sum in dollars to J.P. Morgan & Co., while among the liabilities which the Governor had accepted on behalf of the Bank was a debt of some $85 million to the same firm.

On the whole, the collision seems to have been between personalities rather than policies. It had two distinct phases. The first was in July 1917, after the Governor had returned from a mission to the United States lasting from mid-April to early June, and resulted from a complaint by him to the Chancellor, in extremely strong terms, that the London Exchange Committee, of which he, Cunliffe, was the Chairman, was not being kept properly informed of what the Treasury was doing. This Exchange Committee had been set up by McKenna when he was Chancellor to deal with the many difficult problems relating to foreign currency. Cunliffe told Bonar Law that because of its lack of information it had become 'a mere cypher, entirely superseded by Sir Robert Chalmers and Mr Keynes'. Sir Robert Chalmers, later Lord Chalmers, was one of the joint Secretaries to the Treasury; J. M. Keynes – who in later years, as Lord Keynes, was to be a Director of the Bank – was a young man at the time, though even then so able an economist that he held a Treasury post with direct access to the Chancellor. Cunliffe went on to say that in commercial circles neither was 'considered to have any knowledge or experience in practical exchange or business problems'. Blake says that, in an interview with Bonar Law, Cunliffe demanded the dismissal of both men. If so, the rather cold but habitually mild-natured Bonar Law must have been enraged, but whatever happened there was, after this, a state of open war between the Governor and the Chancellor.

The second incident in the affair happened shortly afterwards. Morgans had cabled that they must at once call in two loans on demand which they had made to Britain, one to the Treasury and the other – the $85 million loan already mentioned – to the Bank. Morgans' request was peremptory, so Cunliffe cabled to Ottawa saying that £17½ million of the Bank's gold there must be paid to them. Sir Hardman Lever, the Treasury representative in America, was also drawing gold from Ottawa. On hearing of this, Cunliffe said that Lever might keep the £2¼ million he had already drawn, but ordered that he must take no more until

Morgans had been paid what the Bank had promised them. All this was done without any reference to the Chancellor.

When the Chancellor at last got to know of it he was very angry indeed. Cunliffe probably realized that he had gone too far and expressed his profound regret if, in blocking Lever, he had injured Treasury credit. He described his action as an unpardonable mistake for which the Court of Directors might censure him. But the Chancellor was not appeased. He considered that what Cunliffe had been doing was by way of reprisal on the officials of the Treasury – that he must have been impelled by the thought that if they would not inform him of their actions, he would not inform them of his. He wrote to Lloyd George that the situation could not continue – either he or Cunliffe must go. The Prime Minister, in conversation with the Chancellor, ruled out the first alternative. This automatically left the second, but Lloyd George liked Cunliffe and got on well with him. He was therefore very loath to see him go. Bonar Law, a fair man and, when not provoked as he had been, an eminently reasonable one, suggested a third solution – that they should both forget their rancour and work together in harmony, but should a difference of opinion arise, the views of the Government, as represented by the Chancellor, must always prevail. The Prime Minister put the Chancellor's proposal to Cunliffe. He invited the Governor to sign a memorandum to the effect that, while the war lasted, the Bank must in all things act on the direction of the Chancellor whenever, in his opinion, the national interest was involved, and must not take any action likely to affect the country's credit without previously consulting the Chancellor. The Governor's reply was that he could not sign such a document without consulting his colleagues. Lloyd George grew stern. He spoke of the Government's 'taking over the Bank'.

The Committee of Treasury was unanimous that it would be 'impossible for the Bank thus to renounce its functions', and suggested that the Governor should again see the Prime Minister, which he did later in the same day, 12 July, but without making any progress. Lloyd George said that if the Bank would not sign the undertaking the Government would have to take over the Bank. Under this threat, the Committee prepared a memorandum desiring the Governor to express his regret that the telegrams relating to the transfer of the Ottawa gold should have been dispatched without previous consultation with the Chancellor, but pointing out that the course taken was the only one which seemed possible in the face of the sudden demand made on the Bank to meet its obligations to Morgans.

Lloyd George thought this memorandum 'pretty stiff'. Cunliffe had earlier made the suggestion that he should take a holiday and leave the negotiations to the Deputy Governor, Brien Cokayne, later Lord Cullen. Lloyd George now advised Cunliffe to do so and later to send, through him, a letter addressed to the Chancellor. A few days later the Deputy Governor reported to the Committee of Treasury that he had seen the Chancellor, who had assured him that he had no personal feeling in the matter and did not want the Governor to resign. With the Committee's agreement the Governor, on 16 July, wrote to the Chancellor, under a covering letter to the Prime Minister, expressing his regret over the matter of the telegrams, assuring him that the Bank fully realized that complete and harmonious co-operation between Bank and Treasury was of paramount importance during the war and that, to achieve this, the Bank would not fail to confer with the Chancellor 'before taking any action during the war involving the general conditions of national credit or substantially affecting the gold holding of the Bank'.

Being the man he was, Cunliffe did not regard this promise as depriving the Bank of its ordinary initiative in controlling the market. On 29 August he told the Committee that it might be necessary to raise Bank Rate, but that he did not propose then or at any time to obtain the Chancellor's special sanction for any change if the Bank considered it to be desirable.

In November 1917 the Committee of Treasury informed the Court of Directors of the names which, in its opinion, should go before the General Court in the following spring for the elections of Governors and Directors. They recommended that Brien Cokayne should be Governor and Montagu Norman his Deputy.

Looking back, it is apparent that this difference must have inevitably arisen in some form or another round about this time, though it is unfortunate that the particular form it took did not allow of more 'sweetness and light'. The Bank was now so great in the nation's counsels that it would soon have to make up its mind, one way or the other, whether it wished to remain master in its own rich but private house or, accepting even greater burdens of responsibility, relinquish some of its independence.

In the world outside it was also being asked whether there should not be a general reappraisal of the Bank of England's duties and functions. *The Economist* of 8 September 1917 summarized the points at issue. It maintained that the Bank was too secretive, suggested that it should make more use of industrialists and bankers, and asked whether it was not dangerous to concentrate so much power in the hands of one man, the Governor, to use wisely or unwisely – what would have happened if Cunliffe had been of a weak or vacillating nature? Criticisms of this kind, together with those arising inside the Bank, led to the appointment, in October 1917, of a Committee to consider the whole position. Lord Revelstoke, son of the first Baron, who had been a Director since 1898, was appointed Chairman, and sitting with him were Huth Jackson, Montagu Norman, R. M. Kindersley and Cecil Lubbock.

In the following February the report of this Committee was approved. Its introductory survey allowed that much of the outside criticism had not been unjustified. It expressed the desire that a Governor should be relieved of any occasion for the exercise of an autocratic control and recommended that it should be obligatory upon him to keep the Committee of Treasury informed of the Bank's affairs. The Committee of Treasury, by custom consisting of the Governors, *ex officio*, and nine or ten Directors, should not, it considered, consist of more than nine members, including the Governors, that there should be at least three members who had not passed either chair and that it should be elected each year by free and secret ballot. It recommended the continuation of the recently established practice of having a Secretary to attend its meetings in order to relieve the Deputy Governor of his traditional task of keeping the minutes.

The Committee had also considered the composition of the Court of Directors and gave good reasons for not abandoning the principle that members of the great clearing banks and of the discount houses should not be eligible for election as Directors. In view, however, of the narrowing field of choice for candidates of the time-hallowed mercantile type, members of British banks with branches in India, the Colonies and South America should be considered eligible. Directors, in future, would be expected to retire at seventy.

In April 1918, after the election of Cokayne and Norman as Governor and Deputy Governor, and of the rest of the Court of Directors, the main recommendations of the Revelstoke Committee were applied without delay. The Committee of Treasury was reconstituted, seven members being elected by ballot, of whom two only – A. C. Cole (Governor, 1911–12) and Cunliffe – had passed the chair. Cunliffe served on this Committee until his death two years later. Sir Gordon Nairne, the Chief Cashier, was appointed Comptroller. This placed him in a unique position. Without being a Director he attended at meetings of the Court, the Committee of Treasury and all Standing Committees, as well as having for his special province the co-ordination of the work of the various offices and Departments. For all purposes within the Bank his signature might replace that of the Governor or Deputy Governor.

He became a Director seven years later when he relinquished the Comptrollership and was elected to the Court. He was the first member of the staff to attain this position. That he did attain it was partly due to a changing outlook, but that he fully merited such a distinction was never questioned. He would in any case have been assured of a place among the 'great' Chief Cashiers. He continued to serve as a Director until 1931 and for a number of years afterwards went on leading an active life in the City. He died in 1945 at the age of eighty-four.

With the entry of the United States into the war the immediate task of finding money to finance it and the struggle to obtain dollars to pay for American supplies came to an end. From March 1918 the new Governor and his Deputy were able to turn to the problems which would face them the moment peace returned. The country, both as regards domestic and foreign expenditure, was living from hand to mouth, an unavoidable result of four years of war, during which the Government had been paying out far more than anything it could collect in taxes. There was little that the Bank could do while the war was still going on, but the warnings it was already giving were reinforced, in April 1918, by the interim report of the Committee on Currency and Foreign Exchange After the War, of which Cunliffe was Chairman. The views and opinions of this Committee and the results of their adoption will be considered in due course; it is enough to say at this point that at the time the Bank and public opinion generally assumed without argument that the aim of any policy must be to restore the pre-war Gold Standard in its essentials.

As for the Bank's own position in the years that lay ahead, the Revelstoke Committee, at the end of its report, had said that the evidence it had considered from outside sources was not in favour of the control or acquisition of the Bank by the State; on the contrary, it was thought desirable in the interests of the commercial world that it should preserve its independent existence. But 'if the Bank is to continue to stand firm on its ancient foundation', the report went on, 'it behoves us to understand the signs of the times and the temper of the community; . . . to take such active and intelligent decisions as may ensure a loyal and united administration of our own affairs and a strengthening of our material relations with outside corporations'.

Under the control of a man who had been a member of this Committee, and had approved its findings, the Bank passed, from 1920 onwards, into what was to prove a new age of very much greater responsibility.

Chapter 8

The Governorship of Montagu Norman

When on 11 November 1918 there ended more than four years of the bloodiest carnage the world has seen, some of the manifestations of relief were almost hysterical. They were, however, short-lived. The men and women of these islands had been promised that their courage and endurance would be rewarded by a fuller, more secure and happier life – and they were determined that these promises should be kept. Nor had the promises been made in any cynical spirit, carrots as it were dangled before the nose of a brave and patient ass. The intentions to rectify the worst of the remaining injustices of the industrial revolution were good ones – and they paved the road to hell. Whatever efforts were made, the harvest was somehow always scanty and blighted. Britain, along with the rest of the civilized world, seemed to be under some irremovable curse, and the disappointed hopes of the multitude led here, as elsewhere, to the most rancorous of political and industrial struggles.

The Government, and those in control of finance and industry, held that an essential requirement for any improvement was that the country must regain, in substantial measure, the wealth and power wasted by an armed conflict costing so much in blood and treasure, even if this meant that belts must sometimes be tightened. The wearers of the belts, who all too literally felt the effects of this decision, were filled with confusion, despair and sullen rage. Millions found no work in a land which they and their fathers had helped to build and fought to preserve; their anger festered and the twenty years between the wars were marked almost throughout by a disrupted economy and turbid unrest. Between the Armistice of 1918 and the General Strike of 1926 labour disputes followed hard upon one another; in the two years 1919 and 1920 there were nearly 3,000. The ostensible reason in each case was a demand for higher wages or better conditions, a protest against 'victimization' or the like, but the underlying cause was the change which the war had wrought in every man's attitude to life itself.

The thankfulness that the war's perils were over and that repair of its ravages could begin led to a brief boom immediately after the Armistice. For a time there was a delusive feeling of prosperity, a sense that once again life could be enjoyed, and this, in itself, irritated the unrest which followed the dashing of these hopes. A climax was reached with the General Strike of 1926. This was defeated. For a moment the nation had come face to face with the ugliness of civil war and a decisive majority, despite an instinctive and not unsympathetic understanding of the sense of outrage causing the catastrophe, had not liked what it saw. Thereafter there was some falling off in the number of industrial disputes, but the unrest, fed by the despair of the workless, persisted until war once again cured unemployment.

What almost certainly saved the country from the last extremities of violence was the newly introduced system of Unemployment Insurance – the maligned 'dole'. To the recipients, the system appeared to be administered meanly and without imagination, saving them from actual starvation, but nothing more. Yet meagre as the individual payments were, collectively they imposed so heavy a burden on the national purse that this was the chief of the causes underlying the great financial crisis of 1931.

The *malaise* was world-wide. The behaviour of one country had, since the dawn of history, always affected the fate of its neighbours. Now, because of the ease and swiftness of transport and communication, all the nations of the earth had become neighbours and the destiny of all would in future depend on the behaviour of all. The new problem confronting man proved too complicated for him to answer. Everywhere, innumerable solutions were offered, but never the right one. At last, in Italy and Germany, two tyrants rose to power. Their solution was the age-old one of conquest by arms and the subsequent destruction or enslavement of the vanquished. In 1939 war again broke out, eventually involving practically the entire world.

These two long decades, full of so much misery and fear, can from one reading of history be regarded as an unbroken period of economic world crisis. The Bank, as the chief regulator of the country's economic machinery, was therefore always in the thick of the trouble. In the circumstances of the time none of its decisions could be perfect, so whatever action it took, whatever policy it advocated, could from one aspect or another always be shown to be wrong. It was fortunate, therefore, that the actions it did take were at least courageous, firm and consistent. The principal reason for this was that, for most of the time, its destiny was in the hands of one man, Montagu Norman. During his Governorship the Bank passed through the final stages of its long evolution into a fully-blown State bank. He was 'the man at the piano' and, not without a certain *bravura*, he did his best – which was infinitely better than anything that could have been done by most of the men who shot at him.

For the Government, the Bank, the City generally, and most others who gave the matter thought, the outstanding economic need was the restoration of the pre-war gold standard as quickly as possible. Modifications of the system might be necessary, but its essential features must be preserved. On relinquishing the Governorship in 1918, Cunliffe had taken up the Chairmanship of the Committee on Currency and Foreign Exchange which the Government had set up – the Cunliffe Committee as it has been known ever since. The Committee's report assumed without question the desirability of the earliest possible return to gold, and its findings had been supported by those of another official inquiry, the Committee on Financial Facilities, formed in the main of representatives of industry and commerce. This Committee had reported in November 1918.

Both Committees had laid down that there could be no effective restoration unless Government borrowing ceased soon after the war; that Bank Rate must be used both to check drains of gold abroad and too speculative an expansion of credit at home; that the principle of the Act of 1844 must be maintained though there should be provision for issue beyond the legal limit, subject as always to Treasury permission; and that the country's gold reserves should be concentrated in the Bank. Meanwhile the Bank itself had appointed a Committee of its own to review the 1844 Act and the existing currency situation. As for the Act, this Committee considered that no amendment was necessary, at least for the time being, and as for the currency, it presumed that the £1 and 10s. notes had come to stay; it considered, however, that sooner or later these notes should be issued by the Bank and not the Treasury. But the main concern was with gold. In one place or another the Bank held over £70 million. For the period of 'reconstruction' this should be kept from returning to the pockets of the general public; it should also, except for a certain amount of till money, be kept out of the banks. The whole gold reserve should be concentrated at Threadneedle Street, to be used as required for the maintenance of the exchanges.

Sir Brien Cokayne, after succeeding Lord Cunliffe as Governor in 1918, served the usual two-year term. On his retirement his Deputy, Montagu Norman, was elected, and served as Governor for the next twenty-four years. To understand how this unprecedented term came about, it is not only the situation that must be considered but the man also.

When the reorganization of the Directorate had been planned in 1917 little or no attention had been paid to the question of the tenure of the Governorship and the importance of continuity in control. Cunliffe's dictatorial handling of the situation from 1914 to 1918 had not been entirely due to the fact that he was a born autocrat. The circumstances had called for a man of this nature and he had been needed for a longer period than the customary two years. In the course of his five-year tenure Cunliffe had seen the work of the Governor become so highly specialized that it would in future be quite impracticable to put it on the shoulders of a man whose own business was impatiently awaiting his return. Nothing but an exclusive attention over a long term would now satisfy the needs of the Bank and the country.

There was, however, a difficulty here. The Governors and Directors had never given up more than a part of their time to the Bank's affairs and their remuneration had been fixed accordingly. In 1695 the Governor and his Deputy had been voted £200 a year each, and each Director £150. These rates were not reconsidered until 1804, when they had been doubled, and in 1884 there had been a further adjustment under which the Governor and Deputy Governor each received £1,000 a year and each Director £500. In 1892 the Governor was allowed £2,000 a year and the Deputy Governor £1,500; these increases were in recognition of the fact that during their terms of office the Bank was now demanding most of their time. It was, however, to be quite a long while before the Directors felt that they could ask the General Court to provide remuneration appropriate for full-time duties to the Bank.

Happily, in the meantime, a man was available who was prepared to serve the Bank exclusively in return for an annual payment which was a great deal less than that received by some of his officers. It had so fallen out that at a moment when his special knowledge and experience could be of particular value both to the Bank and the Government, Norman had been without any private business ties, for at the end of 1915 he had ended his connection with his firm, Brown, Shipley & Co. He then came to the Bank to act as an unofficial assistant to Cokayne, who, in 1915, was Deputy Governor to Cunliffe. He had been added to the Committee of Treasury – at that time an unusual distinction for a Director who had not passed the chair – and was soon accompanying the Governors on their visits to the Treasury. In addition, special duties for the Government were taking him to the War Office as adviser on financial questions arising out of the cable censorship; here his experience of international credit and his knowledge of American and

Dividend Day at the Bank of England, 1850. From an oil painting by G. E. Hicks

Vignette of Britannia, designed by Daniel Maclise, RA, for Bank Notes first issued in 1855

George Joachim Goschen (Viscount Goschen). A Director from 1858 to 1865. Chancellor of the Exchequer in 1887. From a *Vanity Fair* cartoon of 1869

The Garden Court in the old Bank of England, showing one of the lime trees planted *circa* 1782 and the statue of St. Christopher by Richard Goulden, 1921. From a photograph

continental business had been of the greatest value. He gave up this work in March 1918, upon his election as Deputy Governor.

By nature and disposition Norman was quite as independent as Cunliffe, but he had directly witnessed the sort of dangers to which Cunliffe had exposed himself by going his own way without regard for the opinions, feelings and even the rights of others. He was always careful, therefore, to carry with him the informed knowledge and support of his colleagues on the Committee of Treasury, which, in its reorganized form, provided him with his principal advisers and helpers within the Bank. As Governor he reported each week on all the questions he had dealt with and in particular always asked for approval of any action which he had been obliged to take on his personal responsibility. He also shared with the Committee of Treasury the wealth of information he gathered from his 'outside' sources—the chairmen of the clearing banks, the partners of the larger private banking houses and other City leaders whom he was constantly meeting.

This then was the man who was elected Governor in 1920, who was re-elected for a third, a fourth, a fifth and many subsequent times until he had held the office for nearly a quarter of a century and, with it, the confidence of the Directors and of successive Chancellors of the Exchequer.

On the afternoon of Armistice Day 1921, in the Garden Court of the Bank, the Governor unveiled a memorial to those members of the staff who had lost their lives in the war, a memorial raised by their surviving colleagues. It was a life-size statue of St Christopher, by Richard Goulden, cast in bronze. The statue now stands in the new Garden Court at Threadneedle Street. It came unscathed through the war of 1939–45.

At the end of the First World War it was the wish of the Directors that all the work of the Bank should again be concentrated at Threadneedle Street, and it was estimated that this could be done if a large modern building of some six or seven storeys were erected in place of the Soane buildings. There was, however, a general desire that Soane's perimeter walls should be retained, nor was this for the sake of sentiment alone, for they still made a magnificent protection. It was hoped also that his top-lighted banking halls, lying immediately behind them, could be included in the new building. In 1921 Sir Herbert Baker was asked to draw up plans incorporating these ideas: he had just returned from India, where, with Sir Edwin Lutyens, he had been an architect of the New Delhi.

Demolition of the old Bank began in 1925 and the new building was completed at almost the last moment before war broke out again in 1939. Most of the clay sub-soil had had to be excavated to a depth of 60 feet in order to underpin the high building and the old exterior walls, the original foundations of which were nowhere more than 12 feet deep. The whole work was a vast and complicated engineering project as well. From this aspect, Baker and his partner, Herbert Scott, owed much to Dr Oscar Faber, to whom Baker pays a tribute in his autobiography *Architecture and Personalities*. Among his other collaborators, particular mention must be made of Charles Wheeler, the sculptor (now Sir Charles Wheeler, PRA), and Boris Anrep, the eminent Russian mosaic worker.

Thus was transformed, almost beyond recognition, what perhaps had been, save for St Paul's, the City's most familiar landmark. It could not but cause grief, especially to those whose first concern was with the preservation of ancient beauty rather than the provision of modern banking facilities. Dr Nikolaus Pevsner has said in his work *The Buildings of England*, 'The virtual rebuilding of the Bank of England in 1921–37 is – in spite of the Second World War – the worst individual loss suffered by London architecture in the first half of the twentieth century. We may mourn for many a parish church and many a town house, for whole squares, and for the Adelphi and Lansdowne House. But Soane's Bank was unique in a different way. It was the only work on the largest scale by the greatest English architect of about 1800, and one of the greatest in Europe. To preserve the screen-wall only and to scoop out all the rest strikes one as peculiarly distasteful. The use of Soane's masterwork as the footstool of a Herbert Baker seems unforgivable.'

Dr Pevsner's feelings, as one of Soane's greatest admirers, can be understood, but he did not have to try to work in a building that had become far too small for its purpose. Nor must it be forgotten that Soane himself would not have hesitated to destroy Taylor's lovely Court Room had the Directors allowed him to, and that he had built on ground which had once borne a work of Wren's. It may well be that, when the present building is felled in its turn to make way for a cloud-capped tower perhaps half a mile in height, some Dr Pevsner of the future will lament as vehemently the passing of Baker's Bank.

The false dawn of the postwar boom faded in the summer of 1920. Exports started to shrink, the demand for industrial capital slackened, agricultural prices fell sharply and the Labour Exchanges began to present scenes which became sickeningly familiar during the next twenty years – crowds of the workless, at first hopefully seeking employment and, later, listlessly drawing their pittances. The Bank had foreseen what must happen when the economic momentum of war and its after-math had spent itself and had taken what it held to be the necessary corrective steps. Bank Rate had been raised from $5\frac{1}{2}$ per cent to 6 per cent on 6 November 1919. In April 1920, after consultation with the Chancellor of the Exchequer, it had been put up to 7 per cent, and it remained at that figure until the following April, by which time there was a real measure of depression. Cause and effect were confused. Dear money was a symptom only, but in many quarters the Bank's policy was blamed for having itself led to the slump. From the preceding December there had been pressure on the Bank to reduce the rate, but action had been deferred. One reason was that, rightly or wrongly, Norman was hoping that the effect of the high rate would be to bring about a reduction in the cost of living – at its prevailing level he thought that, among other considerations, the miners, then on strike, were being asked to accept an unreasonable reduction in wages, as Sir Henry Clay tells in his *Lord Norman*. The rate was reduced to $6\frac{1}{2}$ per cent on 28 April 1921, and two months later, when it was clear that a nation-wide stoppage in the coal-mines was about to end, to 6 per cent. In July it went down to $5\frac{1}{2}$ per cent and in November 1921 to 5 per cent.

The country's, and the world's, plight was also reflected by the state of the exchanges. The New York rate, by the end of December, was $3.75, nearly 23 per cent below par. The Paris exchange, over which control was no longer being exercised, opened in 1920 at about 41, in place of the old 25.22 for the gold franc, and at the close of the year was nearly 60. The Italian exchange, in 1913 roughly the same as the French, opened in 1920 at about 50 and ended at over 100. The German, formerly about 20 marks to the £, opened the year at about 188, fluctuated considerably and closed the year at 258, though this was almost nothing compared with what was to come two or three years later. With currencies so utterly out of step with each other there was small chance of the hoped-for return to an international gold standard. Moreover, the position inevitably led to gambling with the exchanges and to the development of what was eventually a large market in forward exchange.

Forward dealings affected the machinery of Bank Rate in its international aspect. Before the war one of the main purposes of a high rate had been to draw gold to London; all that a rise in London did now, at any rate immediately, was to cause an adjustment between the forward rates and the spot rates in the world's various money markets. But in any case, gold was not so easily attracted in the postwar world. Every country but one was keeping a tight grasp on it and that one, the United States, did not need to – it was far more likely to attract gold than to export it. In Britain the powers which the Government had taken in wartime to control the export of gold were extended, in May

1920, by means of a Gold and Silver Export Control Act. This Act was to expire on 31 December 1925, so until that date, or the prior rescinding of the Act, there could be no return to the gold standard here.

In the spring of 1920 a concerted approach was made by the world's leading bankers and businessmen to their respective Governments to ask them to convene an international financial conference. A council of this kind was held in Brussels in September, but it was marred by the American Treasury's refusal to co-operate. Norman felt it would be improper to act as the British delegate himself, but he persuaded Lord Cullen (formerly Sir Brien Cokayne), his predecessor as Governor, to represent this country. The Council, when it reported, attributed the inflationary rise in prices and the weakening of the European exchanges to excessive Government expenditure everywhere. This should be reduced, all borrowing should cease and a start should be made in the funding and repayment of past borrowings. Countries which had lapsed from a gold standard should return to it and to facilitate this, central banks should henceforth be freed from any political pressure. If a country had no central bank, it should establish one.

In October 1922, Lloyd George's coalition ministry disintegrated. He resigned and Bonar Law was called upon to form a new Government. A General Election in November confirmed him in office and on 27 December his Chancellor of the Exchequer, Stanley Baldwin, left for America to arrange for the settlement of the £978 million British war debt to the United States. Norman accompanied Baldwin as his technical adviser. As with all post-war debt settlements and arrangements, obloquy was subsequently cast upon the measures agreed upon, and if this was deserved, Norman, as technical adviser, must bear his share of it. Nevertheless, the settlement was very much more of a political than a financial one and was vital for the maintenance of Britain's credit in the world. It is now generally agreed, also, that the hands of the American negotiators were tied to a great extent by the fear that Congress would disapprove of any settlement considered 'soft', and that, in consequence, they had to drive as hard a bargain as they could, consonant with justice. The terms eventually agreed upon for the funding of the debt fixed the interest on it as 3 per cent for the first ten years and at $3\frac{1}{2}$ per cent for the remaining fifty-two. This involved an immediate annual payment of £34 million, at the then existing rate of exchange.

There was, at the time, relatively little opposition to the settlement in this country, the general feeling being that we had 'hired' the money as Calvin Coolidge put it, and had said we would pay it back. If the Americans wanted it, then they must have it; if things turned out as they should, it would be no more than a book transaction anyway, since we had debtors of our own, owing us more than we owed the Americans. There were, however, a number of powerful and influential opponents, the chief of whom, and one of the most bitter, was Bonar Law himself. McKenna, a former Chancellor, supported him, as did the young John Maynard Keynes whose magnificent powers of analysis, coupled with the ability to express them in forceful and lucid prose, were already making everyone concerned pay attention to what he had to say. In the Press, Lord Beaverbrook's newspapers voiced an uncompromising disapproval from the start.

In those days, of course, Keynes did not bear the responsibility of having to make a decision, but when, as will be recorded later, he was leader of the British Delegation to Washington in 1945 and found himself, like Baldwin, faced with a choice between a settlement he thought oppressive and no settlement at all, he used his influence to persuade the Government to accept what terms there were.

But what overshadowed the whole problem of postwar finance was the question of reparations. In 1921 the financial liability of Germany was ultimately fixed by the Reparation Commission at £6,600 million, to be paid in quarterly instalments at the rate of £150 million a year, partly in cash and partly in kind. Germany made a start in paying off this vast sum: large quantities of coal were sent to France and Belgium – one of the main results of which was to throw French and Belgian miners out of work – and some £284 million was paid, mainly in goods. It should have been foreseen, but had not been, that these deliveries would disrupt international trade. Of cash itself, the creditors received very little. The mark gave way under the strain and by the end of 1921 was at 1,020 to the pound. In 1922 the Reparation Commission declared Germany to be in default, and on 8 January 1923 the French Army marched into the great industrial district of the Ruhr. With this, the collapse of the mark was complete: it fell to 80,000 to the pound. By 30 September it stood at 19 billion, totally meaningless figures except to the wretch whose life savings had, in a few hours, been reduced to the price of a single meal.

The Bank was at no time directly concerned with any of the negotiations regarding these reparations. When in 1923 the Government wished Norman to serve on an international committee of experts appointed to examine Germany's capacity to pay, the Committee of Treasury took the view that there was a paramount need for the Governor to devote himself entirely to Bank affairs. A Director, Sir Robert Kindersley, was one of the two British experts on the Advisory Committee, the other, Sir Josiah Stamp (later Lord Stamp) – by whom the Committee's unanimous report was largely written – was to become a Director in 1928 and serve until his death in an air-raid in 1941. This was the 'Dawes Committee', which took its name from its American Chairman, Charles G. Dawes. It recommended that Germany's currency should be stabilized on a gold basis, that greatly reduced payments should begin again in 1926 and – what was to set a rather unhappy precedent – that an international loan of £40 million should be made to Germany to aid recovery there, so that in time the German debts could be paid. Payments were duly made from 1926 until 1929, but these came virtually out of the creditors' own pockets – a fact sufficiently demonstrated when they declined to make further loans and the plan immediately collapsed.

The second Labour Government of the inter-war years was returned to power in 1929 and, as in the first, the Chancellor of the Exchequer was Philip Snowden, a radical of the old school who, in matters of finance, almost out-Gladstoned Gladstone. He asked the Bank to handle the London *tranche* of the Dawes Loan, amounting to £12 million, 'to avoid the break-up of Central Europe'. On 24 September, after long discussions in the Committee of Treasury, the Bank agreed. A subscription to the loan, from the Bank's own funds, was also voted, from the feeling that, as in the case of the American debt settlement, a good example should be set regarding the proper conduct of debtor-creditor relationships in the international field.

The Dawes Plan having collapsed, it was followed in 1930 by another, the Young Plan. The Young Plan collapsed. Then, in 1932, under the Lausanne Agreement, Germany was relieved of all liability, subject to a final capital payment of £150 million. So the victorious Allies were left 'holding the baby' in the shape of their various obligations to one another, and the complete failure of all schemes to 'make Germany pay for the war' was yet another of the many disillusionments engendered by the Versailles Treaty.

In the early twenties, despite the postponement and eventual failure of the attempt to convene a meeting of Central Bank Governors in order to formulate a Monetary Convention, there was a large and welcome increase in informal discussion and co-operation between all the central banks. The importance of a general return to an effective international gold standard, as a safeguard against inflation and as a basis for international trade, had been solidly affirmed both at Brussels and Genoa.

In 1924 it was decided to make one more effort to return to gold. The conditions seemed favourable – the British war debt had been settled, the interest on it was being paid regularly, the Dawes Plan had achieved at least a temporary solution to the Reparations problem and trade had somewhat improved both in this country and the USA. A Committee appointed in 1924 had unanimously recommended restoration; its Chairman had been Sir Austen Chamberlain, an ex-Chancellor, and with him had been Lord Bradbury and Sir Otto Niemeyer of the Treasury, Gaspard Farrer of Barings and Professor Pigou – and as three of these had been on the Cunliffe Committee it would have been strange if their recommendations had been other than they were. Further recommendations were that the two note issues, the Bank's and the Treasury's, should be amalgamated, that other bankers should pay any gold they held into the Bank of England and that there should be no prolongation of the prohibition on gold exports once the Gold and Silver Export Control Act of 1920 had expired at the end of 1925.

With a return to Conservative government in November 1924, it fell to Winston Churchill, as Chancellor of the Exchequer in Baldwin's second Cabinet, to announce the return to gold. This he did in his Budget speech of 28 April 1925. A simple statement was enough, to the effect that the embargo on gold exports would not be renewed at the end of the year and that, in the meantime, licences for its export would be granted. The change was embodied in the Gold Standard Act 1925.

It was, however, to be a gold standard without a gold circulation, an arrangement for which Ricardo had once argued. Bank notes and currency notes were to remain legal tender, but the bank was not bound to cash either in coin. Only the Bank might take gold to the Mint in future. As it happened, no one else had done so for many years, but the Coinage Act of 1870 had continued to permit its being done. The Bank was bound to sell, for any legal tender, gold in bars of not less than 400 ounces, Troy weight – at £3 17s. 10½d. an ounce – the old price. In this way gold movements were to be kept in the Bank's hands.

The immediate results of the restoration were satisfactory. Prices fell, but not disastrously, in the following year, though this must perhaps be attributed to domestic troubles – for it was the year of the General Strike – rather than to exchange policies. However, for the next few years bankers and traders had the satisfaction of knowing once again how much they could get for their pounds in the field of exchange – albeit this was a field limited to those markets where gold had resumed its reign.

The decision was therefore generally welcomed in the banking and business worlds. The financial Press approved; *The Economist* of 2 May 1925 showered congratulation all round on the Chancellor, the Government and the Bank; the *Bankers' Magazine* agreed that the time had been ripe for a return and had a special word of admiration for the thorough way in which the preparations had been made. Among the dissentients Keynes was to the fore. In a pamphlet, *The Economic Consequences of Mr Churchill,* he directed his criticism not at the gold standard as such but to its having been restored in circumstances which could not but lead to a painful readjustment of all money values. 'Mr Churchill's policy of improving the exchange by ten per cent,' he said, 'was sooner or later a policy of reducing everyone's wages by two shillings in the pound.'

The immensely varied questions posed by the state of the post-war economy, both at home and abroad, were obliging the Bank to assume, more and more, the role of Britain's central bank to the exclusion of all others. At home, in addition to its constant preoccupation with first restoring and then maintaining the gold standard, it found itself being drawn into a number of problems arising from the reorganization of industry on a peacetime basis. Abroad, no sooner had the matter of the American debt been settled than the Bank became involved in negotiations regarding other inter-allied debts and the various loans sponsored by the League of Nations.

As to the domestic problems, it was almost by accident that the Bank became the Treasury's agent in unravelling a number of difficulties. One of the great armaments firms which were struggling against adversity in the shape of peace was Armstrong-Whitworth, and Armstrong-Whitworth happened to be customers of the Bank's Newcastle branch. By 1926 Armstrongs were in extreme difficulty. The Bank – one of whose prime concerns was always to do what it could to prevent or stem unemployment – stood by the firm when it undertook a thorough reorganization of its affairs. In February 1929 the company was reconstructed by means of a scheme which *The Economist* called 'the greatest achievement of financial salvage ever recorded'.

Having come into close and direct contact with one basic industry, the Bank almost automatically became concerned with others. Various projects for their 'rationalization' – as the schemes for reorganization and amalgamation were known – were being forced upon its attention. In 1929 the Governor devised a private company, under the name of the Securities Management Trust, to handle the numerous securities which had devolved upon the Bank in the course of these reorganizations.

As the Bank had done in the case of Armstrong-Whitworth, other banks had, from a sense of duty to the country, made advances not in accordance with the strictest canons of banking in order that the production of war materials might not be impeded. Therefore, in the way that the Bank had acquired an interest in Armstrongs, they had acquired interests in all sorts of concerns, of which the Lancashire Cotton Corporation was one important example. This led to the formation of a second private company, the Bankers' Industrial Development Co. Ltd, the Directorate of which was a mixed body of industrialists and financiers, the Governor having a seat on the Board. Under his encouragement practically all the deposit banks, merchant bankers and finance houses contributed towards its capital.

As regards the Bank's concurrent foreign operations, these were very much a legacy of the pre-moratorium bills of 1914 for which, under Treasury guarantee, it had accepted responsibility. They included some millions of pounds of acceptances by foreign, dominion and colonial firms, and banks with branches or agencies in this country, and among them were the acceptances of the London office of the Anglo-Austrian Bank. The break-up of the old Austrian Empire had brought that office many difficult problems, and it was decided, after an accountant's investigation, that they could best be dealt with it if were reorganized as an English bank.

The Bank of England was prepared to assist; it accepted deferred stock in place of the settlement of its prior claims; put up some new money and effected the reorganization with the help of a London board and a Central European expert, Peter Bark, formerly Vice-Governor of the Imperial Bank of Russia. Its new interest in Austria led the Bank and the Governor into extensive negotiations not only there but in central Europe generally, where the economic troubles, common to all countries, were, of course, bedevilled during the whole inter-war period by rancid political conflicts and nationalistic eruptions. As the course of history was to show all too tragically, these ills proved incurable, but some remedy had to be tried, and that could only be an economic one – hence the establishment of various central banks and, in 1930, of the Bank for International Settlements, which can best be described as a central bank for central banks.

Round about 1930 Norman felt that the time had come when the nature of a central bank should be defined, so with Benjamin Strong, the American banker, he formulated the underlying principles. The first of these was that a central bank should not compete with other banks for general business and in conformity with this the Bank of England continued to disengage itself from all business it now considered to be the province of the commercial banks. It was decided that the branches should not resume their discount business and the West End branch, where a considerable amount of business with the old type of customer was still conducted, was disposed of in 1930 to the Royal Bank of Scotland, the Government accounts there being transferred to

Threadneedle Street. Henceforward any new accounts opened either at Threadneedle Street or the branches were restricted, in the main, to those needed by concerns forming part of the essential structure of the capital market.

The causes of the near-chaotic conditions which universally prevailed between the wars and the measures which might have relieved them are still matters of high dispute between historians, political theorists and economists of varying schools and probably will continue to be as long as history is written. Any attempt to discover them at the time therefore had small chance of success and no answers could be correct or complete. Nevertheless, if any hopes of salvation were to be nursed, the attempts had to be made.

One of the most noteworthy in this country was that of the 'Macmillan Committee' – the Committee on Finance and Industry of 1929, of which the Rt Hon. H. P. Macmillan, K.C., was the Chairman. It was given the task of discovering whether the arrangements in this country for banking, finance and credit helped or hindered trade and industry. Its membership included a number of economists and financial and other experts, among them being Keynes, McKenna, Bradbury, Professor T.E.Gregory and Ernest Bevin, then General Secretary of the Transport and General Workers Union. The Committee's Report presents a comprehensive account of British banking, credit and investment practice at the time: its recommendations were cautious and, when they appeared, they had in some important respects been already overtaken by events, particularly in so far as the gold standard was concerned – the country was then about to 'go off gold', so the Committee's qualified approval of the retention of the gold standard, and its suggestion that the next phase of monetary policy must be to make it work more satisfactorily, were of small avail. Its findings on the Bank's organization were also incomplete, since the Committee of Treasury had thought that it would be premature for the Governor or Deputy Governor, Sir Ernest Harvey, to disclose in evidence certain changes and improvements being contemplated at the time the Committee was sitting, but which had been largely put into practice before the Report, which recommended them, was published.

It is in the printed volumes of evidence given before the Committee that the most valuable information can be obtained of the contemporary Bank and City. Sir Ernest Harvey's account of the Bank, its evolution and day-to-day activities was a comprehensive, clear, and factual one. He also dealt very fully with the duties of a central bank, or as he said he would prefer to call it, a central reserve bank, and the way in which the Bank itself functioned in this capacity. As a witness, Harvey was in a much more fortunate position than Norman: all he had to do was to speak of facts within his expert knowledge. Norman, on the other hand, was asked, later in the proceedings, to explain those facts to theorists who based their questions on a perhaps quite unconscious assumption that monetary policy had an absolute influence upon industry, that industry prospered or languished in direct accordance with the actions of financiers, and that if it was in difficulties then monetary policy must be to blame.

In the face of questioning founded on such assumptions, it is hardly surprising that Norman made a bad witness. The interpretation of events by each of his critics was exact and logical, according to whatever theory the critic happened to favour. Norman, the man with practical experience, was disinclined to generalize. He described his actions as a series of responses to particular situations which were never quite the same. To the crucial question put by the economists, whether in moving the Bank Rate he had in view the results upon the industrial position at home, he answered, 'We have them in view, yes, but the principal consideration is the international consideration.' Pressed by Keynes, who claimed that the Bank Rate was 'effective', in Norman's sense of the term, in correcting an adverse international position only by causing domestic unemployment, he at first demurred, but eventually admitted that the external and internal effects were necessarily linked.

When, however, he was not being required to chop logic with his inquisitors, Norman gave a clear picture of the actual difficulties with which he, the Bank and the City had had to contend since the war and the specific problems which had had to be resolved. There was, for example, 'the troublesome question of perpetual maturities of debt'; the steps taken to help stabilize those European countries which had lost all they had possessed before the war – efforts which had had to be made, but which, in the end, had been so disappointing; and on top of all this, the problems of British industry itself, which the Bank could not ignore, although in theory it was no part of a central bank's business directly to investigate the problems of particular industries or handle their affairs.

At a later date in the proceedings he attended with Sir Guy Granet, his alternate in the Chair of the Bankers Industrial Development Company, in order to explain to the Committee the aims and policies of the Company. In the opinion of an economist of the present day, A. J. Youngson (in his book *The British Economy 1920–1957*), his answers were 'impressive' when he was questioned regarding the problems of 'rationalization'. He made a final appearance before the Committee in company with Dr O. M. W. Sprague, to answer inquiries about the recently constituted Bank for International Settlements, giving his opinions on its prospects of success and what he thought were the limitations inherent in its nature.

In June 1929 the second of the Labour administrations of the inter-war period came to power with Macdonald once again Prime Minister and Snowden Chancellor. Men of all shades of political opinion have since agreed that, whatever its shortcomings or virtues, it was doomed to fail through sheer misfortune, circumstances outside its control forcing it to take decisions so contrary to the apparent interests of the classes it mainly represented that it could not avoid splitting irrecoverably. No Government ever quite deserved to encounter such vile misfortune.

In 1928 the heavy lending to Europe by American investors had ceased and the most feverish speculative boom of all time had taken its place. Investors on the New York Stock Exchange had seen their money doubled and trebled – though usually on paper, for why disturb money which they were confident would double yet again? – and the prospect of quick, unearned wealth was drawing large amounts of European gold and funds across the Atlantic. As Americans, at least, need no reminding, the crash came in late October 1929. In one hectic week 240 securities had declined in market value by $16,000 million. Trade and investment were immediately affected all over the world. Britain's exports, which were £869 million in 1929, fell to £666 million in 1930 and to only £461 million in 1931.

Before the crash, Bank Rate had been raised to 6½ per cent, the highest it had been for eight years. This was done partly to stem the investment flow to America and, partly, a gold drain to France – at that moment there were political differences between France and Britain and to these were ascribed, rightly or wrongly, some of the French withdrawals. A further factor leading to the increased rate was the 'Hatry crisis' which was then shaking the City and alarming the foreign short lenders, for in those troubled days London, like every other capital market, would be suddenly flooded by and as suddenly drained of short-term lendings it would sooner have done without – 'funk money' not knowing where to lay its head and finding a short resting-place in whatever market seemed safest for the time being.

The Bank was not entangled in any way with the Hatry crisis, except in so far as it was the general watcher over credit in the City. Clarence Hatry was the founder and moving spirit of a new issuing house which 'went up like a rocket and down like the stick'. In happier days his undoubted business abilities might well have earned him honourable success. As it was, when he got into difficulties he attempted to extricate himself by fraud. He tricked a famous firm, specializing in the printing of bonds, share certificates and similar commercial and financial paper, into printing bonds, for a perfectly legitimate loan being issued by his house, far in excess of the actual amount of the loan. The additional bonds thus obtained, false but not forged, were put up by him as security for large advances from commercial banks. The Governor had previously met Hatry, who had confided his schemes for industrial reorganization to him, and it was to the Governor that Hatry confessed when he realized that his misconduct must eventually be detected, whatever he did. On the day of Hatry's collapse the whole matter was gone into in the Governor's room at the Bank, the commercial banks concerned were brought in, the co-operation of the Stock Exchange for the clearing up of the affair was sought and obtained, and the same evening everything known was reported to the Chancellor of the Exchequer.

Throughout that autumn gloom reigned over the City. After Hatry came the Wall Street crash. Paradoxically, this strengthened London for a while, since it intensified an inward flow of gold, London having become much safer than New York. Britain, however, could not evade the world crisis for long. The disastrous and long-continued fall in her exports which started almost immediately after the American crash led to an increase in the unemployment rate from 10 per cent to nearly 16 per cent. Profits fell; there was in consequence little fresh money seeking investment and new industrial issues on the London Stock Exchange fell in volume by almost a third.

The nadir was reached in 1931, which saw the greatest financial crisis ever known. It started in Vienna, where the Credit Anstaldt, an old house founded by Rothschild of Vienna in 1855, suspended payment in May. Germany, always closely linked with Austria financially, next felt the strain, and during the whole of June the Reichsbank lost millions of marks in gold and foreign exchange. Despite intensive rescue operations in the shape of credits from New York, where some recovery had by now been made, Paris, the Bank for International Settlements, and the Bank of England, the German economy collapsed.

In July it was the turn of Britain herself – and the recent credits to the Reichsbank did nothing to help her position. From the middle to the end of the month the Bank's gold losses averaged nearly £2½ million a day. Bank Rate, which had been low for some twelve months, had been reduced even further, to 2½ per cent, on 14 May. On 23 July it was raised to 3½ per cent and on the 30th to 4 per cent, but still the drain went on. On 1 August the Bank announced that it had arranged credits of £25 million each with the Bank of France and the Federal Reserve Bank of New York. The fiduciary note issue was increased by

161

£15 million, but after a short lull during the first week of August the drain was resumed.

The Governor's health had broken under the strain and Harvey, his Deputy, was acting for him. It had been hoped that the announcement of the French and American credits would stop the outflow from London but, by a piece of cruel luck, on the very day that they were announced the Report of a Committee on the national finances – the 'May Committee' – was published, and it was a most depressing one. It estimated that there would be a Government deficit of £120 million by April 1932; it proposed that in order to meet the deficit new taxation amounting to £24 million should be imposed and that there should be cuts in Government expenditure of £96 million per annum – £66½ million of which was to be carried by shoulders least able to bear it, since this amount would be saved by reducing unemployment benefit by 20 per cent. The Report was factual, it was attended by no statement of a reassuring nature, and this could only increase the existing fears of foreign observers. On 6 August, Harvey had to tell the Chancellor that in the previous four weeks £60 million of gold and foreign exchange had been withdrawn from London, and that the Bank could not withstand that sort of loss very much longer – if it continued at the same rate, the credits would be exhausted in less than a month.

The recall of the Prime Minister from his holiday retreat in Lossiemouth marked the start of the August crisis which, in less than two weeks, brought down the Labour Government. Snowden's rigid Gladstonian orthodoxy caused him to clash fiercely with most of his fellow-members in the Cabinet. His ruling, deep-seated fear was of inflation – he had seen what it had done to Germany – and he was acutely aware of the country's weak external position and of the dangers then brewing up in Europe politically. In the end he gained the support of the Prime Minister, but almost without exception the rest of his colleagues, perhaps forgivably, could think only of what must happen to the workers, especially the unemployed ones.

Everyone concerned did what he thought was right and whatever was done must have had painful results. The recriminations which followed were therefore of the bitterest kind. The accusation was flung out that the crisis had been engineered by the bankers of this country and of those countries, France and America, from which it was hoped to obtain further credits. Their method, it was said, had been to insist on the cuts in the 'dole', proposed in the May Report, as a prior condition to the granting of the new credits. Hence the whole thing was simply an 'international bankers' ramp' designed to bring down a Socialist Government. This, however, could only mean that Snowden himself had stooped to conspire with the bankers, yet, whatever his sins in the eyes of his erstwhile comrades, it is almost inconceivable that they could have seriously thought that a man of Snowden's character would have deliberately worked for the downfall of a party to which he had devoted himself, heart and soul, all his life. As for the Bank's part in the alleged 'ramp', it had been asked for its advice as the Bank, not as anything else; it could therefore hardly have been expected to reply except upon the strictest of orthodox banking lines, and if it had done otherwise it would have failed in its particular duty.

On Monday, 24 August, the formation of a National Government was announced, though it was far from being a truly national one in the sense that, say, a wartime coalition is. Its title did not so much represent the reality as the image of itself which the Government wished to project. Macdonald was still Prime Minister and Snowden Chancellor; there was a sprinkling of Labour Ministers who followed them and one or two Liberals, but it was the Conservatives who supplied the bulk of the new ministers, with Baldwin at their head as *eminence grise* to Macdonald. In the House, all the Conservative members and – until their party split later over the question of tariffs – all the Liberal members backed the new administration, but practically all the Labour members closed their ranks to form a busy and very hostile Opposition. The sentiment among the people at large followed much the same pattern. They certainly did not support the Government unanimously, especially the men who, after drawing what was always a small and was now to be a smaller amount at the Labour Exchange, had nothing better to do than return to their lounging at drab street corners, while as for those manual workers who were still in employment, the Labour Party and the Trades Union Congress published a joint manifesto, on 3 September, in which 'embittered conflict and industrial chaos' were threatened if any attempt were made to reduce wages.

Confidence was restored to some extent after Snowden was able to announce that fresh credits, of £40 million each, had been obtained from Paris and New York, but the worst of the financial crisis was yet to come. On 10 September, Snowden produced a balanced budget which mainly followed the May Committee's recommendations, but the pound was still very weak and the general international situation was degenerating more and more. Then came the 'mutiny' in the Fleet at Invergordon. It was not a mutiny at all – it was an orderly protest at the cut in their pay which had been suffered by the sailors along with everybody else who drew a salary or wage from Government sources – but 'mutiny' made a more striking headline in the sensational Press. Abroad, the already apprehensive followers of Britain's fortunes became more nervous still. Another, though minor, panic ensued. £30 million of gold was lost in three days and British Government securities were sold heavily. The recent credits of £80 million were near to exhaustion. On 21 September, Bank Rate was raised from 4½ per cent to 6 per cent and, far more important, the Government simultaneously announced that, after consultation with the Bank, it had decided to suspend for the time being the operation of Sub-section (2) of Section 1 of the Gold Standard Act, 1925.

Thus, after six short years, Britain quietly 'went off gold'. The reserves had proved inadequate. They had, in fact, never been large enough, though in 1925, when the die had been cast, there had been a valid hope that they could be gradually built up. This had never been possible, and now, only two months after the Macmillan Committee had – not in very strong terms, it is true – confirmed Norman's testimony that the maintenance of the gold standard was of supreme importance, the Bank had been forced to advise the Government that it must be relieved of its statutory obligation to sell gold at a fixed price.

Although the immediate results of the abandonment of gold were not serious or, indeed, very noticeable, the country had reached a major turning-point in its economic history. It had tried, and had failed, to restore the old nineteenth-century confidence and trust which, with a few occasional tremors, had firmly ruled between the world's great trading nations. The first results of this failure seemed almost entirely favourable to Britain, but the more remote consequences were an increase of international suspicion and hatred, an inflamed nationalism in Europe and, finally, war.

After the general election in 1931, Snowden's task, as he had seen it, was done. A tired man, in constant pain, he relinquished the Chancellorship into the hands of Neville Chamberlain. So far as future financial policy was concerned, Chamberlain was in a not unenviable position, at least to the extent that he was not hampered by having to fulfil any promises, for Macdonald's election manifesto had not contained any – it had been deliberately vague on the subject, saying that the Government would feel itself free to advocate whatever measures it thought best, including the imposition of tariffs if necessary.

To the Government and the majority of its supporters protective tariffs seemed the only way out. All kinds of factors contributed to the decision – international liquidity had disappeared, world prices were falling, many of the country's assets abroad were 'frozen', foreign loans were difficult or impossible to obtain, Britain had abandoned the gold standard, and above all else, she was now the only country undefended by a tariff wall. In February 1932, Chamberlain introduced an Import

Lord Cunliffe, Governor 1913 to 1918. From a painting by Augustus John

Soane's Bank of England, immediately prior to its demolition. From an etching
and aquatint by Kenneth Hobson after Hanslip Fletcher, 1925

Lord Norman, Governor 1920 to 1944

Norman caricatured: Cartoon by Low, 1939, relating to a visit by Walter Nash, New Zealand Minister of Finance, to negotiate loan settlements. Sir John Simon, Chancellor of the Exchequer, feeds Poland, Turkey and Rumania, while Norman puts off New Zealand with book entitled *Benefits of Slimming*

Duties Bill. Its main provisions were the imposition of a general customs duty of 10 per cent on almost all imports, though goods from within the Empire were exempted pending the outcome of an Imperial Economic Conference to be held at Ottawa in the summer.

In June 1932, as already mentioned, there was an International Conference at Lausanne, where the unhappy story of reparations was, for all practical purposes, ended, though Germany remained under obligations to serve the bonds created under the Dawes and Young Plans.

All these matters affected the practices and policies of the Bank to a greater or lesser degree, but the Government measure with which it was most intimately concerned was the clause in the Finance Act of 1932 which set up the Exchange Equalization Account, a Government account to be administered by the Bank. In Parliament, somewhat later, Chamberlain explained its aims: 'To smooth out the variations in exchange caused by three sets of phenomena; firstly, the seasonal fluctuations; secondly, the operations of speculators, which increase those seasonal fluctuations . . . thirdly, the special flight of capital from other countries for the sake of finding a safer place to stop in for a time.' Its prime requirement was an ample fund of gold and sterling administered by officials able to act swiftly, widely, and, above all, secretly.

The foundation of this Account was not the sudden erection of defences for a completely unprotected sterling. As soon as the gold standard had been abandoned steps had been taken to level out exchange fluctuations and to frustrate the forays of speculators. The Exchange Committee set up between the Treasury and the Bank was, in September 1931, already buying and selling dollars and looking for gold. When this Committee was renewed in the December of that year it was made up of three Bank Directors, the Bank's adviser on American matters, a representative of the joint-stock banks and two Treasury representatives. When it became more formally legalized it was operated by officials of the Bank under the general direction of the Treasury.

The Account started its working life on 1 July 1932. Its initial capital assets were £17 million and it had powers to borrow up to £150 million. This maximum was increased by £200 million in May 1933 and by a further £200 million in April 1937. At first its administration was far from easy. At the end of 1932 sterling underwent considerable pressure because of war debt payments due to America; the Account's efforts to support sterling were hampered by insufficient resources, one result of which was that the dollar exchange once fell as low as $3.17 before making a recovery and it had to endure much hostility from abroad, especially from America. Two events in 1933 altered the situation; the first was Hitler's accession to power, the second the troubles which the whole American banking system ran into later that year. Britain suddenly became the safest place in the world in the eyes of the holders of capital; indeed, the extension of the Account's borrowing powers in May 1933 was the direct outcome of its being asked to absorb large amounts of foreign exchange and gold. Thenceforward its resources were always sufficient for it to operate effectively both as a buyer or seller of sterling.

Another great financial operation of 1932 was the conversion of almost all the massive loan of £2,085 million 5 per cent War Stock 1929–47, then constituting 27 per cent of the total funded debt. Bank and Treasury had discussed its possible conversion long before 1929, the year in which the loan first became redeemable. The Government's policy was the promotion of low interest rates – 'cheap money' – aimed at reducing debt charges. The scheme of conversion finally adopted assumed that most holders would accept conversion; they were given three months in which to make up their minds whether to redeem or convert, after which, if they had not demanded repayment, their assent to conversion would be taken for granted.

On 30 June, as a final stimulus, Bank Rate was reduced to 2 per cent – at which it was to remain until 1939. On the same day Chamberlain announced the conversion terms, using along with more traditional channels the then fairly novel medium of communication, the 'wireless' or radio, on which he gave a nation-wide broadcast. The 5 per cent War Loan would be converted to a $3\frac{1}{2}$ per cent stock redeemable in or after 1952 at the option of the Government. When the offer expired at the beginning of December 1932, 92 per cent of the stock, amounting to some £2,000 million had been converted, £165 million only having to be repaid in cash.

So, by the end of 1932, revolutionary changes had taken place in the country's economic organization. The links with gold and with world price levels had been broken and an autonomous independent monetary policy had thereby been made possible. Cheap money had been made available and a general tariff imposed. The country had emerged from a ten-year struggle to re-establish the gold standard, from ten years of dear money and from eighty-five years of Free Trade.

The great changes in the Bank's internal organization carried through during the inter-war years had had small beginnings. Initially, many of them were made because the Governor needed more help in the field of central banking than was afforded by the existing offices.

The first of these new activities were conducted by a special section

of the Chief Cashier's Office; it was formed in order to maintain relationships, business and diplomatic, with other central banks and to
train selected members of the junior staff in some of the responsibilities
entailed by this work. It was thought best that the section should be
organized and directed by an expert from outside the Bank. The man
chosen was H.A.Siepmann, a former Treasury official who had had
some experience of private banking, had worked with the Finance
Member of the Council in India and had subsequently been Adviser to
the National Bank of Hungary. 'Adviser' was also the term adopted to
describe his position in the Bank. It had the advantage that it was one
not used in the existing staff hierarchy, and made it possible to go
outside in order to fill other appointments in the new fields of activity
without obstructing normal promotion to the existing higher positions.
Siepmann was thus the first of the Advisers to be appointed, and under
his leadership the Central Banking Section of the Chief Cashier's Office
expanded into the Overseas and Foreign Department. He was elected
to the Court of Directors in 1945, on which he served until 1954.

Another section which grew from small beginnings was formed to
deal with economic and statistical questions, and to prepare tables and
charts illustrating current economic and financial trends. A further new
duty, deputed to an experienced official versed in all branches of the
Bank's varied interests, was an examination of the Press, at first in order
to ensure that the Governor did not miss any significant item of news;
later this led to the production of a daily News Summary circulated
throughout the Bank.

The annual election of Governors and Directors in 1929 saw an
appointment of exceptional interest. It almost goes without saying that
the onerous duties which the Governor had performed ever since he
was first elected caused a great deal more work to fall upon successive
Deputy Governors. Though Norman's re-election year after year showed
that the Court was aware of the need for his prolonged services, Deputy
Governors had continued to be elected on the old system of rotation.
In fact, three men only had shared the post between 1920 and the spring
of 1929. They were H.A.Trotter, who served from 1920 to 1922 and
again for one year in 1926; Cecil Lubbock, who served for 1923 and
1924 and again in 1927 and 1928; and Sir Alan Anderson, who served
in 1927 only. The days were clearly over when a Director could take
time off from his own business in order to devote himself exclusively to
the Bank for two, or more, years at a time. What was now called for
was a full-time Deputy Governor, who must be a man experienced in
banking and with all the necessary professional qualities – a man who,
as Bagehot had foreseen, many years previously, was both a working

banker and a Director and need not, as he put it, 'say Sir to the Governor'.

The natural choice was Sir Ernest Harvey, who had trod in Sir Gordon Nairne's footsteps, following him in 1918 as Chief Cashier, in 1925 as Comptroller and in 1928 as a Director. Harvey was Deputy Governor until 1936, when he was succeeded by yet another Chief Cashier who had been elected to the Court, B.G.Catterns.

A question which had been avoided for a long time could not, after Harvey's appointment, be put off much longer – the question of what was the proper reward for a member of the Court who gave full-time service. It was settled in September 1932, when the General Court approved an addition to the By-law which governed the remuneration of Directors. This allowed the Court of Directors to engage the exclusive services of any of its members, as from 1 March preceding, and placed an appropriate annual sum at its disposal for their remuneration. On 21 March 1940 the General Court amplified the terms of this order by authorizing a fund to be maintained for the payment of pensions to those giving such services, ordering a corresponding increase in the annual sum allotted.

Progress continued to be made towards a co-ordinated monetary policy within the Empire, and with the very active co-operation of the Bank of England the process of establishing central or reserve banks in all the leading countries of the Empire and Commonwealth was completed. As early as 1920 the first of these, the South African Reserve Bank, had been set up, with a Bank of England man, W.H.Clegg, as its first Governor; in 1924 Australia had introduced legislation which enabled the Commonwealth Bank to conform more closely to the conception of a central bank than it had hitherto done; but it was the year 1934 which saw some of the most conspicuous advances in Empire central banking.

In India a Reserve Bank had been under consideration ever since it had been first recommended by a Commission on Indian Currency and Finance which had sat in 1926. Its establishment had now become a vital necessity in view of impending constitutional reforms – the India Office considered that the creation of an Indian central bank must precede any transfer of financial power to a Minister in India. Accordingly, an Indian Bill was introduced in 1933 constituting a Reserve Bank; this was signed by the Governor-General in March 1934, and the new bank was opened the following month. In the same year banking law in Canada was altered and a Bill to establish a central bank was introduced. It was to be the banker for the Dominion, to give financial advice to its Government and to regulate internal credit and the exchanges. At Canada's request, another Bank of England man, J.A.C.Osborne, was released to act as its first Deputy Governor, a young Canadian banker being the Governor. In New Zealand the Reserve Bank opened its doors on 1 August 1934, its first Governor again being a Bank of England man, Leslie Lefeaux. It had had much advice from London, aimed principally at stabilizing the New Zealand pound on sterling. Sterling, it had been agreed, should be the currency in which the Empire conducted its external transactions.

Indeed, the stability existing all through the thirties between the various Empire currencies and sterling was the best proof of the success of the Empire's central banking policy. Its members had confidence in sterling and were always prepared to hold it even though it was no longer tied to gold. For the Bank, acting through its Governor, this meant a constant attention to Empire business. In London itself bankers and the heads of issuing houses were continually visiting Threadneedle Street in order to discuss the needs for loans of the various Empire territories; Governors and officials of the now firmly-established central banks were frequent and welcome visitors, while the Overseas Department, by letter and cable, maintained unbroken contact with them.

At home, the stubborn and heart-breaking problem of unemployment was little nearer solution. From 1929 to September 1932 more and more men had lost their work. Thereafter there was a gradual but painfully slow recovery. By the autumn of 1934 the numbers employed had crept back to the 1929 figure, itself a grave enough one. By 1937 this figure had improved by a further 10 per cent, for by then the war clouds were gathering and rearmament had begun. In the Press that year 'situations vacant' began being advertised for such men as jig and tool-makers, whose long-neglected skills were now needed for the fashioning of the machines without which weapons could not themselves be fashioned.

Recovery was, therefore, in the air in 1933 and by 1935 was beginning to be noticeable. Unfortunately, it was very uneven, for despite improvements in the domestic markets there was none in the export trades. Exports continued to diminish, and where an industry's prosperity had mainly depended upon them there was always great distress – coal-miners, textile workers, shipyard men, dockers and seamen were among the worst sufferers. Agriculture, too, was in a depressed state: the traditional policy, now nearly a hundred years old, was still being followed of importing cheap food from abroad as the best means of checking wage demands by the industrial workers, and this, of course, made the lot of those working on the land an unenviable one. The expansion was in the new industries largely dependent on the home market – chemicals, rayon and motor vehicles – and in one or two of the old – steel, china and railways.

That the 'hungry thirties' were a period of abject and unrelieved poverty for all the nation's workers was, therefore, a myth sedulously cultivated in later years for purposes of political propaganda. That does not mean that there was not very real hunger and distress in the extensive 'depressed areas' where old basic industries had once flourished. The indignation and anger of the 'hunger marchers' from such places as Tyneside and South Wales were only too understandable – but they marched towards a quite well-fed London. Whether in depression or recovery, the standard of living fell very little for those in work. Imports were maintained, and at a much lower cost than before. In effect, the quite comfortable condition of the many millions still employed was at the expense of the foreign importer and of their unemployed fellow countrymen.

This decrease in exports while imports were being maintained at their former level had dire results on the country's balance of payments. In 1937 and 1938 the deficit averaged over £50 million, and on the eve of war Britain was meeting part of the cost of its imports by realizing overseas assets, though the seriousness of this course of action was not to become apparent until after hostilities had ended.

One of the principal attempts made to solve the problem of the 'depressed areas' was, of course, the 'rationalization' policy with which the Bank was so closely associated. It was far more the Governor's own contribution towards helping industry than it was the Bank's, though Norman could never have taken the many steps he did without its status, reserves and implicit consent behind him. His achievements here were impressive and things would have undoubtedly been far worse but for his efforts; nevertheless, because of his constitutional habits of reticence, all that he had done was obviously unknown to those Members of Parliament who poured so much acid scorn on him when the nationalization of the Bank was being debated in 1948.

What he did do is well set out in Sir Henry Clay's biography: 'Considered as an exceptional and abnormal task, undertaken with an improvised policy and improvised staff, limited by the co-operation he could secure from a reasonably suspicious capital market and a properly cautious Court and Committee of Treasury, and lacking any powers of coercion, to have saved the armament capacity of Armstrongs and Beardmores, established one efficient large-scale unit in the cotton-spinning industry, restored a large part of British liner traffic to profitable operation, helped to save the greater part of shipbuilding from bankruptcy and closing down, and prevented from collapse the experiment of establishing a modern, technically efficient steel-sheet industry . . . was a considerable achievement.' It is even more remarkable, Clay continues, when it is remembered that its author's main work, the maintenance of stable monetary conditions, was at the same time requiring his care and attention.

With central banks on the Continent – France, the Netherlands, Belgium, and to a more limited extent, Switzerland – and in all cases where a central bank conducted its exchange operations free from interference by its Government, co-operation was more intimate and continuous than it had been in the time of the gold standard. The Bank had, perforce, to be more distant in its relationships with those central banks which were under strict Government control, that is, those of Nazi Germany, Communist Russia, and the United States under the 'New Deal'. Even so, the regular communications with these banks, made necessary by exchange dealings, led to personal acquaintanceships which tended to ease the difficulties arising from differences of principle. The Governor, for example, felt able to continue a personal relationship with Dr Schacht, President of the Reichsbank, even though his abhorrence of Schacht's masters, the Nazis – 'the gangsters' as he called them, as early as 1934, in his talk to the Bank staff at the annual Library meeting – grew in intensity as the years went by.

Throughout the period British policy was based on the importance of maintaining a free market in London for currencies and as far as possible for securities as well. Such a market was vital to the country's foreign trade, to the imports on which its economic life depended and to the exports by which they could be paid for. The central bank governors of Europe recognized the London market as the one place where international payments on a large scale could still be negotiated, an indispensable element in maintaining an international economic community.

A most disagreeable 'incident' for the Bank came at the very end of the inter-war period. In the spring of 1939 there occurred the affair of the Czech gold, which inflamed public opinion and led, both in Parliament and Press, to a series of attacks on the Bank, its Governor and on Sir Otto Niemeyer, formerly of the Treasury, a Director of the Bank since 1938, who was associated with Norman as a representative of the United Kingdom on the Board of the Bank for International Settlements.

At that time the country was generally coming to appreciate that, sooner or later, although appeasement was still the Government's policy, Hitler's arrogant pretensions to universal dominion could be stopped by arms alone. On 15 March he had torn up the Munich Agreement by invading Czechoslovakia, occupying Prague and declaring

'Bohemia-Moravia' to be a German Protectorate. Less than a week later, on 21 March, the Bank had received instructions from the Bank for International Settlements to transfer an amount of gold, of about £5·6 million, which stood in that bank's name at the Bank of England, from one of its accounts to another. In itself this was an ordinary enough transaction which the Bank of England, or any other bank, would not think of questioning. The instructions were perfectly in order and the transfer was made the same day. Although it was none of its business, the Bank was fairly certain, however, that the account from which the gold was transferred was one which the Bank for International Settlements operated on behalf of the National Bank of Czechoslovakia and that the other account belonged to the German Reichsbank.

The Bank consulted the Government and the opinion of the Law Officers to the Crown was sought. The legal position was clear. When the Bank for International Settlements had been set up in 1930 it had been granted, as a non-political body, a general immunity from interference by any Government which was a party to the original agreement. The British Government could therefore take no action. If they did so they would be breaking their treaty obligations in a time of peace.

The central fact, the transfer of the gold, leaked out, though the surrounding circumstances were unknown. Searching questions were asked, but the answers were evasive. The Bank itself could naturally say nothing. The Government was still clinging to a thin thread of hope that its appeasement policy might succeed. This policy would be imperilled if it were driven into taking any action or even talking of doing so. Press and public seized the chance to enjoy a fine burst of moral indignation with Norman and Niemeyer, the agents who had actually conducted the transaction, as the pre-ordained victims.

Recriminations and evasions went on all through May, but gradually the real picture emerged. On 3 June *The Economist* was able to say, 'The truth and commonsense of the matter seems to be that the decision was the B.I.S.'s and that once Bâle had accepted the instructions it received from Prague, the Bank of England had no real option in the matter, however distasteful it might be to see Czech gold go to Germany . . . That the affair has still further restricted the scope of the B.I.S. cannot be gainsaid. The statutes of the B.I.S. have been shown to have a painful imperfection.' The article went on to allow, however that 'even as no more than a central bankers' club the B.I.S. is a body which it is well worth while keeping alive . . . The greatest need of the moment is to prevent anti-aggressive ardour from destroying all sense of proportion.'

On 5 June the Chancellor of the Exchequer, Sir John Simon, communicated to Parliament the advice previously received from the Law

Officers and on the 7th the *Financial Times* summed up the situation: 'Misconceptions which need never have existed concerning the Government, the B.I.S. and the Czech gold transaction have now been lengthily and painfully cleared away. The episode is an object lesson in how such matters should not be managed. Much confusion of thought and undignified altercation might have been avoided. The task of rehabilitating the B.I.S. is bound up with the task of restoring political sanity and confidence to the world.' Unfortunately, with a madman in the saddle in Germany, such hopes of 'restoring political sanity' were vain. They grew fainter as the summer wore on until, on 3 September 1939, with the German invasion of Poland, Britain was once again at war.

The Bank was infinitely better equipped for dealing with war finance than it had been twenty-five years earlier. During the twenty years of Norman's Governorship a vastly different Bank had emerged, one which was far more in advance of the 1914 Bank than the latter had been in advance of the Bank of Pitt's day. It had kept pace with the great changes brought about by war, reconstruction, depression and recovery, the new demands upon it being met by modifications in its structure and by important, though not always conspicuous, adjustments of its functions. The change in its outward appearance was there for all to see – from behind the familiar outer walls the high buildings rose, white and new, above the stream of City traffic. What was not so publicly apparent was the new banking instrument within. This was very largely of Norman's own creation, ready and able to undertake the many tasks which were to fall to it in a world at war.

The City, too, was far less taken by surprise than it had been in August 1914, and more prepared to accept the changes and restrictions which total war must inevitably bring. With the experience of the First World War behind it, there was little of the hesitation, delay and makeshift improvization which had marked its behaviour in the opening stages of the former conflict. The breathing-space since the Munich crisis had given it time in which to make thorough preparations. As a result, the main City markets went on functioning without interruption, the Stock Exchange closed for a few days only – from 1 to 6 September – and minimum prices were fixed. The necessary controls, including Exchange Control with the dollar at 4.03 to the £, were imposed at once. Bank Rate, which had been raised as a precaution to 4 per cent on 24 August, was reduced to 3 per cent on 28 September, and on 26 October returned to 2 per cent, at which figure it remained, a financial instrument not to be used again until 1951. One most important result of this greater preparedness was a much firmer control of prices.

In the six years between 1913 and 1919 the wholesale index had risen from 100 to 246 and the retail from 100 to 220, with further rises, a year later, to 375 and 276 respectively. In the corresponding six years between September 1939 and August 1945 these indexes rose only to 173 and 132.

So far as finance was concerned, however, what contributed most to the defeat of Germany and Japan was the embodiment in the Defence (Finance) Regulations of stringent measures of foreign exchange control. These were administered by the Bank as agent for the Government. There had been little such control in the earlier war, since both the Treasury and the Bank had then wished to preserve freedom of exchange and to maintain London's position as an open market for gold. As a result of what, after the event, can be recognized as a mistaken policy, large reserves were needlessly frittered away. Even when the danger was realized and the London Exchange Committee was formed in November 1915, with wide powers, it was never put into a position to exercise them.

This time the machinery was already there, it was in good working order, and the authorities had no qualms about using it. Back in 1926 a Foreign Exchange Section had been originally set up in the Bank; in 1929 the first official intervention had been made in the dollar exchange; in the great crisis of 1931 operations had been conducted on a large scale and the scope of these had been widened in 1932 when the Bank was authorized to administer the Exchange Equalization Account. Preparatory discussions regarding wartime control had been held with the Treasury between July 1937 and August 1939. By the latter date the Bank had had seven years' experience of running the Exchange Equalization Account, and it considered that a full control on the transfer of sterling into other currencies could be put into effect immediately. Incidentally, it also considered that a high degree of State interference in every branch of economic life would be inevitable should a major war break out. The Treasury had to be convinced, but in the end accepted this view, though with some reluctance; as for exchange control, it feared that there would be objections from America and other countries and was unwilling to endanger the prospects of obtaining the financial aid from America which it knew it would have to ask for, sooner or later, in the event of war.

Some of the Regulations were put into force before the war actually began, though at a time when it could be seen to be all but inevitable. This was on 25 and 26 August, when the Treasury issued Statutory Rules and Orders requiring the registration of securities marketable outside the United Kingdom and empowering the Treasury to take them over. On 3 September a large number of restrictions were introduced, their immediate objects being to prevent capital transfers abroad by residents in this country and to forestall any speculation in foreign exchange. To help the achievement of the second of these objects, the export of banknotes was prohibited, though it was recognized that the success of this particular measure would in the main depend upon the efficiency of the censorship. The import of bank-notes was forbidden later, on 20 August 1940, by which time many European countries had been overrun by the enemy: it was known that large stocks of sterling notes of high denominations, estimated to amount to between £10 million and £20 million, had been held in these countries, and this prohibition was designed to prevent Germany from getting the benefit of them. In the latter stages of the war this particular prohibition also came in useful in a manner probably not foreseen when it was first framed. Germany had forged Bank of England notes on a massive scale in the hope that they would disrupt the currency if they could be clandestinely introduced here. They were magnificent imitations, but the prohibition helped to keep most of them out.

An elaborately centralized system of control had been avoided. It was thought better that, so far as possible, its operation should be dispersed, the ordinary day-to-day working being put into the hands of the banks, with the Bank of England always there to be referred to for guidance if required. It was, moreover, realized that too stringent a system would require a vast and wasteful bureaucracy for its operation, interfering with and delaying vital trade and business. When evasions were detected they could best be dealt with by tightening the particular regulations or procedure which had been found to be defective.

The first step taken, in 1939, at Head Office to cope with these large and important wartime duties was the gathering, from the various offices of the Cashier's Department, of all those men with any previous experience of foreign exchange work. They were augmented, almost from the day war broke out, by a number of temporary officials who had been members of the Foreign Exchange Market and whose services were available owing to that market's immediate closure. Because of their expert knowledge and experience these men were of particular value.

For the convenience of local banking and commercial communities separate Branch Controls were set up at most of the Bank's branches; at Plymouth and Southampton the control was operated by the existing staff after they had been instructed at Head Office. Additional Exchange Control Offices were established in Belfast, Liverpool, Nottingham, Birmingham and Cardiff.

Thus, then, was forged a mighty but keen and flexible weapon for the confounding of the nation's foes which must have delighted the shade of that first great financial warrior, William Pitt the Younger. There was, perhaps, one result of Exchange Control which would have surprised even him, while the effect it would have had upon the old Bank Directors with whom he worked and quarrelled is almost impossible to imagine. In March 1941 the Bank ventured into the field of 'public relations'. In order to make sure that accurate information should be available to satisfy the public interest in the Bank, and its Governor in particular, and to provide the Press with current information regarding the numerous Government regulations it was then the Bank's duty to administer, a new Adviser was required. He obviously had to be a man with a first-class knowledge and experience of the newspaper world, able to keep a close watch on the accuracy, and wider implications, of any item of news concerning the Bank. A former Editor-in-Chief of Reuters, J.B.Rickatson-Hatt, was invited to undertake these duties, and to help him in his work he was given the services of an official conversant with the Bank's business in all its many aspects.

Co-operation between the Bank and the Treasury was, over the whole of the war period, close, cordial and outstandingly successful. There were differences of view, of course. As we have seen, they arose when the Exchange Control was being devised during the summer of 1939, and there was yet another difference over general wartime monetary policy.

'Left-wing' critics of the Bank as it was in those days have, for their own purposes, always chosen to regard the Bank, and Norman, as being concerned only with the preservation of the capital and profits of financiers and industrialists and have always been careful, then and since, to forget that it was the Bank which so often put forward the more 'advanced' view in its discussions with the Treasury. Urged by its Governor and supported independently by Keynes, it pressed from the start for a cheap-money policy with an unvarying Bank Rate of 2 per cent. Before the war, and for almost the whole of its first year, the Treasury could not quite believe that this would be practicable. But Norman was not to be deflected from his purpose. He pointed to the 6 per cent Exchequer Bonds of 1917 as a particularly outrageous example of what must be avoided and was a determined advocate of moderate interest rates for the inevitable war borrowings. His declared aim was a '3 per cent war' and his attainment of it is reflected in the much lower cost of Government borrowing compared with that incurred between 1914 and 1919. When, therefore, the first War Loan – £300 million at 3 per cent, maturing 1955 to 1959 – was issued in March 1940, Norman insisted that a public statement should be simultaneously made that more generous terms would not be offered for any later loans.

The policy's success was convincingly demonstrated in January 1944, when the Government was able to repay, at the first possible date, the 5 per cent Conversion Stock 1944–64, the only high-interest Government loan outstanding from prewar days. There was no conversion offer, but the importance of the prompt re-investment of the redemption money in one of the current Government issues was stressed. As it happened, although the total capital of this stock was £318 million, only £89 million was by then actually in the hands of the public, the Bank's Issue Department and the National Debt Commissioners having, over the years, gradually bought up the rest in the open market as favourable opportunities offered.

The 3 per cent War Loan was followed by a series of 'tap' loans – National War Bonds at 2½ per cent and Savings Bonds at 3 per cent. In order to organize a system which would attract small savings not suited to such bond issues, Sir Robert Kindersley returned to his 'first war' post of Chairman of the National Savings Committee.

Work on the first issue of 2½ per cent National War Bonds began in London in September 1940, but on the night of 9–10 September the Bank was damaged by two high-explosive bombs. The incident, which will be recorded in greater detail later, was inconvenient rather than serious, but to ease demands on space the 'tap' was turned off at Threadneedle Street and turned on at Whitchurch in Hampshire.

Whitchurch and its environs was the 'emergency location' of the Accountant's Department. In common with many Government departments and large business houses the Bank had made arrangements, in the months immediately preceding the war, to remove as much of its work as possible from a capital which would almost certainly be subjected to air-raids and possibly to poison-gas attacks. Those parts of the Bank's work which could most conveniently be conducted away from London were a large amount of its printing and most of the operations of the Accountant's Department. The most obvious place for a wartime Printing Works was the village of Overton, three or four miles from Whitchurch, since it was here that Messrs Portals, who had manufactured the paper for the Bank's notes for some two centuries, had their mills. The Dividend Preparation Office, which had long occupied premises in Old Street adjacent to the Printing Works, would also go to Overton. Two 'shadow factories' – as such buildings, erected away from London and other large centres against an 'emergency', were then known – had accordingly been built, ostensibly as additional stock-rooms for Portals, and they were ready for occupation when war broke out.

One very large office of the Accountant's Department having thus been accommodated, it was thought that the remainder might very well be situated in the same vicinity. A large field, forming part of the grounds of the mansion at Hurstbourne Priors, near Whitchurch, was therefore acquired, and in this a 'camp' had been established. The 'covered wagons' which had never had to be used for the evacuation of the Bank in the days of Napoleon now took the twentieth-century form of a fleet of lorries, and these, over the weekend which saw the outbreak of war, transported the accounts, records and chattels of almost the entire Department from Finsbury Circus, through the southern English countryside, to Hurstbourne. The camp consisted of a large office block of some 40,000 square feet on one level, sixteen large living-huts and a canteen.

Work at Head Office, though greatly increased as already described, went on more or less normally until the Battle of Britain and the heavy air assault upon London in the late summer and autumn of 1940 and after. The direct hit on the Bank on the night of 9–10 September had the effect, if anything, of improving morale. Shattered glass filled the offices and corridors, but it was felt that if the building could stand up to that it could stand up to almost anything – the strength of Faber's engineering and Holloways' construction could not have been demonstrated in a more spectacular way. The bomb hit a raking beam formed of two parallel girders, the space between which had been filled with concrete. The beam was severed completely. It was over the telephone room on the seventh floor, below which was the kitchen supplying meals for the Directors. Both rooms were wrecked, but actual structural damage did not extend more than fifty feet or so from the point of impact. There were no casualties. The Directors had to be content with cold meals for a few days; for an even shorter time the telephones were silent and the Bank went back to pre-Cunliffe conditions. An emergency exchange, which had previously been installed in the vaults, was quickly prepared for service. For what seemed a long while more a sinister tinkle, proceeding from the shovelling up of heaps of shattered glass, continued.

Work, especially at night, was driven more and more into the three underground floors. Space in the security and store vaults was taken over for office work, much of the less valuable of their contents being moved above ground, where they would have to take their chance. As the dislocation of rail and road services was making the daily journeys to and from the suburbs uncomfortable and difficult, a staff of 500 worked, fed and slept in the vaults; an underground canteen provided the evening meals.

A certain amount of further damage was suffered, though it was slight compared with that done by the high-explosive bomb. During the first night raids a number of unexploded anti-aircraft shells fell on the buildings; later, a number of incendiary bombs landed, but all of these, except one, were promptly rendered harmless by the Bank's own fire-fighting detachment. The 'one that got away' went through one of the windows of a room on the first floor, where it damaged furniture and fittings before it was extinguished. Many of the Bank's other premises, in London and elsewhere, also suffered. On the morning of 19 July 1944 a flying-bomb fell on Bank Buildings, at the corner of Princes Street and Gresham Street, the site on which 'New Bank Buildings' had been erected after the widening and straightening of Princes Street in Soane's day. Nos. 1, 2 and 3 and the adjacent National Debt Office at 19 Old Jewry were rendered uninhabitable. The Bank's Head Gate Porter, who lived in Bank Buildings, was seriously injured and some twenty other people were hurt by flying glass. The branch buildings at Manchester, Liverpool, Birmingham, Bristol and Plymouth were all damaged more or less seriously; the new building at Southampton, where bombing was particularly severe, stood up well under the attacks and there the damage was relatively slight.

The transfer to Overton of a large part of the Printing Works was entirely successful. The printing of the £1 and 10s. notes was simplified by the substitution of offset lithography for the long and complicated process of plate printing. These notes could therefore be produced in the Overton 'shadow factory'. The change of method robbed the notes of some attractiveness in appearance. There was also a change in the colour of the ink in the main design, so the new notes were immediately distinguishable. They would undoubtedly have been easier to imitate but for the embedding of a metal thread in the paper, an invention of S. B. Chamberlain, General Works Manager.

The demands of war added greatly to the volume of printing work both at Old Street and Overton. More than 4,000 million bank-notes were produced, over half of them at Overton. In London, in addition to Treasury Bills and many special documents, the huge supplies of forms required for the working of the Exchange Control had to be printed. Later in the war the British Military Authority required currency for the troops in occupied countries and 400 million notes were produced for this purpose. A great deal of work was done which was never seen by the public; for example, large quantities of 5s. and 2s. 6d. notes were prepared against a possible shortage of coin, and these, of course, were never required.

Notes of all denominations above £5 ceased to be issued in April 1943; in 1945 such notes were called in. They had proved rather too handy for tax-dodgers, evaders of the foreign exchange regulations and Black Market operators.

The position in which British industry would find itself at the end of the war and the necessity for adequate funds to ease the transition from war to peace were matters constantly in the mind of the Governor during the war's later stages. He could all too easily recall the Herculean labours which had to be attempted because of the failure to solve this problem after 1918, and was determined to do all he could to prevent the same thing from happening again. In March 1943 he set up a Committee within the Bank, charged with reporting on what it considered the best methods for ensuring co-operation, between the Government on the one side and the Bank, the bankers generally and other lenders upon the other, adequately to meet the country's postwar financial needs. The Committee was to have particular regard to what measures would be necessary for an effective control of the economy in what he knew would be a difficult period. These would include the methods by which the validity of demands for capital, especially from new industries, could be judged; how allocation of capital and available materials could be co-ordinated; how to deal with the needs of industry generally in such a way as to encourage full employment, and finally – a constant preoccupation of Norman's – how to undertake the most fruitful methods of industrial research. The Committee reported in the autumn of 1943. It assumed that post-war conditions would require the maintenance of low interest rates and of as much stability in commodity prices as could possibly be attained. It also assumed that the great majority of controls already in force would have to continue – exchange and import controls would be needed to keep imports down to a level which could be paid for without depressing the sterling exchanges; capital issues would have to be controlled to prevent the unregulated export of capital and the various controls imposed on commodities would be necessary so long as shortages remained. Prompt relaxation of controls would, however, be vital as production increased, for an unnecessary rigidity would deprive the consumer of the benefits of the higher standard of living which he ought then to enjoy.

The poor state of Norman's health had obliged him to decline to stand for re-election as Governor in April 1944. It was therefore his successor, Lord Catto, who in August of that year informed the Committee of Treasury that progress had been made on the proposal that the clearing banks and the Bank of England should form an organization to finance businesses, large and small, to the share capital of which organization the Bank itself would subscribe, as would the other banks

Lord Catto, Governor 1944 to 1949. From a photograph

Cartoon by Lee on the Bank passing into Public Ownership on 1 March 1946. The caption reads 'So much for Nationalisation. This is what 'appens when one of the OWNERS asks for a few quid till Friday.'

The Bank of England, as rebuilt by Sir Herbert Baker. From a photograph

and the great insurance corporations. Hence was born the Finance Corporation for Industry, registered on 19 May 1945, and the Industrial and Commercial Finance Corporation on 20 July following. The second of these concerns was for aiding small businesses and the one on which Norman had particularly set his heart; the purpose of the first was the granting of loans of over £200,000.

Mr Norman – he was never 'Sir Montagu', although he was often erroneously referred to in this way in the Press and elsewhere – was with some difficulty persuaded by his colleagues to accept, on his retirement, the peerage which he had declined some twenty years earlier for the characteristic reason that 'he could be of more use without it'. His barony was announced on 27 July 1944, the day on which the Bank celebrated the two hundred and fiftieth anniversary of its foundation.

To his work in the Bank and in the worlds of finance and industry this chapter is itself a short and necessarily inadequate tribute. He was a man who would have been remarkable in any walk of life and was, without doubt, the most outstanding of all those who, for two and a half centuries, had contributed to the making of the Bank of England. That he happened to become a Bank of England man was mainly due to the fact that he sprang from families long associated with banking, the City and the Bank itself. His paternal grandfather, George Warde Norman, a Director from 1821 to 1872, played a leading part in the counsels of the Bank during his exceptionally long service; his mother, who lived to see her son's achievement, was a daughter of Sir Mark Wilks Collet, a Director from 1866 to 1905, and Governor in 1887 and 1888. From this grandfather he learned at first hand the history of the Bank since the time of the Overend, Gurney crisis on 'Black Friday' 1866; and Sir Mark Collet had sat at the Court Room table with men who remembered, as Directors, the resumption of cash payments after the wars with Napoleon.

At the Bank, to those who had no personal contact with him, he seemed aloof and unapproachable, a dedicated man who regarded himself as being set apart by destiny to perform a great task. To some extent this impression was shared even by those who knew him more closely. His personal appearance and bearing contributed to this feeling. They were, in the most exact sense of the word, singular without being outlandish or eccentric. They were certainly a gift to the cartoonists.

Tall and upright, in his movements he was unhurried and strangely graceful; at rest, he was completely immobile. His head, with its broad, magnificently modelled brow and full but neatly pointed beard – worn at a time when beards were practically unknown in England – was unforgettable. Outdoors he usually wore a black felt hat, as did thousands of City men at the time, but it was pushed back from his forehead to form a kind of dark halo; a loose, unbuttoned overcoat hung from his shoulders like a cloak. That he was aware of his difference from the usual run of businessmen – 'sound' or shrewd or brilliant – and that he cultivated an outward appearance which emphasized that difference cannot be denied, but what that difference was and the complexity of character from which it sprang are hard to define, nor will any attempt to define them be made here. It has been done convincingly in the chapter entitled 'The Man' in Sir Henry Clay's biography.

He made only one public appearance in the Bank after his retirement. It was at the dedication of the wreath, on the plinth of the statue of St Christopher, which commemorated the Bank men and women who had fallen in the Second World War. A representative gathering, from the Court of Directors down, was there. The Bishop of Stepney, Rector of the old parish of St Christopher-le-Stocks, was there to pronounce the dedication and trumpeters of the Guards to sound the Last Post and Reveille, when the 'old Governor' entered to take his place among his former colleagues; with his entry the gathering seemed to be made complete in a way it had not been before.

More extensive preparations were made for marking the Bank's two hundred and fiftieth anniversary than for any previous one. In anticipation of the event Professor J.H. Clapham (later Sir John Clapham) had been invited in January 1938 to write his history of the Bank, which was published in time for the celebrations; these took place on 27 July 1944, the Bank's Charter having been sealed on the same day in 1694.

Also in the field of historical studies, the Directors ordered the setting up of a Trust Fund for the promotion of research into the historical development of business and finance, a branch of learning which they felt was poorly endowed in this country compared with many others. The Fund, for which a sum of £100,000 was provided, was to be known as the Houblon-Norman Fund. The income was to be used for awarding fellowships and making grants in aid of research in those departments of economic and social science covering the Bank's own field of operation, that is to say, in the study of business and financial institutions and conditions, past and present, particularly in relation to the problems of central banking. Grants to assist publication of the results would, of course, also be made.

The Directors also subscribed towards a personal gift to the Bank which would be a permanent memento of the anniversary, the money to be used, after the war, to provide an inkstand for the Court Room table. In due course, in 1951, this took shape as a handsome and attractive piece designed and made by Mr Leslie Durbin, MVO.

On the day of the anniversary itself a luncheon was held in the Court Room, it being felt that, in wartime, the guests should meet in private and be small in numbers. Among those who attended were the Chancellor of the Exchequer, Sir John Anderson, and the Lord Mayor of London, Sir Frank Newson-Smith. In his speech of welcome the Governor, Lord Catto, referred to a dinner which had been held in 1794 to celebrate the Bank's first centenary. The records of this dinner, he said, were not very complete, though the list of guests survived and was of some historic interest. The Lord Mayor of London had been present, as was his successor in office that day, so were the Masters of the two ancient guilds with which the Bank had had long associations, the Mercers' and the Grocers' Companies. Also present on that occasion, as now, were the Governors of the Royal Exchange Assurance and the London Assurance, and then, as now, the guest of honour was the Chancellor of the Exchequer – in 1794 it had been William Pitt.

In the evening Lord Catto made a broadcast speech, in the concluding passage of which he outlined the principles which guided those in whose hands the affairs of the Bank lay two hundred and fifty years after its foundation.

'From time to time,' he said, 'the Bank is accused of having undue power. But neither the Bank nor any other body working for the Government can determine policy: the power to do that is the prerogative of Government and Parliament alone. What the Bank does is to give independent and candid advice based upon experience. . . . The Bank has influence, of course, and rightly so, for that comes from experience and service and the confidence not alone of the Government, but also of the financial communities of the Nation, the Empire and of the world; and above all the confidence of the man in the street, as summed up in his own phrase – "Safe as the Bank of England".'

Chapter 9

Public Ownership and After

The end of Montagu Norman's long Governorship and his succession by Lord Catto in the spring of 1944, followed by the celebration of the Bank's two hundred and fiftieth anniversary in the same summer, seemed as it were to close an important chapter, though only a chapter, in its long history. None could have known, and few foreseen, that these were, in fact, the final events of an era.

The victory in Europe, in May 1945, was marked for the staff by the early return of the Accountant's Department to the City. It was found possible for the Department, by effecting a straight 'swap' with the Pay Corps, who had been in occupation throughout the war, to regain possession of the offices in Finsbury Circus from which it had been evacuated. There was no longer any possibility of the Department's taking up possession of the banking halls at Threadneedle Street which Sir Herbert Baker had designed for its occupation – they had by now been put to other uses; for example, the work of Exchange Control was being done in a large part of the accommodation originally intended to house the stock ledgers. However, the business of the Accountant's Department no longer demanded the personal attendance of stock-brokers, nor of the general public.

While the staff were settling down again, as best they could, into an accustomed routine, and while the Bank was preparing for the problems of a post-war world by encouraging the setting up of the Finance Corporation for Industry and the Industrial and Commercial Finance Corporation, a general election on 5 July 1945 brought the Socialist Party into power with a large majority. The main issue of the election had been that of private enterprise versus nationalization, and it immediately became apparent that, whatever the exact future of the Bank of England might be, its days as a private institution were numbered.

Nationalization of the Bank was not, of course, a new concept. It had been advocated in one guise or another since at least as early as mid-Victorian times. Of all the central banks that had operated in the pre-war world two only were not, to a greater or lesser degree, State institutions. One was the Bank of England, the other the German Reichsbank – a juxtaposition which did not pass unnoticed by the Socialists. At almost any time during the previous thirty years, the Government might have decided to 'take over' the Bank. In 1917, as we have seen, it came very near to doing so. Furthermore, proposals to nationalize not only the Bank but the country's whole banking system had been in the programme of the earlier Socialist Governments, though they had lacked either the power or a suitable opportunity to carry their ideas into effect.

The Bank itself was well aware of a weakness derived from its 1694 constitution which might in some circumstances have led to a 'take-over' far more embarrassing than any by the Government. This weakness lay in the continued existence of the General Court of Proprietors. As former pages have shown, it was only in the Bank's very first years that the General Court had had any say in the shaping of policy or in the control of day-to-day activities. From the early years of the nineteenth century it had been little more than an historic link with the past. But its voting powers remained: in theory and in practice it continued to elect the Governors and Directors annually, and while Bank stock remained a market commodity there was always a possibility, remote but real, that some market conspiracy might concentrate in wrong or undesirable hands the votes adhering to all holdings of £500 stock and over, and so bring about the election of Governors and Directors whose aims and objects might be very different from those of the men they had ousted. The character of the Proprietorship being what it was, such a *coup* would have been immensely difficult to organize: it would doubt-less have been detected at an early stage and would almost certainly have been combated as decisively and skilfully as had been the bid of the Tory Party to gain control in the days of Queen Anne. Nevertheless, while the possibility existed it engendered a not completely unfounded sense of insecurity.

This possible danger and what was, in effect, more important – a feeling that the natural development of the Bank from a commercial institution to a central bank called for some such adjustment – resulted in there being a general acquiescence in the Government's plans, and what would have horrified earlier generations in the City was quietly agreed to. And when it became clear, on publication of the Bill's terms, that three vital principles had been safeguarded, the general sense within

185

the Bank itself was one of readiness to accept the new dispensation and make it work. These vital principles were, of course, that the Proprietors should be properly compensated, that the day-to-day relations of the Bank *vis-à-vis* the Treasury and the Government should continue on the same footing as before, and that the Directors, though appointed by the Crown and no longer privately, should, subject to directions in the public interest, continue to keep their own house in order. A willingness to concur with the Government's intentions ran through the whole Bank and was common to officials and staff as well as the Directors. The evidence of Lord Catto before the Special Committee of the House of Commons on the Bill, and his action in speaking in the Lords in its support, had much to do with this.

The Bank of England Bill was one of the first measures introduced by the new Government in the autumn of 1945. Its purpose was set out as being '. . . to bring the capital stock of the Bank of England into public ownership and bring the Bank under public control, to make provision with respect to the relations between the Treasury, the Bank of England and other banks . . .' It consisted of four main clauses. The first related to the transfer of Bank stock to a Government nominee (the Treasury Solicitor) and the compensation of the Proprietors by their being allocated an amount of stock created by the Treasury for the purpose (3 per cent Treasury Stock, 1966 or after), to yield them an equivalent income; the second clause concerned the constitution of the Court of Directors; the third contained such constitutional amendments as were necessary and the fourth, the most debated, set out the relationship between the Treasury, the Bank and 'other banks'. At the second reading, on 29 October 1945, it was described by the Chancellor of the Exchequer, Hugh Dalton, as 'a model, a streamlined Socialist statute, containing the minimum of legal rigmarole'.

The debate gave rise to much discussion on the peculiar status of the Bank and of the services or – according to the speaker's geographical position in the House – disservices it had rendered in the past both to the community and the Government. The Chancellor dwelt on the strange anomaly that it should still be, in law, a private institution owned by a rather miscellaneous body of private stockholders. It was only a tribute to British common sense that this state of affairs had continued so long without serious trouble. That it had, however, worked effectively he conceded by allowing that 'no day-to-day interference by the Government or Treasury with the ordinary work of the Bank was intended: that would be left, with confidence, to the Directors and their efficient and well-trained staff'.

Some other Members were not so complimentary. There was much adverse comment on the Bank's actions between the wars and many repetitions of the popular misconception that it was the Bank and not the Government that had shaped the economic policies of the period; the blame was laid on the Bank for a large part of the sufferings endured by the industrial areas during the long depression. Mr Gaitskell attacked Lord Norman unworthily, presenting the worst possible picture of him, characterizing him as a 'mysterious figure who travelled about the world incognito (Mr Skinner) – though, he remarked, there was always a press photographer to take pictures of him – not the kind of public servant we shall require for this important office'. Another Member bluntly called the Bank 'a racket'. 'No other concern', he said, 'had ever established so complete a monopoly with as much State backing as had the Bank of England.'

So, from tradition and prejudice, most of the Government's supporters found little good to say, but the Bank – and Lord Norman – were, of course, not without their champions on the opposite side of the House. Mr I. J. Pitman (now Sir James Pitman, KBE), who, up to his election in July as Member for Bath, had been a Bank Director, made it clear that the return to the gold standard in 1925, which Labour members had held up as a particularly diabolical contribution by the Bank to the great interwar depression, had, in fact, followed a report of a Committee on which the Bank had not even been represented. In his endeavour to 'put the record straight' Mr Pitman also pointed out that the much-criticized foreign loans under the Dawes and Young Plans were international, not domestic, issues and as much the responsibility of Foreign Secretaries as of Chancellors of the Exchequer, and that, moreover, the Foreign Secretaries and Chancellor concerned were members of a Socialist Government led by Mr Ramsay Macdonald. Regarding Lord Norman, he submitted that he 'had built up at the Bank a magnificent machine; gathered round himself a staff of great quality; had led this organization with distinction, and won the respect, admiration and affection of the whole staff'. Another Member spoke on the 'almost proverbial' phrase 'as safe as the Bank of England': a saying which had grown into history, since governments might come and go and policies change with changing governments, but the policy of the Bank had remained, steady and progressive, guiding this country throughout its history and development.

In the House of Lords, Lord Catto offered no apology for speaking on a matter of such urgent and public importance, though, as he said, it was unusual for a Governor of the Bank to address the House and still more unusual for a Governor to speak on matters directly concerning the Bank. He particularly stressed the clauses in the Bill which ensured the continuation on the existing lines of the relationship between the Treasury and the Bank and, as to the future management of the Bank, he was pleased that the staff would not become a part of the Civil Service and that their existing salary and pension rights would remain undisturbed.

Lord Swinton spoke of the possible danger that political considerations might affect such banking functions as the granting of advances: the Bank could, for example, sustain a loss of confidence if it were seen that these were being made to co-operative concerns in preference to individual traders. The Bank, he said, was unlike the ordinary central banks created in other countries – its strength lay in its ability to attract confidence to itself and to transmit that confidence to the whole banking system of the country. Lord Piercy approved the Bill: there was much to be said for the Bank at last becoming a State institution now that it was a fully developed, fully responsible Central Reserve Bank, leading the world in that capacity. The Bill might easily have been of a totally different character, attempting, in a most unsuitable way, to break down a living body of practice into a code and to hedge it round with definitions and prohibitions. 'Some time hence,' he concluded, 'this whole measure will be seen in its proper perspective as a wise and timely step in the evolution of our banking system.'

The Act received the Royal Assent on 14 February 1946. It comprised four main clauses, already outlined, and two schedules. The first schedule set out incidental and supplemental provisions as to the management, etc., of the Government stock by the Bank and sums payable by the Bank to the Treasury in lieu of dividends on Bank stock; the second contained supplemental provisions regarding the Court of Directors. The 'appointed day' for transfer to public ownership was, by Treasury Order, to be 1 March following.

On 26 February the composition of the new Court was announced. Under the Act it had to consist of sixteen instead of twenty-four Directors as hitherto, headed by a Governor and Deputy Governor. This reduction in numbers was not unwelcome – when Lord Catto had given evidence before the Special Committee of the House of Commons on the Bill, he had made it clear that this step would have been taken earlier if it had not involved the necessity of introducing special legislation to vary the terms of the Bank's original Charter. Of the initial sixteen Directors, four were to retire after the first year, four after the second and so on, but Directors so retiring would be eligible for reappointment. The term of office of the Governor and Deputy Governor was to be of five years.

Nothing like a clean sweep happened. Six of the members of the 1945

Court who stood down would have done so in any case, since they had reached the age limit set by the Revelstoke Committee. Among them were Sir Alan Anderson, who had been Deputy Governor in 1925 and 1926; G. M. Booth, who had been Chairman of the Rebuilding Committee during the greater part of the time it had been in operation; the first Lord Kindersley, who, as Sir Robert Kindersley, had been one of the guiding spirits of the National Savings Campaign of the First World War; and Arthur Whitworth, who for many years had been Chairman of the Printing Works Committee, the 'Committee on St Luke's'. The Governor, Lord Catto, and the Deputy Governor, C. F. Cobbold (who had been appointed in place of B. G. Catterns on his resigning the office in the previous summer) were unchanged, as were thirteen of the Directors who had sat on the old Court. Only three new Directors were therefore required to make up the statutory sixteen. Those appointed were Lord Piercy, the economist and statistician, who had spoken in favour of the Bill in the Lords; George Gibson, a prominent trade union leader; and R. E. Brook, one of the younger 'City men', who had served in the Army during the war, reaching the rank of Brigadier.

The new Royal Charter, granted under the terms of section 3 of the Act, was dated 1 March 1946. The former Charters were revoked except in so far as, first, they incorporated the Bank; second, constituted its capital stock; third, authorized it to have a common seal, to hold land and other property, and to sue and be sued. The capital stock was to vest in a nominee of the Treasury.

A schedule to the Charter set out the forms of declaration to be made by members of the Court on being appointed. These, as was fitting, were in time-honoured terms, and Directors of the nationalized Bank, as did their predecessors of the first Court of 1694, pledged themselves that they would be 'indifferent and equal to all manner of persons' and that in the execution of their office they would 'faithfully and honestly demean themselves according to the best of their skill and understanding.'

The disappearance of Bank of England stock as a market security caused a change of minor but interesting historic significance in the Accountant's Department – the Bank Stock Office had to be renamed. The office had come into being when, as a result of the building of various transfer offices by Sir Robert Taylor between 1765 and 1770, the work of the original Accountant's Office had been split up between a number of newly formed offices. The Bank Stock Office took its title from the principal stock it housed – a practice which over the years became a usual one when an office dealt with more than one security. Its new title – the Funding Stocks Office – was therefore derived from the most important of the securities then being managed there. Some two years later, in July 1948, in a general rearrangement of the offices in the Department, the newly named office lost its separate identity, being merged with the Colonial and Corporation Stocks Office; then, once again, the changing times dictated a change of name – in April 1954 the word 'Colonial' with all its implications, was dropped and the office became the Commonwealth and Corporation Stocks Office. Incidentally, it may be mentioned that in the 1948 reorganization the two specifically named 'Transfer by Deed' offices disappeared – by then transfer by deed had been, for nearly ten years, the only method available and the maintaining of separate registers for 'deed' stock and the former 'inscribed' stock was no longer needed. In former times the great advantage of holding inscribed stock had been that the holder's capital was immediately available, but by now the banks, the Stock Exchange and the Bank of England had jointly worked out methods which extended this advantage to a holder of 'deed' stock also.

It is as yet too early to place in proper historical perspective the events of the period of some twenty years which has elapsed since the Bank passed into public ownership. An account, year by year, of the country's financial struggles during this time would be necessarily incomplete, since the material, particularly that relating to the part played by the Bank, is not yet fully available. At first the battle raged round the 'Dollar Gap', while every administration since the end of the war has been painfully aware of the menace of uncontrolled inflation. The fight to keep prices within reasonable limits, while at the same time building up and then maintaining a prosperous economy, yet without jeopardizing full employment, has been the problem overriding all others. The period has also seen an immense activity in the field of international finance; this was foreshadowed in the months immediately following the nationalization of the Bank, when the International Monetary Fund and the International Bank for Reconstruction and Development were formally inaugurated.

The first meetings of the Boards of Governors of these two bodies were held at Savannah, Georgia, between 8 and 18 March 1946. The Chairman was Mr Vinson, the United States Governor on both. The United Kingdom Governor was Lord Keynes. At these meetings it was laid down that both Bank and Fund should operate from Washington, DC.

The two institutions were the outcome of the Bretton Woods meetings of 1944, in which the Bank of England had not been intimately concerned. Lord Keynes, who had led the British delegates, was, it is true, a Bank of England Director, but it was as the Treasury's nominee that he had put forward his plan for an international clearing union. In his life of Lord Keynes, R. F. Harrod is of the opinion that the Bank of England was 'never sympathetic' to the Bretton Woods proposals: 'At the time', he says, 'it was far more concerned with immediate post-war problems than with far-reaching schemes; and it would not be human if its approach to such schemes was not influenced, even if unconsciously, by some degree of jealousy of a rival central banking institution, which might, in certain circumstances, poach upon its domain.' Not unnaturally, in view of the immensely strong economic position of the United States, the ideas of its delegates had very largely prevailed over those formulated by Lord Keynes. The deliberations had been international in scope, but the Fund and the Bank born of them were, Mr Harrod says, essentially the product of British and American brains, valuably assisted by the Canadians. There had, of course, been differences, some very hotly contested, one of the chief of which had been about location. The British had first of all favoured the idea of operating both the Fund and the Bank somewhere outside the United States: the American plan had initially contained a proposal that the headquarters should be in New York, where they would be in daily contact with all the activities of one of the world's great financial centres. Upon the insistence of the American Treasury, however, it was finally decided, at Savannah, that the location should be at Washington, DC. Lord Keynes was not alone in fearing that this decision might mean that political pressure rather than purely economic considerations might become the dominating influence on both institutions.

Ratification of the Bretton Woods Agreement by Britain was one of the conditions attached to the granting of an American loan of $3,750 million needed so sorely by a country drained of its resources by long years of war. This ratification had been carried through Parliament in December 1945 and meant that Britain had accepted both the International Monetary Fund and the International Bank for Reconstruction and Development.

Lord Keynes's tenure of the Governorships of the Fund and the International Bank was cut short by his death on 21 April 1946, a few weeks after his return to this country. Soon afterwards these offices, to which no remuneration is attached, were taken over by the Chancellor of the Exchequer. They have since been held by successive Chancellors, though at the time of writing the Governor of the Bank, Lord Cromer, is the present United Kingdom Governor of the International Bank. A Bank of England Director has customarily been Alternate Governor for Britain on the Fund and an officer of the Treasury Alternate Governor on the Board of the Bank. The United Kingdom's Alternate Executive Director on the Fund is a senior Bank of England official.

Lord Keynes's death at a comparatively early age was a loss his country – and, for that matter, the world – could ill afford. The Bank never enjoyed any very full share in the benefit of his great gifts during the four and a half years of his Directorship; there had been too many other calls on his time and services. Nevertheless, he was a man who left some mark of his genius on everything he touched, and this was felt in many quarters of the Bank, as, for example, on the Staff Committee, membership of which is a duty devolving upon all new Directors. He took a very strong interest in the Bank's history, an interest not surprising in so notable a student of the humanities. In the period between the wars he had been a critic – and a critic whose thrusts no one could ignore – of the Bank's administration and policies, but if any high feelings had ever crept into the controversy they must have been long forgotten on both sides, and he must have felt himself as being fully identified with the Bank and his fellow Directors by the time of the Bank's two hundred and fiftieth anniversary, for he celebrated that event, in July 1944, by giving a dinner in Ottawa. His approach to finance and economics was an unusual and refreshing one in so great a master of these subjects – though never irresponsible, it was never ponderous or oversolemn, and his writings effectively demonstrate that such a mastery need not automatically exclude an ability to manage one's native language gracefully. The writer of the notice of his death in the *Annual Register* did well to emphasize Lord Keynes's belief that 'the day is not far distant when the Economic Problem will take the back seat where it belongs and that the arena of the heart and head will be occupied, or reoccupied, by our real problems – the problems of life and of human relations, of creation and behaviour and religion'.

Events have happily shown that the fears of Lord Keynes and others were exaggerated regarding the possibility that the potentially beneficent economic actions of the International Fund and the World Bank might be bedevilled by politics. The thanks for this must, in the main, be given to the integrity of their Boards and to the wise and statesmanlike restraint displayed by the United States. Nevertheless, in the world as it is, economic considerations must always be conditioned by more potent political ones.

As is well known, the Socialist Government nationalized also the railways and other transport undertakings, coal, gas and electricity, and iron and steel. The various shareholders were compensated by being given holdings of newly created Government stocks corresponding in value to the shares they had surrendered, and it has been estimated that in this way nearly two million accounts were added to the Stock Registers maintained by the Bank. This swollen volume of work fell on the Accountant's Department and there was insufficient room to deal with it in the building at Finsbury Circus. Premises therefore had to be sought elsewhere.

The Accountant's Department had almost come to regard it as a condition of existence that its work should be carried out in widely scattered offices. After the upheavals caused by both wars, as many as possible had been concentrated at Finsbury Circus, but there was never enough room here for the whole Department, and for more than thirty years it had failed to enjoy the advantages to be derived from having a single roof over its head. To achieve this had now become the Bank's aim, and the devastation of the City was, in this respect, something of a blessing in disguise, for the tenure of sites larger than any obtainable before the war was now possible. Such a site was acquired at the western end of Cheapside, almost in the shadow of St Paul's Cathedral. Its area of just over two and three quarter acres was adequate and the building erected upon it affords a pleasant contrast to much of the more up-to-date architecture of the rebuilt City. In deference to its great neighbour, the Architects, Messrs Victor Heal and Smith, have given it an unobtrusive semi-traditional form; modern in size and function, but Georgian in manner, it provides a dignified 'backcloth' to the Cathedral, with its warm red Buckinghamshire brick relieved by Portland stone dressings discreetly, if unadventurously, enriched by carvings. The building is always referred to as New Change, though strictly it is 'the Bank of England, New Change', since its main frontage, facing the Cathedral, stands on a freshly constructed thoroughfare which has been named 'New Change' by the City authorities. It began being occupied in March 1958, though it was not fully completed for another two years.

Towards the end of 1948 the Bank came into the public eye in a rather unenviable way when one of its Directors, Mr George Gibson, was called before a tribunal set up by the Government to investigate 'allegations reflecting on the official conduct of Ministers of the Crown and other public servants'. The inquiry, which was presided over by Mr Justice Lynskey, showed that those against whom the allegations had been made had been the victims of a Mr Sydney Stanley, a man described in the Tribunal's report, when it was published in January 1949, as one 'who will make any statement, whether true or untrue, if he thinks it to his advantage to do so'.

Mr Gibson was, it will be remembered, one of the three new Directors appointed under the Act of 1946. He had been the General Secretary of the Confederation of Health Service Employees, a trade union affiliated to the TUC. In the year of his appointment to the Court of the Bank he had appeared in the Honours List as a Companion of Honour. His great misfortune seems to have been that, by sheer accident, he was introduced to Mr Stanley in a railway carriage. The Tribunal found that he had assisted Mr Stanley and that he had done so in the hope of material advantage to himself, though, in fact, all that he had received, apart from some trivial gifts, was a present of a suit of clothes. This, in a period of rationing when most of the population had not been able to buy a decent new set of clothes for many years, loomed to a perhaps unduly large extent. Mr Gibson's case was a tragedy, not least because of its trivial and somewhat ludicrous circumstances; he resigned his Directorship and died a short while afterwards.

In February 1949, on the eve of his seventieth birthday, Lord Catto retired from the Governorship and was succeeded by Mr C. F. Cobbold, the Deputy Governor. The place of Lord Catto is secure on the roll of Governors who have made significant contributions to Bank history: he was the last Governor under the old régime and the first under the new. He saw the Bank through the first three years after its nationalization without courting any of the troubles which might then have so easily arisen and – although he was not without his critics for taking too passive a line – he achieved a smooth passage in a way few others could have done. When, some ten years later, he died, it was written of him in an obituary notice that 'the extent to which the independence necessary to the Bank's effective daily operation was preserved, while the principle of public ownership was fully accepted, owed much to his leadership and grasp of essentials in a relatively novel field'. Five years had been all too short a time for Lord Catto to arrive at the position which his predecessor Lord Norman had attained in his term of nearly twenty-five years. By long association in work and in many of their recreational activities as well, Lord Norman had come to know and be known by large numbers of the Bank staff. Lord Catto's term was not long enough for him to have met very many in this way, but those who did have the opportunity of working with him will not readily forget his great abilities and the essential kindliness of his nature.

By September 1949 the battle of the 'Dollar Gap' had reached the point where despite earlier – and, in the circumstances, necessary – protestations by the Government that no such solution could be contemplated, the situation was relieved by devaluing the pound from $4.03 to $2.80; this led, in the following year, to a considerable improvement in gold and dollar reserves. In his Budget speech Sir Stafford Cripps, the Chancellor, was able to announce that industrial production was rising and that devaluation had eased the country's competitive trading position in international markets without there being any pronounced rise in internal costs.

A general election in February saw the Socialist Party again returned to power, but with so small a majority that they could carry on the Government only with great difficulty. A further appeal to the country in October 1951 resulted in a return of the Conservatives, though their majority also was a small one. The first weeks of their administration saw a change which brought the Bank into greater public notice – the new Chancellor of the Exchequer, Mr R. A. Butler, announced that the struggle against inflation demanded the use of a more direct and active monetary policy than had been the system of mere guidance to the banks employed since the war. He considered that, at 2 per cent, the Bank of England rate of discount had been quite ineffective and that the requirements of the money market had been supplied at too low a rate. On 7 November Bank Rate was raised to $2\frac{1}{2}$ per cent, the first change since October 1939 and, disregarding the abnormal alterations caused by war emergencies, this was, in fact, the first change since 1932. Mr Butler also foreshadowed a relaxation of the controls which the Socialists had continued from wartime. 'Set the People Free' had been a Conservative slogan during the election campaign and, perhaps as an earnest that their promise would be redeemed, on 17 December 1951 the Foreign Exchange Market, which had been closed immediately on the outbreak of war, was reopened.

That Bank Rate had been an idle weapon for so long had been due to a combination of circumstances. During the 'thirties the 2 per cent rate had been maintained chiefly as a stimulant to trade revival; during the war monetary policy was almost entirely subordinate to the Government's borrowing needs and Bank Rate in itself was of no significance: then, in the period immediately following, it had been necessary to continue the official controls of wartime, since the scarcity of capital was acute.

Professor Sayers, the author of *Central Banking after Bagehot*, is of the opinion that these money-market changes of 1951 and the raising of the Bank Rate must, in general, be regarded as symbolical and pre-paratory – they were intended to give the world a shock and succeeded in doing so. Because of London's long tradition, Bank Rate has always had 'news value' in the world's financial centres and the rise of one half per cent was a symbolical rather than an effective measure.

But it was another matter entirely when, on 13 March 1952, Bank Rate was raised to 4 per cent – Mr Butler said that this step was an essential part of the Government's campaign to fortify the currency. Although Professor Sayers thinks it doubtful that it exercised any direct check upon inflation at home, it had at least one important effect on the economic situation of the whole world in so far as it foreshadowed tighter and dearer money all round and a general weakening of commodity prices in 1952. This world-wide downward movement was of great importance to the country's internal situation, since it put something of a brake on the rising cost of living, which, in its turn, has always figured largely in wage bargaining: a policy of 'wage restraint' was therefore now likely to have some chance of being considered.

The general election of May 1955 saw the return of the Conservatives with an increased majority. During their first period of office improving conditions had enabled them to remove a number of the more harassing controls: the last vestiges of food and clothes rationing had gone and Mr Butler's Budget of 1953 had been the first since the war to contain neither proposals for new taxation nor for increases of existing taxes. Later in 1955, however, came the 'credit squeeze', when the Government called for postponement or reduction of expenditure by central and local government authorities and by the nationalized industries. In December 1955 Mr Butler was succeeded as Chancellor by Mr Harold Macmillan.

In January 1957 Mr Macmillan succeeded Sir Anthony Eden as Prime Minister; the new Chancellor of the Exchequer was Mr Peter Thorneycroft. On 7 February Bank Rate was reduced from $5\frac{1}{2}$ to 5 per cent, but on 19 September exceptionally heavy drains on sterling occasioned a 'crisis' rise to 7 per cent, at which figure it remained until March 1958.

This particular rise, though in itself sufficiently sharp to be recorded as an indication of the country's immediate economic position, had consequences affecting the Bank far more closely than any of a purely economic kind. In various quarters charges were made that certain persons had been given prior knowledge of the coming rise and had turned this information to their own advantage. Questions implying that this had happened had been asked in the House of Commons, and in the end a public inquiry was held upon the whole general circumstances surrounding any alteration in Bank Rate and in particular regarding all those persons who are privy to an impending change.

A private inquiry into the allegations was made by the Lord Chancellor, and his conclusion that they were without foundation should have satisfied those making them, but party feeling was running high and the Opposition pressed for the appointment of a Tribunal of Inquiry: this was conceded and the Tribunal, under the chairmanship of Mr Justice Parker, sat on 2 December 1957 and on eleven subsequent days. Much of the evidence heard and reported upon in the Tribunal's

Report was found to be of no significance and, indeed, to be entirely irrelevant, founded as it was upon mere scandalous gossip regarding alleged conversations overheard in all manner of places, in trains and on railway platforms, at luncheon and cocktail parties, including one excited discussion about the impending rise between two Japanese in their native tongue. The sole justification for collecting what turned out to be so much worthless evidence was the implication that the secret had been no secret at all, and that all manner of unauthorized persons had had access to it. The Report brought out quite clearly, however, that everyone who had, in fact, been in possession of authentic information had in no way divulged it.

Nevertheless, the Report disclosed that, on this occasion, the circumstances attending the change of rate had been complicated by the fact that it was only one of a number of various restrictive measures forced upon the Government by the financial situation generally. Mr Thorneycroft, as Chancellor, was having to leave the country on 20 September, the day following the official announcement of the rise, in order to attend a meeting of the International Monetary Fund in Washington, and during the week before his departure he had met representatives of the Press, the Conservative Central Office, trade unions and employers, including the nationalized industries, to whom he had conveyed the terms of all these measures, except the change in Bank Rate: to this he had made no reference.

The Bank had followed the customary procedure. The Governor and Deputy Governor had discussed the matter and the Governor, following traditional practice had, on the Monday and Tuesday, 16 and 17 September, asked some of the senior Directors for their views on an increase. Early on the Wednesday he had obtained the Chancellor's agreement that in the circumstances a rise to 7 per cent would be justified, and at its meeting the same day the Committee of Treasury approved the necessary resolution. On the Thursday, at its normal weekly meetings, the full Court of Directors gave its approval, and at 11.45 a.m. notice of the increase was made public through the usual channels.

Among the Directors consulted by the Governor were Lord Kindersley, who had succeeded his father in 1954, and Mr W.J.Keswick: Lord Kindersley was Chairman of Lazard Brothers and Governor of the Royal Exchange Assurance, Mr Keswick a Director of Matheson & Co. Ltd. Both of them thus had City connections of the kind which Directors have had throughout Bank history, and both of them, because of the offices they held, might have been in a position to advise upon the immediate desirability, or otherwise, of selling gilt-edged securities at this critical time. The evidence clearly showed, and the Report of the Tribunal as clearly bore out, that they had both behaved with the utmost discretion and that there was no justification for any allegation that either of them had disclosed in any way their knowledge of an impending change, whether intentionally or otherwise. As 'part-time' Directors, with commitments outside the Bank, they had, in fact, conducted themselves in the best tradition, always giving their outside associates to understand that they were not 'approachable' for consultation regarding such matters as, say, investment policy, when information derived from their position within the Bank might cause them 'embarrassment'. The Tribunal did feel, however, that the general circumstances of such cases and, in particular, the fact that difficulties of this kind might arise, should be referred to the Radcliffe Committee on the Working of the Monetary System, then sitting.

In concluding its Report the Tribunal referred to observations made by the Governor on the effect abroad of the very holding of the Inquiry. The rumours which had led to its being held had, he pointed out, prejudiced the financial reputation of London and so of the national credit. 'If you should conclude,' he went on to say, 'that these rumours are baseless, I do earnestly hope that the final result of this Tribunal may be not only to maintain, but actually to enhance, the reputation of London for financial integrity.' The Tribunal endorsed these hopes of the Governor.

The Radcliffe Committee, mentioned in the Report, had been set up by a Treasury Minute of 3 May 1957 to conduct a comprehensive inquiry into the working of the monetary and credit systems – it was the first of its kind since the Macmillan Committee. Its Report described the country's principal financial institutions, analysed the monetary system and discussed its efficiency as a factor controlling the economy. Its general conclusion was that monetary measures alone cannot be relied upon to keep in nice balance an economy subject to major strains from both within and without.

Of the Committee's recommendations those most directly concerning the Bank dealt with the appointment of part-time Directors with outside commitments and with changes in Bank Rate. On the first question the findings of the Committee showed a clear appreciation of the value, both to the Bank and to the working of the financial system, of there being a number of Directors who did not act merely as consultants, but who were – as they have been throughout the Bank's history – men also having a concurrent active and practical contact with the business world outside. In the Committee's view the Bank would be considerably weakened by the absence of such Directors, though – as Sir Oscar

Hobson pointed out in a criticism of the Report – it then went on to make other recommendations which, if carried out, would largely stultify those it had just made. Sir Oscar, it may be noted, was also critical of those aspects of nationalization which tended to make the Bank merely the financial agents of the Treasury. 'I would like', he wrote, 'to see the Bank given a status as independent as it is possible to make it. A status as independent in the sphere of monetary policy, as autonomous as the status of the judiciary or the Comptroller and Auditor-General in their respective spheres. They, too, can be overridden by the Government in the last resort, but most governments would avoid any unnecessary head-on collision with them.' Sir Oscar Hobson's opinions appear in *Not Unanimous. Comments on the Radcliffe Committee's Report* published by the Institute of Economic Affairs.

As to the Committee's recommendations regarding Bank Rate, it considered that any change should be made in the name of the Chancellor of the Exchequer, upon his authority, and preferably by his explicit direction. The Government's view on this particular recommendation was not, however, a favourable one, a view expressed by the Chancellor, Mr Amory, in the course of a House of Commons debate on the Report which took place in November 1959. He preferred that when a change 'is agreed to be desirable, the Governor will make a formal written proposal to me on the day before the change is to be made and I shall convey my formal approval in writing on the same day'. He was not prepared, either, to accept a further recommendation that a standing committee of representatives of the Bank and the Government should be set up 'to advise the authorities on all matters relating to the co-ordination of monetary policy as a whole'. He was, however, willing to arrange for the Bank to be permanently represented on the various existing committees which formulated and co-ordinated advice to Ministers regarding economic policy. He also favoured the Committee's recommendations for improving the presentation of financial statistics and for increasing the statistical information given by the Bank to the public.

The Bank was ready to adapt itself to the Government's wishes. On 30 October 1959 it announced the formation of a new Department. Entitled the Central Banking Information Department, it was designed to provide the increased services called for in the field of information and statistics, covering the situation both at home and abroad, and including information as to the Bank's relations with other central banks. The Department was to be operational in character, in a way which would entail many more activities than those covered by such headings as 'intelligence' or 'research'. It would naturally work in close association with the team of Advisers initially recruited in the days of Norman's Governorship. The new Department merged the existing Overseas Department and the Statistics Office, and in its final form, in addition to a General Office, it comprised an Overseas Office, a Balance of Payments Office and a Home Intelligence Office. In effect this was a rearrangement of existing offices and sections, though their staffs would carry out duties of an enlarged scope: it involved little recruitment of new personnel. As an outcome of experience in working the arrangement the Department was dissolved in February 1964 and two new Departments substituted: an Overseas Department, which included the Overseas Office, the Exchange Control Office and, incidentally, the Glasgow Office, and the Economic Intelligence Department, which absorbed the remaining offices above mentioned.

The first intimation to the public that the new Department was functioning was the issue, in July 1960, of an expanded issue of the Bank's now customary Annual Report: on this occasion it contained far more information and analysis than ever before. In the following December there appeared the first number of a new publication, the *Quarterly Bulletin*, though in this instance the period covered was one of six months in order that continuity might be preserved with the similar material published in the Annual Report of the preceding July. Such a bulletin normally contains a description and assessment of the current conditions in which monetary policy must operate, followed by an analysis of the principal financial statistics for the period under review. If the Governor has made any public speeches, the text of these is usually printed and there are a number of articles on special subjects as well. The result is the presentation, to an extent never previously attempted, of a picture of the whole financial situation – a notable departure from the Bank's traditional reserve and a complete change from the old atmosphere of mystery and secrecy which surrounded all its doings.

Allowance must, of course, be made for the inborn handicap of any quarterly publication – always some weeks, at least, behind the events with which it deals, yet too near to them to see them in perspective, it falls uneasily between the two stools of journalism and history. It was perhaps because of the Press's failure to appreciate this that the reception of the first *Bulletin* was a somewhat cool one and it may also be that the compilers had not yet got into their stride. The chief complaint was that much of the material was, in any event, available from other sources, and that the information given, while invaluable to the economic historian, was not sufficiently up to date or generally informative to fill the need pointed out by the Radcliffe Committee. In subsequent issues steps were taken to meet these criticisms, and later issues of the

Bulletin have been hailed by the leading economic journals in far more complimentary terms.

On 23 November 1960 Mr C. F. Cobbold was created Baron Cobbold of Knebworth, and on 30 June in the following year he retired from the Governorship. In the Bank, with which his association began when he was appointed an Adviser in February 1935, he will be remembered by the staff with affection for the ease and friendliness which always characterized his dealings with them. On retirement he could look back to having successfully completed the transition of the Bank from the old system to the new, which his predecessor, Lord Catto, had so well begun. His days as Governor had not been free from periods of difficulty, as the case of the Bank Rate Tribunal had shown, but he had guided the Bank with distinction in such circumstances and had seen that its position and functions were well represented to the Radcliffe Committee. He had been elected to the Court in 1938, and was Deputy Governor from May 1945 until his appointment as Governor in 1949.

He was succeeded by the Earl of Cromer, who had been appointed a Director in January 1961. Lord Cromer, the third Earl, a member of the Baring family, was born in 1918, and on his appointment was the youngest Governor for at least a century. His predecessor had been forty-four when appointed in 1949: Montagu Norman had been forty-eight in 1920. Lord Cromer, Managing Director of Baring Brothers & Co. Ltd from 1947 to 1961, had, while on leave from his firm from 1959 onwards, been Head of the Treasury Delegation and British Economic Minister in Washington. He had also extensive acquaintance with the International Monetary Fund and with the International Bank for Reconstruction and Development, of which bodies he was United Kingdom Executive Director.

In a work of this general nature no attempt has been made to provide more than an outline, devoid as far as possible of technicalities, of the Bank's duties and functions as they have originated and evolved, and no more will be attempted at this point when, as a fitting conclusion, its present-day functions are summarized. The most easily consulted source for any reader wishing to obtain a fuller account of the working of the Bank and its existing position in the City, the country, and the world, is the Radcliffe Committee's Report.

The Bank's modern role, in brief, is that of the central bank of the United Kingdom. No one of its functions operates in complete isolation: each is essential to this main duty – a duty indicated in one particularly cogent sentence in the Radcliffe Report, which states that 'the practical working of the Bank revolves on the one hand round the business of exchanging sterling for other people's currency, and on the other hand round the business of putting sterling into or out of the domestic banking system in the course of managing the Government's current financial business and the National Debt . . .'

The Report divides the Bank's work into its external and its domestic business. Externally, it says, the Bank has five tasks. It ranks as the first of these the management of the Exchange Equalization Account. This Account, it will be remembered, was set up by the Finance Act of 1932 to provide a fund, under the control of the Treasury, to purchase and sell gold and foreign currencies in order to prevent excessive day-to-day fluctuations in the exchange value of sterling. The Account is now the custodian of the country's reserve of gold and foreign currencies, and the Bank's operations as manager of the Account are largely determined by the exchange rate policy of the Government authorities. As a condition of membership of the International Monetary Fund the United Kingdom has undertaken, as have all the other member countries, to ensure that exchange-transactions within the territories covered by the Fund do not differ by more than 1 per cent either way from the parities declared to the Fund by the respective members. The Bank itself operates in the market in order to keep the rates of exchange within these limits: as manager of the Account it is also at liberty to operate in those foreign exchange markets where the Government is not under any obligation to keep rates inside prescribed limits.

The second external task is the administration of the foreign exchange control. The Exchange Control regulations, introduced in 1939, were consolidated by the Exchange Control Act of 1947, which gave the Treasury wide powers of control over transfers of sterling into other currencies and also over the disposal of amounts in foreign currencies coming into the hands of residents in the United Kingdom. The administration of this control is centred at the Bank and the policy determining that administration is one agreed between the Treasury and the Bank. Certain commercial banks, numbering a hundred and twenty or so, are authorized dealers in foreign exchange; the Bank may delegate to them a measure of freedom to enter into transactions covered by the Act, indicating to them, according to the policy currently in force, the type and size of transactions permissible without its prior approval.

Those overseas territories which base their currencies on sterling comprise what is known as 'the sterling area'. So far as transactions with bankers and traders within the sterling area are concerned, the Bank of England keeps in close and constant touch with the area's central banks, and other monetary authorities, upon a wide range of questions, embracing both operational procedure and general policy. The conduct of this *liaison* is the Bank's third external function. Its fourth is a complementary one – the maintenance of a similar relationship with central banks outside the sterling area, in particular the Federal Reserve System of the United States, the Bank of Canada and the major European central banks: this relationship is founded on the underlying banking connections. The Bank of England provides services for these other central banks, such as the holding and managing, on their behalf, of their reserves of sterling, and in many cases the relationship also extends to a regular and intimate exchange of views and information.

The fifth external task of the Bank is its participation in the work of various international financial institutions. In the case of the International Monetary Fund, as we have already seen, the Chancellor of the Exchequer is the United Kingdom's Governor, the Treasury provide this country's Executive Director, the Alternate Governor for the United Kingdom is an Executive Director of the Bank of England and the Alternate Executive Director is one of its senior officials. The Bank also has representatives, and plays an important part, in other international organizations, such as the International Bank for Reconstruction and Development – of which Lord Cromer is (1966) the United Kingdom Governor – the Organization for European Economic Cooperation and the European Monetary Agreement. It also continues to be a member of the Bank for International Settlements: apart from close daily connections, the periodic meetings of the Board of Directors provide opportunities for the Governor and his senior colleagues to have regular and intimate discussions with their 'opposite numbers' in other central banks.

The Radcliffe Report emphasizes that, in this external field, it would be misleading to say that the Bank undertakes no more than technical operations and the related international negotiations. 'It is inevitable', it states, 'that the Bank should also be making an important contribution to the formation of policy in this field.'

As regards the 'domestic' side of the Bank's business, we have seen how, over the years, it has become the 'banker's bank' and the bank to the Government. The term 'banker's bank' indicates that the principal banks of the United Kingdom deposit with it their reserves of cash: these balances afford the clearing banks some of the advantages a private customer derives from an ordinary banking account. They can make payments to each other, or to the Exchequer, by cheques drawn on their accounts at the Bank of England and they can draw out the notes and coin they require. Others that keep accounts with the Bank are the more specialized institutions of the London money market, the banks whose principal business is overseas and, as already mentioned, the Bank's own overseas customers – the other central banks of the world. In addition, there is a small ordinary banking business for commercial and industrial firms, a vestige and a reminder of former days when the Bank of England was the largest bank in the City. During the present century business of this kind has been shed gradually and deliberately, the only new accounts accepted now being charitable ones such as Lord Mayor's Appeal Funds and the like, or others with some special public interest. The only personal accounts are those of members of the Bank staff. Set against the vast amounts passing through other accounts, this business is of little significance, but it does serve the useful purpose of giving the members of the Bank staff an opportunity of remaining acquainted with ordinary banking routine.

As the Government's banker, the Bank renders the services which any bank offers its customers, not the least important of which is advice in monetary matters. It performs certain other specific services to the Government as well:

First, it keeps the accounts of the Public Departments, a service which originated in the keeping of accounts for certain of the officers of state during the eighteenth century. All money received by the central Government must be paid into, and all payments authorized by Parliament must come out of, the Exchequer, the central account of the Government kept by the Treasury at the Bank of England.

Second, the Bank arranges to meet the Government's fluctuating needs for short-term finance, which are met by borrowing from the money market: every Friday it receives, and allots, tenders for the weekly issue of Treasury bills.

Third, the Bank manages the Government stocks that form the bulk of the National Debt. We have seen how this originated in the eighteenth century, since when long-term borrowing by stock issue has been a constant method of financing the Exchequer. Not only does the Bank issue these stocks, but it keeps the registers of stockholders and pays them their dividends as they fall due. This work as Registrar is a gigantic task and in terms of staff employed is the largest of the Bank's activities. In addition to Government stocks the Bank manages stocks of certain other long-term borrowers, principally the nationalized industries, Commonwealth Governments and local authorities.

Fourth, the Bank is responsible for the issue of bank-notes: it is the only issuing bank in England and Wales. Its 10s. and £1 notes are legal tender in the whole of the United Kingdom, its £5 and £10 notes in England and Wales (during the Second World War it ceased issuing notes of higher denominations). They are printed at the Bank's large modern Printing Works at Debden, near Loughton, in Essex. From there the millions of notes printed each week find their way to the public through the commercial banks; to the magnitude of this task are added the accompanying processes of designing the notes and destroying them when their useful life is over.

These, then, are the main duties of the Bank today. A multitude of supplementary tasks might be added, performed by Directors, officials and members of the staff; many of them are of too little significance to be detailed, though mention must be made of those without which the Bank would soon cease functioning, the maintenance of the fabric of its various buildings and installations, the appointment and payment of the staff and the abiding attention to their welfare which the Bank authorities have shown, in increasing measure, throughout the years.

This care of the Bank for its own calls for particular mention in the closing passages of a work devoted to its history. More than anything else it shows that, despite the vast and impersonal nature of its present activities the Bank of England remains, in this and other respects, a 'humane' institution in the finest sense of that often-abused term. Though it is no longer in such immediate contact with the general public, though it no longer welcomes its stockholders within its doors to receive their dividends or sees so large a number of customers across its counters, it retains, if anything in fuller measure, that spirit of service which always tries to remember that institutions like itself are made for mankind, not mankind for them. It is still the same bank of which Addison wrote in 1711, in No. 3 of *The Spectator*, when he expressed himself as being 'not a little pleased' with 'that just and regular Oeconomy'.

Bibliography

Books, Pamphlets, etc. consulted

Bank of England

ACRES, W. MARSTON *The Bank of England from within*, O.U.P., 1931
ANDRÉADÈS, A. *History of the Bank of England*, P. S. King & Son Ltd., 1909
CLAPHAM, SIR JOHN H. *The Bank of England: a history*, C.U.P., 1944
CLAY, SIR HENRY *Lord Norman*, Macmillan, 1957
MACKENZIE, A. D. *The Bank of England note*, C.U.P., 1953
PHILLIPS, MABERLY *The token money of the Bank of England, 1797 to 1816*, Effingham Wilson, 1900
ROGERS, J. E. THOROLD *The first nine years of the Bank of England*, Oxford, Clarendon Press, 1887
STEELE, H. R. & YERBURY, F. R. *The old Bank of England*, Ernest Benn, 1930

General Works

ANDERSON, A. *An historical and chronological deduction of the origin of Commerce, 1764* Revised ed. 1787/9 Printed at the Logographic Press by J. Walter
BAGEHOT, WALTER *Lombard Street*, 14th ed. 1915 (many reprints), John Murray
BAKER, SIR HERBERT *Architecture and Personalities*, Country Life, 1944
BEAVERBROOK, LORD *Men and Power*, Hutchinson, 1956
BLAKE, ROBERT *Ths unknown Prime Minister: the life and times of Andrew Bonar Law*, Eyre & Spottiswoode, 1955
BOSWELL, JAMES *Life of Samuel Johnson*, 1835 edn.
CHURCHILL, SIR WINSTON *The world crisis*, T. Butterworth
COURTNEY, JANET E. *Recollected in Tranquility*, Heinemann, 1926
DE FRAINE, H. G. *Servant of this House*, Constable, 1960
DEFOE, DANIEL *A Tour through England and Wales*, 2 vols., Dent's Everyman Library
DE ROOVER, R. *Money, Banking and Credit in Mediaeval Bruges*, Mediaeval Academy of America, Mass., 1948
FISHER, H. A. L. *History of Europe*, E. Arnold, 1936
HARGREAVES, E. L. *The National Debt*, E. Arnold, 1930
HARROD, R. F. *The Life of John Maynard Keynes*, Macmillan, 1951

HENRY, J. A. and SIEPMANN, H. A. *The first hundred years of the Standard Bank*, O.U.P., 1963

HIBBERT, C. *King Mob: the story of Lord George Gordon and the Riots of 1780*, Longmans, 1958

HORSEFIELD, J. K. *British Monetary Experiments, 1650–1710*, London School of Economics *and* G. Bell, 1960

LLOYD GEORGE, D. *War memoirs*, 6 vols., Nicholson, 1933–1937

LUTTRELL, N. *A brief historical relation of State Affairs from Sept. 1678* 1678 to April 1714, 1857 edn.

MACAULAY, T. B. *History of England* . . . [Ed.] C. W. Firth, 6 vols., Macmillan, 1913–15

MARRIOTT, SIR J. A. R. *Modern England, 1855–1939*, 2nd ed., Methuen, 1942

MITCHELL, B. R. and DEANE, P. *Abstract of British historical statistics*, C.U.P., 1962

MOWAT, C. L. *Britain between the Wars, 1918–1940*, Methuen, 1955

PALGRAVE, R. H. I. [editor] *Dictionary of political economy*, 3 vols., Macmillan, 1901

PATERSON, WILLIAM *The Wednesday's Club Dialogues*, Printed for A. & W. Bell, 1717

PEVSNER, N. *The Buildings of England series*, Penguin Books

RICARDO, DAVID *Plan for the Establishment of a National Bank*, John Murray, 1824

SAYERS, R. S. *Central banking after Bagehot*, Oxford, Clarendon Press, 1957

SELDON, ARTHUR [editor] *Not unanimous. A rival verdict to Radcliffe's On Money*, Institute of Economic Affairs, 1960

SCOTT, W. R. *The constitution and finance of English, Scottish and Irish Joint Stock Companies to 1720*, 3 vols., C.U.P., 1910–1912

TAWNEY, R. H. *Religion and the rise of capitalism*, Murray, 1929

TEW, BRIAN (Pamphlet) *The International Monetary Fund: its present role and future prospects*, Princeton University, 1961

TREVELYAN, G. M. *England under Queen Anne*, 3 vols., Longmans, 1930–4

WITHERS, HARTLEY *War and Lombard Street*, Smith, Elder & Co., 1915

YOUNGSON, A. J. *The British economy, 1920–1957*, Allen & Unwin, 1960

Tracts

BRISCOE, JOHN *Reasons humbly offered for the Establishment of the National Land Bank*, 1696

DEFOE, DANIEL *The Villany of Stock jobbers detected and the cause of the late run upon the Bank and Bankers discovered and considered*, 1701

KEYNES, J. M. *The Economic Consequences of Mr Churchill*, Hogarth Press, 1925

Parliamentary Reports, Periodicals and Works of Reference

Annual Register
Architectural Magazine and Journal
Bankers Almanac
Black Dwarf, The
Calendar of State Papers
Calendar of Treasury Papers
Dictionary of National Biography
International Monetary Fund, The first ten years of the (Report)
Journal of the House of Commons
London Chronicle
Report of the Committee on Finance and Industry ['Macmillan Report']
Report of the Committee on the Working of the Monetary System ['Radcliffe Report']
The Old Lady [Staff Magazine of the Bank of England]

Economic Journal
Economica
Economist, The
Genealogists Magazine, The
Gentleman's Magazine
Hansard
Illustrated London News

Books for further reference

ASHTON, T. S. *and* SAYERS, R. S. [editors] *Papers in English monetary history*, Oxford, Clarendon Press, 1953

ASHTON, T. S. *An Economic History of England: the 18th Century*, Methuen & Co. Ltd., 1959, (An economic history of England; edited by T. S. Ashton)

ASHWORTH, W. *An Economic History of England, 1870–1939*, Methuen & Co. Ltd., 1960, (An economic history of England; edited by T. S. Ashton)

BANK FOR INTERNATIONAL SETTLEMENTS *Eight European central banks: organization and activities of Bank of England . . .: a descriptive study*, George Allen & Unwin Ltd., 1963

BISSCHOP, W. R. *The rise of the London money market, 1640–1826*, P. S. King & Son Ltd., 1910

BRITTAIN, SIR HERBERT *The British budgetary system*, George Allen & Unwin Ltd., 1959

CLAPHAM, SIR J. H. *An economic history of modern Britain* [1820–1914], C.U.P., 1930/1938, 3 vols.

COPPIETERS, E. *English bank note circulation 1694–1954*, Published by the Louvain Institute of Economic and Social Research, and by M. Nijhoff, The Hague, 1955

CRICK, W. F. and WADSWORTH, J. E. *A hundred years of joint stock banking* [*1834–1934*], Hodder & Stoughton Ltd., 1936

DACEY, W. MANNING *The British banking mechanism*, 5th rev. ed., Hutchinson & Co. (Publishers) Ltd., 1964

DAY, A. C. L. *Outline of monetary economics*, Oxford, Clarendon Press, 1957

DILLEN, J. G. VAN *History of the principal public banks*, The Hague, M. Nijhoff 1934, Reprinted by Frank Cass & Co. Ltd., 1965 [Contains chapter entitled 'The first fifty years of the Bank of England, 1694–1744' by R. D. Richards, *and* 'Modern bibliography of banking and currency (British Empire) from the XVth century to 1815' composed under the direction of Sir J. H. Clapham]

EINZIG, P. *Primitive money in its ethnological, historical and economic aspects*, Eyre and Spottiswoode (Publishers) Ltd., 1949

FEAVEARYEAR, SIR A. E. *The pound sterling: a history of English money*, 2nd edition revised by E. Victor Morgan, Oxford, Clarendon Press, 1963

GREAT BRITAIN. CENTRAL OFFICE OF INFORMATION *The British banking system* (Reference Pamphlet No. 65), HM Stationery Office, 1964

GREAT BRITAIN. ROYAL MINT *The Royal Mint: an outline history* compiled by H. G. Stride [new ed.], HMSO, 1953

GREGORY, SIR T. E. [editor] *Select statutes, documents and reports relating to British banking 1832–1928*, O.U.P., 1929, 2 vols., Reprinted Frank Cass & Co. Ltd., 1964

HANSON, J. L. *Monetary theory and practice*, 2nd ed., Macdonald & Evans Ltd., 1962

HOBSON, SIR OSCAR R. *How the City works*, 7th rev. ed., Dickens Press, 1962

HOLDEN, J. MILNES *The history of negotiable instruments in English law*, (University of London Legal Series) Athlone Press, 1955

INSTITUTE OF BANKERS *The Bank of England today; being the Ernest Sykes Memorial Lectures 1964*, Institute of Bankers (Pamphlet)

JONES, G. P. and POOL, A. G. *A hundred years of economic development in Great Britain* (1840–1940), G. Duckworth & Co. Ltd., 1940

JOSSET, C. R. *Money in Britain: a history of the currencies of the British Isles*, F. Warne & Co. Ltd., 1962

JOURNAL OF THE INSTITUTE OF BANKERS, Articles written for 'the young banker' in vols. 79 and 80, 1958 and 1959, entitled 'The history of banking'

KING, W. T. C. *History of the London discount market* [to 1913], G. Routledge & Sons Ltd. (now Routledge & Kegan Paul Ltd.), 1936

DE KOCK, M. H. *Central banking*, 3rd ed., Staples Press, 1954

MACRAE, N. *The London capital market: its structure, strains and management*, 2nd ed., Staples Press, 1957

MINTS, L. W. *A history of banking theory in Great Britain and the United States*, University of Chicago Press, 1945

MORGAN, E. V. *A history of money*, Penguin Books, 1965

MORGAN, E. VICTOR *The theory and practice of central banking, 1797–1913*, C.U.P., 1943

PALGRAVE, SIR R. H. INGLIS *Bank rate and the money market in England, France, Germany, Holland and Belgium, 1844–1900*, John Murray Ltd., 1903

POWELL, ELLIS T. *The evolution of the money market (1385–1915)*, Financial Times, 1915

PARKER, J. B. *Banking*, English Universities Press, 1953 (Teach Yourself Books)

PRESSNELL, L. S. *Country banking in the Industrial Revolution* [1750–1844], Oxford, Clarendon Press, 1956

QUIGGIN, A. H. *A survey of primitive money: the beginnings of currency*, Methuen & Co. Ltd., 1949

RICHARDS, R. D. *The early history of banking in England* [to 1833], P. S. King & Son Ltd., 1929, Reprinted Frank Cass & Co., Ltd., 1958

SAYERS, R. S. *Bank of England operations, 1890–1914*, P. S. King & Son Ltd., 1936

SAYERS, R. S. *Modern banking*, 6th ed., Oxford, Clarendon Press, 1964

SYKES, J. *The amalgamation movement in English banking, 1825–1924*, P. S. King & Son Ltd., 1926

THOMAS S. E. *The rise and growth of joint stock banking* Vol. I [*Britain: to 1860*], Sir Isaac Pitman & Sons Ltd., 1934

THORNE, W. J. *Banking*, 2nd ed., O.U.P., 1962 (Home University Library)

Index

Abney, Sir Thomas: 13

Accountant, the Chief: 19, 60–1, 63, 104, 124, 129

Accountant's Department: 35, 69, 177–8, 184, 189, 192–3

Ackermann's Gallery: 81

Acres, W. Marston: 14, 124

Acts of Parliament

Bank Charter Act, 1694 (5 & 6 Wm. & Mary C. 20): 9–12

Recoinage, 1696 (7 Wm. III C. 1): 28–9

Bank of England Act 1696 (1st April 1697) (8 & 9 Wm. III C. 20): 32

Riot Act, 1715 (1 Geo. I Stat. 2 C. 5): 41

Consolidation of Annuities, 1752 (25 Geo. II C. 27): 55

Calendar (1750) (24 Geo. II C. 23): 55

Acquisition of Properties, Threadneedle Street, etc. 1764 (4 Geo. III C. 49): 57

Acquisition of Glebe Lands of St. Christopher's Church 1766 (5 Geo. III C. 91): 58

Bank Notes, Scotland 1765 (5 Geo. III C. 49): 64

Vesting in Bank of St. Christopher's Church 1781 (21 Geo. III C. 71): 68

Reduction of National Debt 1786 (26 Geo. III C. 31): 72

Annuities 1797 (37 Geo. III C. 57): 77

Imperial Loan 1797 (37 Geo. III C. 59): 77

Restriction of Cash Payments 1797 (37 Geo. III C. 45): 75–6

Acquisition of Properties, Princes Street & Lothbury 1800 (39 & 40 Geo. III C. 89 Public, Local & Personal): 86

Resumption of Cash Payments 1819 (59 Geo. III C. 49): 80

Country Bankers Act 1826 (7 Geo. IV C. 46): 92

Bank of England Act 1833 (3 & 4 Wm. IV C. 98): 94–5

Bank Charter Act 1844 (7 & 8 Vict. C. 32): 98–9, 101, 107, 109, 114, 121, 125, 135, 147

Post Office Savings Banks 1851 (24 Vict. C. 14): 117

Treasury Notes 1914 (4 & 5 Geo. V C. 14): 135

Gold & Silver Export Control Act 1920 (10 & 11 Geo. V C. 70): 152, 155

Gold Standard Act 1925 (15 & 16 Geo. V C. 29): 155, 164

Coinage Act 1870 (33 & 34 Vict. C. 10): 155

Exchange Equalization Account (Finance Act 1932) (22 & 23 Geo. V C. 25): 165

Bank of England Act 1946 (9 & 10 Geo. VI C. 27): 188

Exchange Control Act 1947 (10 & 11 Geo. VI C. 14): 202

Addington, Henry, later Viscount Sidmouth: 77

Addison, Joseph: 205

Advances, to Customers: 4, 5, 65, 96, 113, 114, 120, 129, 135, 188; to Government: 14, 30, 36, 38, 40, 54, 75, 79, 137; 'long term': 74

Advisers: 165, 167, 176, 201
Aislabie, John: 45
Alexander, William, & Sons: 65
Althorp, Lord (John Charles Spencer, afterwards 3rd Earl Spencer) Chancellor of the Exchequer: 94
America *see* United States of America
'American Houses': 97
American Independence, War of: 66
Amiens, Treaty of 1802: 77
Amory, D. H., Chancellor of the Exchequer: 199
Amsterdam: 2, 56, 64, 131
Anderson, Sir Alan: 167, 189
Anderson, Sir John (later Lord Waverley) Chancellor of the Exchequer: 183
Andréadès, A.: 97
Anglo-Austrian Bank: 157
Anne, Queen: 36, 39–41, 94, 185
Annual Report of the Bank: 200
Anrep, Boris: 150
Antwerp Agency: 21
'Appeasement': 172
Arbuthnot, George, Treasury Official: 115
Argentine: 126–7
Armstrong-Whitworth: 156, 170
Asgill, John: 27
Ashurst, Sir William: 12
Aslett, Robert: 84–5
Asquith, H. H. (later Lord Oxford & Asquith): 135, 139
'Assignats': 74
Audit Department: 129–30
Australasia, Bank: 95
Australia: 112
 Commonwealth Bank of: 168
 Royal Bank of: 95
Austria: 121, 133, 157, 161
Austrian Succession, War of: 53

'Baby Bond' *see* War Savings Certificates
Bacolet: 65
Bagehot, Walter, 118–21, 167–8
Baily, George: 107
Baker, Sir Herbert: 58, 69, 86, 149, 184
Balance of Payments: 170
Baldwin, Stanley (later Lord Baldwin) Chancellor of the Exchequer: 152, 155, 163
Bank Annuity Society: 104
Bank Charter Act 1844 *see* Acts of Parliament

Bank Coffee House: 57
Bank Dollar: 78
Bank ink: 105
Bank of England
 Title: 2
 Established 1694: 12
 Difficulties of 1696: 26–31
 Granted exclusive privileges 1709: 38
 Agent for Government lotteries 1710: 38
 As Banker to the Government and Registrar of Government Stocks: 95
 Manages the National Debt: 95, 204
 Cash payments restricted 1797: 75–6
 Cash payments resumed 1821: 80
 Privileges, limited 1826: 92
 Branches established 1826: 92–3
 Privileges further limited 1833: 94–5
 As the Bankers' Bank: 95
 As the 'lender of last resort': 95
 Separation of its Issue and Banking Departments: 97–8
 Issue of Notes limited 1844: 98
 Required to publish a weekly summary of accounts: 99
 Duties and functions considered 1917: 142–3
 Disengages itself from most commercial business: 157
 Manages the Exchange Equalization Account 1932: 165, 202
 Changes in internal organization 1920–39: 166–7
 Passes into Public Ownership 1946: 188
 Carries out changes recommended by the 'Radcliffe Committee': 199–200
 Its duties and functions at the present day: 201–5
Bank of England Library *see* Library and Literary Association
Bank of England Notes *see* Notes, Bank of England
Bank of England Stock *see* Bank Stock
Bank of Ireland *see* Ireland, Bank of
Bank of Sweden *see* Sweden, Bank of
Bank Post Bills: 47
Bank Premises, Threadneedle Street *see* Threadneedle Street
Bank Provident Society: 103–4
Bank Rate
 on Bills and Notes with less than 3 months to run, exempted from the Usury Laws: 94–5
 ordered to be fixed weekly: 107

fluctuations: 108–9, 113–14, 118, 120–1, 126, 128, 131, 134, 136, 151, 159, 160, 161, 164, 166, 173, 195–6, 197, 199
Bank Rate Tribunal: 196–8, 201
Bank Restriction Note: 89
Bank Sealed Bills *see* Notes, Bank of England
Bank Stock *see also* Capital of the Bank
  Subscribed: 12
  Qualifying holdings of for Governors and Directors; 13; for Voting rights: 13; Bank offers to lend on: 43; offer withdrawn: 43
  Foreign holders of: 99–100
  Danger of, as a market security: 185
  Vested in a nominee of H.M. Treasury: 189
  Dividends on: 30, 31, 59, 73
  Fluctuations in price of: 26, 31, 32, 44–5, 73
Bank Stock Office: 63, 105, 189
Bank Street: 57
Bank tokens, of 3s. and 1s. 6d.: 78, 80
Bank Volunteers *see* Volunteers
Bankers' Almanac, The: 63
'Bankers' Bank': 95, 203
Bankers' Industrial Development Co. Ltd.: 157, 159
Bankers' Magazine, The: 155–6
Bankers 'Ramp': 162–3
Banking
  nature of: 2; in England before 1694: 4–8; developments 1750–1800: 63; in Scotland: 63–4; enquiry into the system 1832: 94; practice reshaped 1833–1844: 95; in London 1833–1844: 95
Banking methods and practices: 46, 93, 95, 111, 121–2, 125, 129–30
Bankruptcies: 9, 44, 56, 64, 73, 91–2, 108, 113, 119, 131
Barbon, Dr Nicholas: 27
Barclay, Bevan & Co.: 119
Barebones, Praise-God: 27
Baring Brothers & Co.: 120, 126–8, 201
Baring Crisis: 126–8
Baring, Francis I (1793): 74
Baring, Francis II (1890): 126
Baring, John, 2nd Lord Revelstoke: 143
Bark, Peter: 157
Barnard, Sir John: 52
Barnett, Hoares & Co.: 119
Bartholomew Lane, Bank's premises in: 50, 57, 85
Bateman, Sir James: 13–23, 43, 45

Battle of Britain: 178
Beardmores: 170
Belfast: 175
Belgium: 135, 171
Belgium, National Bank of: 138
Bell Yard: 125
Bere Mill: 56
Berlin Decrees: 79
Bertie, Charles: 20
Betting and Gaming *see* Staff, Rules and Orders for
Bevin, Ernest: 158
Bill Transactions *see* Staff, Rules and Orders for
Bills of Exchange: 6, 22, 32, 47, 55, 63, 65, 73, 75, 94–5, 99, 119, 135, 157
'Bills of Property': 11
Bi-metalism: 80
Birmingham: 93, 114
Bish, Mr, Lottery Office Keeper: 84
Black Dwarf, The: 89
'Black Market': 180
'Black Friday': 120, 181
Blake, Robert: 139
Blaythwayt, William: 31
Blomfield, Sir Arthur: 125
Boddington, George: 13
Boddington, Thomas: 74
Boer War: 130–1
Bomb damage
  at Head Office: 178–9
  at Bank Buildings: 179
  at the Branches: 179
Booth, G. M.: 189
Bosanquet, Samuel: 74
Boulton & Watt, Messrs: 78
Bowen, H. G.: 129
Bradbury, Sir John (later Lord Bradbury): 136, 155
Branches of the Bank: 92–3, 124–5, 157, 175
Brazil: 118
Bretton Woods: 191
Bridges, Brook: 13
Brindley, James: 88
Briscoe, John: 27
Bristol: 2, 73, 93
Bristol Branch: 93, 97
Britannia, as the badge of the Bank: 17–8, 34, 51, 58, 82, 112
British North America, Bank of: 95
Brook, R. E.: 189
Brown, Shipley & Co.: 148
Browning, Robert: 63
Brunel, I. K.: 88

Brussels, Financial Conference at: 152, 154
'Bubble' Companies: 43–4
Bubble, South Sea *see* South Sea Company
Building Committee: 107
Buildings of England, The: 150
Bullion, dealing in: 4, 47–8
Bullion Broker, the Bank's: 47–8
Bullion Committee 1810: 78–9
Bullion Yard: 103
Buonaparte *see* Napoleon Buonaparte
Burke, Edmund: 71, 73
Butler, R. A., Chancellor of the Exchequer: 195–6
By-Laws of the Bank: 23–4

Campbell, W. M.: 136
Campo Formio, Treaty of 1797: 77
Canada, Bank of: 168–9, 203
Capel Court: 105
Capital of the Bank: 12, 30, 32, 38, 54–5, 80, 186
Cashier, the Chief: 19, 60, 61, 84, 103, 112, 121, 122, 128–9, 132, 143–4, 168
Cashier's Department: 34–5, 167, 175
Catterns, B. G.: 168, 189
Catto, Lord: 180, 183, 186, 187–8, 189, 194
Central Bank and Central Banking: 91, 95, 121–2, 138, 154, 156, 158, 166–7, 168–9, 171, 185, 199, 201
Central Banking after Bagehot: 195
Central Banking Information Department: 199
Chalmers, Sir Robert (later Lord Chalmers): 140
Chamberlain, Sir Austen, Chancellor of the Exchequer: 155
Chamberlain, Neville, Chancellor of the Exchequer: 164–5
Chamberlain, S. B.: 179
Chamberlen, Dr Hugh: 27
Chambrelan, Charles: 23
Chancery Office: 125
Change Alley: 54
Charles Edward, the 'Young Pretender': 54
Charles I, King: 7
Charter of the Bank
  Sealed 1694: 13
  Term of, Extended: 32, 37, 53, 71, 94, 98
  of 1946: 188

Chartism: 110–11
Chatham, Lord (William Pitt, Earl of Chatham): 56
'Cheap-Money' Policy: 176
Cheapside: 67
Cheer, Henry, Sculptor: 51
Cheque books: 93
Cheques: 18–19, 46, 111, 123
Chief Accountant *see* Accountant, the Chief
Chief Cashier *see* Cashier, the Chief
Chile, Bank of: 138
China: 118
Chitty, Sir Thomas: 53
Cholera, in London: 104
Churchill, Lord Randolph: 125
Churchill, Sir Winston: 71, 133, 155–6
City Corporation: 106
City of London Bank: 2
C.I.V., City of London Imperial Volunteers *see* Volunteers
Clapham, Professor J. H. (later Sir John Clapham): 4, 10, 22, 27, 30, 60, 70, 77, 121, 182
Clarke, Edward: 13
Clay, Sir Henry: 139, 170, 182
Clearing House, the Bankers': 122
Clegg, W. H.: 168
Clerks *see* Staff
Clerks' Widows Fund: 104
Clifford & Sons, of Amsterdam: 65
Clutterbuck, Charles: 62–3
Cobbold, C. F. (later Lord Cobbold): 189, 194, 197–8, 201
Cockburn, Sir Alexander, Lord Chief Justice: 118
Cockerell, C. R.: 106, 111
Coinage, the
  High 'rating' of gold, in terms of silver 1695: 22
  Re-coinage of 1696: 28–9
  Shortage of 1763: 56
  Shortage of 1793: 76
  Royal Mint resumes coining: 80
  See also Gold Coin
Cockayne, Sir Brien (later Lord Cullen): 142–3, 147, 152
Cole, A. C.: 143
Colenso, Battle of: 131
Collet, Sir Mark: 181
Collier, James: 61
Colonial and Corporation Stocks Office: 190
Colours of the Bank Volunteers: 82
Commissary-General, the: 82

Commissioners for the Reduction of the National Debt: 72
Commissioners of Sewers: 107
Committees, Special
of the Bank: 21, 23–4, 69, 71, 81, 92, 129, 143–4, 180
Parliamentary (or Government): 94, 97, 109–10, 114–15, 144–5, 147, 155, 162
on Finance & Industry 1929 see Macmillan Committee
On the Working of the Monetary System, 1957 see Radcliffe Committee of Bankers of London 1793: 74
Committees, Standing
of the Bank: 59–60, 107, 129–30
For Audit see Audit Department
For House and Servants see House and Servants Committee
Treasury see Treasury, Committee of
Commonwealth and Corporation Stocks Office: 190
Compensation for certain Issuing Bankers: 99
Comptroller: 143, 168
Conferences, International, etc.
Brussels: 152, 154
Genoa: 154
Ottawa: 165
Lausanne: 154, 165
Conservative Central Office: 197
Consols: 55, 108, 126
Coolidge, Calvin: 152
Cope, Sir John: 23
Cost of living: 61, 123
Costan, Matthew: 106
Cotton, William: 98, 111
Country Bankers: 63, 91, 92, 93, 96, 99, 122–3
Country Clearing: 122–3
Court Room: 50, 58, 69
Court of Directors: 13, 17, 25, 47, 59, 107, 186, 188–9
Courts of Justice: 125
Cowell, J. W.: 97
Credit: 2, 31
'Credit Squeeze': 108, 196
Credit Anstaldt, the: 161
Crimea, War in: 113, 123
Cripps, Sir Stafford, Chancellor of the Exchequer: 194
Crises
Crisis of 1763: 56; of 1772: 64–5; of 1793: 73–5; of 1825: 91; of 1847: 108–9; of 1857: 113–5; of 1866: 118–21; of 1890: 126–8; of 1907: 131; of 1914: 134–7; of 1931: 161–4; of 1957–8: 196
Cromer, Lord: 191, 201, 203
Crown Tavern: 50, 57
Cruikshank, George: 90
Cullen, Lord see Cokayne, Sir Brien
Culloden, Battle of: 54
Cunliffe, Walter (Lord Cunliffe): 134–7, 139–43, 147–9, 155
Cunliffe Committee, on Currency and Foreign Exchange: 147, 155
Currie, Bertram: 127
Curtis, T. A.: 105, 108
Customer, the Bank's, origin of: 19
Czech gold: 171–3
Czechoslovakia, National Bank of: 172

Dalton, Hugh, Chancellor of the Exchequer: 186
Darien Scheme: 26
Dawes Plan, of Reparations: 154, 165, 187
Day they Robbed the Bank of England, The film: 106
Daylight Saving: 55
de Koning, Jacobus: 21
Defence (Finance) Regulations: 174
Defoe, Daniel: 46
Denew, James: 13, 21
Departments of the Bank: 19, 97, 130, 167, 169, 199
'Depression, The': 160
Devaluation, of the £: 194–5
Devonshire, Duke of: 39
Directors' Charitable Fund: 104
Discount and Discount Policy: 4, 8, 47, 64, 65, 73, 94–5, 96, 108–9, 118, 119–21, 125, 131, 134
Discount, the Rate of, see Bank Rate
'Dividend Day': 123
Dividend Pay Office: 106
Dividend Preparation Office: 177
Dividend Warrant Office: 106, 111
Dividends on Bank Stock see Bank Stock
Dobree, Bonamy: 120
Dodd, Samuel: 36, 37
'Dole, The' see Unemployment Insurance
'Dollar Gap': 190, 194
Doorkeepers: 34
Dowdeswell, Thomas: 60
Dowgate: 107
Drawing Office: 19
Drawn Notes see Cheques
Dual Control: 84

Dundas, Henry (Viscount Melville): 81
Durbin, Leslie: 183

East India Company: 40, 43, 64–5, 113
Economic Consequences of Mr Churchill, The: 156
Economic Intelligence Department: 200
'Economic Man': 16
Economic and Statistics Section: 167
Economist, The: 118, 119, 121, 129, 133, 142, 155, 156, 172
Eden, Sir Anthony (Lord Avon): 196
Egypt: 118
Elections, General *see* General Elections
Electro-metallurgy: 104, 112
Electrotypes: 112
Emperor of Germany *see* Imperial Loans
European Monetary Agreement: 203
Exchange Committee 1931: 165
Exchange Control: 173–6, 179
Exchange Control Regulations: 174, 202
Exchange Equalisation Account: 165, 174, 202
Exchequer & Audit Roll: 72
Exchequer, H.M.: 7, 8, 52, 95, 203
Exchequer Bills: 27, 30, 38, 40, 52, 71, 74, 84, 108
Exchequer Bonds: 127
'Exclusive Privilege': 32, 92, 94
Executive (Full-time) Directors of the Bank: 168
Exeter Branch: 168
Exeter 'Change: 28
'Ex-Directors', of the Bank: 24
Exports, Britain's: 160, 170

Faber, Dr Oscar: 150, 178
Failures, *see* Bankruptcies
Farrer, Gaspart: 155
Fleet Street: 125
Fiduciary Note Issue: 161–2
Finance Corporation for Industry: 180–1, 184
Financial Conferences *see* Conferences, International
Financial Times, The: 173
Finsbury Circus, Bank Premises in: 184, 193
Fisher, Sir Warren: 136
Foley, Paul, Speaker of the House of Commons: 27
Fontency, Battle of: 54
Fordyce, Alexander: 64
Foreign Banks, in London: 130

Foreign Exchange: 6, 7, 8, 74–5, 153, 174–5, 195
see also Exchange Control
Foreign Exchange Market: 174–5, 195
Foreign Exchange Section: 174
Forgery of Bank Notes: 32, 77, 89, 173
'Forward Exchange': 151
Fox, Charles: 20
Fox, Charles James: 73
France: 73, 131, 171
France, Bank of: 127, 138, 161, 171
Francis, John: 68
Franz Ferdinand, Archduke: 133
Free Libraries: 103
Free Trade: 166
French Revolution: 73
'Fund of Perpetual Interest': 9–11
Funding Stocks Office: 189
Furnese, Sir Henry: 13, 23

Gaitskell, Hugh: 187
Gamble, William, Silversmith: 31
Garraways Coffee House: 54
Garden Court, Bank: 68–9, 149
Gate Porter: 34
General Court of Proprietors: 13, 23, 24, 30, 31, 41, 55, 59, 72, 117, 142, 168, 185
General Elections: 1741: 53; 1922: 152; 1931: 164; 1945: 184; 1950: 195; 1955: 196
General Strike 1926: 145, 155
Genoa, Bank of: 2
Genoa, Conference at: 154
George I, King: 41
George II, King: 76, 81
German Mark, collapse of: 153
Germany: 121, 131, 135, 146, 153, 171, 173, 175
Gibson, George: 189, 193
Gillray, James: 81, 88
Gladstone, W. E., Chancellor of the Exchequer: 116–17, 120
Gloucester Branch: 92, 97
Glyn and Halifax: 64
Glyn, Mills, Currie and Co.: 127
Goddard, Thomas: 13
Goderich, Viscount *see* Robinson, F. J.
Godfrey, Sir Edmondbury: 22
Godfrey, Michael: 9, 13, 21, 22, 23
Godolphin, Lord (Sidney, 1st Earl of Godolphin): 26, 37, 39, 40
Gold: 1, 4, 22, 47–8, 112, 130–1, 140–2, 154–5, 165–7, 171–2, 174
    Drains of: 74–5, 113, 160, 164

Reserve: 74, 91, 121, 131, 134, 137, 147, 164
Runs on: 113, 134–6
Bullion: 78–9
Gold Coin
  Guineas, 1663–1694: 22
  7s. pieces: 56
  Sovereigns and Half-Sovereigns: 80
  light coins: 111
  coin-weighing: 111
  in circulation 1851–7: 112–13
Gold Standard: 144, 147, 151–2, 154–5, 158, 164, 187
Gold Weighing Room: 103
Goldsmiths, the London: 7–8, 10, 63
Goldsmith's Hall: 76
Gordon, Lord George: 67
Gordon Riots: 66–70, 110
Gore, Sir William: 13
Goschen, G. J. (Viscount Goschen), Chancellor of the Exchequer: 118, 125–7, 131
Goulburn, Henry, Chancellor of the Exchequer: 98
Gould, Nathaniel: 24
Goulden, Richard, Sculptor: 149
Government, Advances to see Advances
Government Expenditure: 152
Government Stocks
  Bank as Registrar of: 95
  Payment of dividends on: 116–7
Governors and Directors
  Qualifications for office: 13
  Election of 1694: 13
  Proportion of retiring Directors allowed to be re-elected annually: 24
  Members of the Staff as Directors: 143–4, 167–8; as Deputy-Governors: 167–8, 201
  Remuneration of: 148, 168
  Age of Retirement: 188–9
  Terms of office (Act of 1946): 188
Governors' Leave see Leave of Absence
Gower, A. L.: 108
Granet, Sir Guy: 159
Grahame, Kenneth: 132
Gray, G. E.: 124
Great Bursted Church, Essex: 69
Great Hall: 50–1, 54, 76–7, 106, 111
Greene, B. B.: 127
Gregory, Peter: 70
Gregory, Professor T. E.: 158
Grenada: 65
Gresham, Sir Thomas: 7, 106

Grey, Earl (Charles Grey, 2nd Earl Grey): 94
Grocers Company: 19–20, 183
Grocers Hall: 19–20, 25, 33–5, 38, 46, 49
Guest, William: 62
Guineas see Gold Coin

Half-Sovereigns see Gold Coin
Halifax, Earl of, see Montagu, Charles
Hambro, Sir Everard: 126
Hamburg, Bank of: 2
Hamburg: 56, 74–5, 137
Hampstead Waterworks: 26
Hankey, Thomson: 103
Hanover: 121
Harcourt, Sir William, Chancellor of the Exchequer: 129
Hardwick, Philip: 122
Harley, Edward: 27
Harley, Robert (1st Earl of Oxford): 27, 37, 39–40, 42
Harrison, George: 51
Harrison, Samuel: 82
Harrod, Sir Roy: 190–1
Harvey, Sir Ernest: 121, 158–9, 162, 168
Hatry, Clarence: 160–1
Head Gate Porter: 34, 105, 179
Heath, J. B.: 98
Heathcote, Sir Gilbert: 13, 16, 29, 32, 39, 41
Heal, Victor, & Smith, Messrs: 193
Hedges, Sir William: 13
Hicks, G. E.: 123
Hill, Richard: 21
Hitler, Adolf: 166, 171
Hobson, Sir Oscar: 198–9
Holloways, Messrs: 178
Holy-days Observed at the Bank: 35; Reduced in numbers: 100–1
Houblon, Abraham: 13, 21
Houblon, Sir James: 13, 21
Houblon, Sir John: 13, 29, 31, 49, 84, 182
Houblon, Dame Mary: 49
Houblon-Norman Fund: 182
Hours of business: 35, 100, 102
House and Servants, Committee for: 34, 59
'House Money': 117
Huband, Sir John: 13
Huddersfield: 93
Hungary, National Bank of: 167
Hurstbourne Priors, Hants.: 178
Hyett, D.: 124

Imperial Economic Conference, Ottawa: 165

Imperial Loans to Emperor of Germany 1794: 75, 77

Import Duties Bill: 164–5

Ince, John: 19

Income Tax: 80, 98, 123

Incorporated Law Society: 125

Indemnity, Bill, or letter of: 77–9, 109, 114, 120, 135

India: 118, 131, 137, 149, 168

India, Reserve Bank of: 168

Indian Mutiny: 113, 123

Industrial and Commercial Finance Corporation: 181, 184

Industrial Research: 180

Industrial Revolution: 78, 89, 110

Inflation: 22, 136, 190, 195

Inscribed Stock: 197

International Bank for Reconstruction and Development: 190–1, 201, 203

International Conferences see Conferences

International Loans: 75, 77, 154, 156

International Monetary Fund: 190–2, 197, 201–2

International Settlements, Bank for: 157, 160, 161, 172–3, 203

Invergordon: 163

Ireland: 108, 114, 133

Ireland, Bank of: 96

Issue, its place in banking: 4; contention over, in proposals for the Bank: 10–11; statutory regulation of: 64; the Bank's in 1793: 74; usefulness of local issues realised to be passing: 95–6; restrictions on (Act of 1844): 98–9; by Government 1914 see Notes, Treasury, amalgamation of Bank and Treasury Issues: 155

Issue Department of the Bank: 97–8

Issue, a National or State Bank of considered: 114–15

Italy: 146

Italy, Bank of: 138

Jackson, Adrew, President of USA: 96

Jackson, F. Huth: 143

James, the 'old' Pretender: 41

Janssen, Theodore: 13, 21, 43, 45

Jews, the first Bankers in England: 5

Johnson, Dr Samuel: 63

Joint-Stock Banks: 92–3, 94, 111, 122, 123, 127–8, 130, 156–7, 175

Kennet, Brackley: 66

Kennington Common: 110

Kenrick, John: 19

Keswick, W. J.: 197

Keynes, J. M. (later Lord Keynes): 140, 153, 156, 158, 159, 190–2

Kindersley, Sir Robert (1st Lord Kindersley: 138–9, 143, 153, 177, 189

Kindersley, H. K. M. (2nd Lord Kindersley): 197

Knickerbocker Trust Company: 131

Labour Governments, etc. see Socialists

Lamb, Charles: 45

Lancashire Cotton Corporation: 157

Lancaster: 93

Land Bank: 26–8

Langport, Somerset: 93

Lausanne Agreement: 154

Law, Andrew Bonar, Chancellor of the Exchequer: 139–42, 152–3

Law Courts Branch: 125

Law Officers of the Crown: 117, 172

Lazard Brothers: 197

League of Nations: 156

Leave of Absence: 101–2, 124

Leeds: 114

Leeds Branch: 93

Lefeaux, Leslie: 164

Legal Tender: 11, 96

'Lender of last resort': 95

Lethieullier, Samuel: 13

Lever, Sir Hardman, Treasury Official: 140–1

Lewis, Sir G. C., Chancellor of the Exchequer: 114, 117

Library and Literary Association: 103, 132–3, 171

Lidderdale, William: 126–8

Life Assurance: 103–4

Liverpool: 73, 74, 96, 113

Liverpool Borough Bank: 113

Liverpool Branch: 93

Liverpool, Lord (R. B. Jenkinson, 2nd Earl of Liverpool): 92

Liverpool Royal Bank of: 109

Lloyd George, D., Earl Lloyd George: 71, 133, 139–42, 152

Lloyd, Rev. Richard: 82

Loans, see also Advances, War Loans, International Loans: 7, 21, 23, 71, 96–7, 140, 191

Lombard Street: 6

Lombards as bankers in England: 5–7

London Assurance: 183
London Bank: 91
London Chronicle: 64
London, the City of: 1–2, 73, 171, 173
London Exchange Committee: 140, 174
London Gazette: 36, 54, 73
London Joint Stock Bank: 95
London and Westminster Bank: 94, 95, 119, 122, 128
Lordell, John: 13
Lord Mayor's Appeal Funds: 204
Lord's Cricket Ground: 81–2
Lords Justices (the Council of Regency for William III): 22, 29
Lossiemouth: 162
Lothbury: 50, 85
Lothbury Court: 60
Lotteries, State: 38, 64
Lowe, Robert (1st Viscount Sherbrooke): 123
Lowndes, William, Secretary of the Treasury: 37–8
Lowth, Robert, Bishop of London: 68
Lubbock, Cecil: 143, 167
Lubbock, Sir John (later Lord Avebury): 135
Lutyens, Sir Edwin: 149
Lynskey, Mr Justice: 193

Macadam (McAdam), J. L.: 87
Macdonald, J. Ramsay: 160, 162–3, 164, 187
Macdonnell, Thomas: 61
McKenna, Reginald, Chancellor of the Exchequer: 139, 153, 158
Maclaine family: 83
Maclise, Daniel, RA: 112
Macmillan, Harold, Chancellor of the Exchequer: 196
Macmillan, Rt Hon. H. P., KC: 158
Macmillan Committee 1929: 158–9, 164, 198
Madockes, Thomas: 61
Mail Robberies: 46–7
Manchester: 92, 96
Manchester Branch: 92, 132
Mansion House, Meeting of Bankers and Merchants 1797: 76
Maria Theresa, Empress: 53
Marlborough, Duke of (John Churchill, 1st Duke): 36, 38
Marshall, Matthew: 103, 122, 132
Martin, Francis: 75
Matheson and Co. Ltd.: 197

'May Committee' (on the Public Finances): 162, 163
May, Frank: 128–9
Mayne, Jonathan: 34, 51
Medical Officer to the Bank: 104
Mercer, Thomas: 19
Mercers Chappell *see* Mercers Hall
Mercers Company: 183
Mercers Hall: 12–13, 19, 38
Merchants: 4, 9, 10, 12, 54, 63, 76, 121
Messengers, Bank *see* Staff
Metcalfe, John: 88
Microcosm of London: 51
Middleton, H.: 81
Military, the
    Garrison the Bank during the Gordon Riots: 67
    Nightly guard at the Bank: 68
    Garrison the Bank 1848: 110
Miller, Bowler: 62
Million Bank, the: 26
Minden, Battle of: 56
Mine Adventures Company: 37
Minorca: 56
Mint, the Royal: 7, 29, 80, 155
Mocatta and Goldsmith, Messrs: 47
Monetary Convention: 154
Moneylending: 2–3
Montagu, Charles (later Earl of Halifax), Chancellor of the Exchequer: 9, 11, 27, 28, 29, 30–1, 37
Monteagle, Lord (Thomas Spring-Rice, 1st Baron): 115
Moorfields: 66
Moratorium: 135, 157
Morice, Humphry: 48–9, 128
Morice, Mrs Katherine: 49
Morgan, J. P. and Co.: 140
Morris, James: 108
Mortgages: 65–6
Munich Agreement: 171, 173

Nairne, Sir Gordon: 121, 143–4, 168
Napier, D. and Son, Messrs: 111
Napoleon Buonaparte: 70, 77, 79, 81, 97, 178, 181
National Debt, the: 9, 10–11, 35, 52, 56, 66, 116, 125, 130–1, 166, 204
    Management of, by the Bank *see* Remuneration
National Debt Office: 179
National Government: 163
'National Land Bank': 26–8
National Provincial Bank: 95, 128

National Savings Certificates: 138–9, 177
National Savings Committee: 177
National War Bonds: 138
Nationalization
of the Bank: 115, 141, 144, 170, 184–90
of Railways, etc.: 192
Neale and Co., Messrs: 64
Netherlands, Bank of the: 138, 171
New Change: 193
'New Deal': 171
New York: 113, 131, 137
Clearing House Association: 31
Federal Reserve Bank of: 161
Stock Exchange: 137, 160
New Zealand, Reserve Bank of: 169
Newcastle Branch: 114, 156
Newcastle, Duke of: 39
Newgate Prison: 66–7, 85
Newland, Abraham: 84
News Summary: 167
Newson-Smith, Sir Frank: 183
Niemeyer, Sir Otto: 155, 171–2
Norman, G. W.: 181
Norman, M. C. (Lord Norman): 132–3,
142, 150, Chap. 8 passim 187, 194, 201
Northey, Sir Edward, Attorney General:
35, 37, 48
North, Lord (Frederick North, 2nd Earl
of Guildford): 68
Northern and Central Bank of England:
96
Norway, Bank of: 138
Norwich: 93
'Not Unanimous': 198–9
Notes, Bank of England
Running Cash Notes: 18–19, 46
Drawn Notes see Cheques: 18–19
Bank Sealed Bills: 21, 36
Specie Notes.: 30, 35
for printed amounts: 46
for £10 and £15 issued: 57
for £25 issued: 57
Improvements in design, etc.: 57, 112
for £5 issued: 74
for £1 and £2 issued: 76
for £1 and £2 discontinued: 90–1
for £1, a number returned to circulation, 1825: 91
legal tender, under Act of 1833: 96
Export of, prohibited 1939: 175
Import of, prohibited 1940: 175
Metal thread in: 179
for the British Military Authority:
179
for 5/- and 2/6 printed: 179

for denominations above £5, called
in: 179–80
Issue at the present day: 204
Forgery of, death penalty imposed for:
32
extensive forgery of £1 and £2 notes:
77, 89
death penalty abolished: 90
Notes, Treasury of £1 and 10s.: 135–7,
147, 155

Oaths
Taken by Governors and Directors: 15
see also Declarations
Ohio Life Insurance & Trust Co.: 131
Old Lady of Threadneedle Street, The:
88, 129
Organization for European Economic
Co-operation (OEEC): 203
Orphans' Fund: 25–6, 27
Osborne, J. A. C.: 169
Ottawa: 137, 140, 165, 192
Overend Gurney and Co.: 118–19, 120,
126, 181
Overseas and Foreign Department: 167,
169, 200
Overton, Hants.: 177, 179

Palmer, J. Horsley: 96
Palmerston, Lord (Henry John Temple,
3rd Viscount): 113–14
Paris, Peace of 1763: 56
Parker, Mr Justice: 196
Parliamentary Committees see Com-
mittees
Parlours, the Bank's: 33
Paterson, William: 9, 13, 25–6
Pawnbrokers: 7
Pax Britannica: 87
Pay Hall see Great Hall
Payne, John: 63
Pearse, John: 79
Peel, Sir Robert: 97–8, 107, 109, 110, 116
Pells, Clerk of the: 95
Pensions
for Staff, see Staff
for full-time Directors see Executive
Directors
Pepys, Samuel: 8, 18
Perceval, Spencer, Chancellor of the
Exchequer: 79
Pevsner, Dr Nikolaus: 150
Philadelphia: 97

Pieces of Eight: 76
Piercy, Lord: 188, 189
Pig Street: 67
Pigou, Professor: 155
Pitman, Sir James: 187
Pitt, William: 52, 70–5, 77, 88, 176, 183
Plumer, Thomas: 61–2
Plymouth Branch: 93
Pocket scales and balances: 112
Poland: 173
Pole, Sir Peter & Co. (Pole, Thornton, Free, Down & Scott): 91
Pope, Alexander: 16
Post Office Savings Banks: 117
Postal Orders: 135
Portal, Henry: 56
Portals, Messrs: 56, 177
Porters see Staff
Portland, Earl of: 12
Portsmouth Branch: 93
Poultry, the: 67
Poultry Compter, the: 84
Powell, David: 127
Prague: 171
Press, the: 167
Prestonpans, Battle of: 54
Pretenders see James, the old Pretender; Charles Edward, the young Pretender
Prices, Control of: 173–4, 195–6
Princes Street: 85–6
Princes Street Gate: 110
Printing Works, the Bank's: 136, 177, 179, 204–5
Private Drawing Office: 106
Privilege of the Bank see Exclusive Privilege
Privy Council, H.M.: 75, 78
Property Tax: 77, 79, see also Income Tax
Proprietors see General Court of Proprietors, see also Bank Stock
'Protestant Ethic': 73
Prussia: 121
Public Departments, Accounts of the: 204
Pugin, C. A.: 51
Punch: 101, 129

Quarterly Bulletin: 200
Queen's Arms Tavern: 67

Race, Daniel: 61–2
Radcliffe Committee 1957: 198–9, 200, 201–3
Raikes, Thomas: 81

Railways: 96, 108, 192
Ranelagh, Lord, Paymaster for the Army: 20
'Rationalization' of Industry: 156–7, 159, 170–1
Raworth, Robert: 13, 22
Re-armanent: 169
Recoinage see Coinage
Record Office, the Bank's: 132
Reform Bill 1832: 93–4
Reichsbank: 161, 172, 185
Reid, Irving and Co., Messrs: 108
Reid, Sir John: 108
'Remisses', Committee for: 21–3
Remuneration, of the Bank (for Management of the National Debt): 71–2, 117
of Governors and Directors: 148, 168
Reparations: 153–4, 165
Residents at the Bank: 34
Restrictions of Cash Payments: 75–81
Revelstoke, Lord (E. C. Baring, 1st Baron): 126
Revelstoke, Lord (John Baring, 2nd Baron): 143
Revelstoke Committee: 143, 144, 189
Retirement, age of; see Staff—Pensions; see also Governors and Directors
Ricardo, David: 115, 155
Richards, James: 124
Richardson, Sir Albert: 59
Richmond, Frances Stewart, Duchess of: 18
Rickatson-Hatt, J. B.: 176
Riot Act: 41, 66
Riots
The Gordon: 66–8, Reform Bill 1831: 93–8
Rivière du Chemin: 65
Robinson, F. J. (later Viscount Goderich): 92
Robinson and Co., Messrs: 108
Robinson, William R.: 108
Roehampton: 132
Roettier, John: 18
Roman Catholics: 60–1
Romilly, Sir Samuel: 89
Rothschilds, Messrs: 92, 161
Rotunda, in the Bank: 57, 105
Rowlandson, T.: 51, 81, 105
Royal Army Pay Corps: 189
Royal Bank of Scotland: 157
Royal Engineers: 110
Royal Exchange, the: 1, 7, 19, 57, 105, 106
Royal Exchange Assurance: 183, 197

Royal Mint *see* Mint, The Royal

Rules and Orders for the Staff *see* Staff

Running Cash Notes *see* Notes, Bank of England

'Runs' on the Bank: 29, 41, 54, 73, 75, 94

Russell, Lord John: 109

Russia: 127, 171
  Imperial Bank of: 157

Ryswick, Treaty and Peace of: 35–6

Sacheverell, Dr Henry: 39, 41

'Safe as the Bank of England': 1, 183, 187

St Christopher, Statue of; *see* War Memorial

St Christopher-le-Stocks Church: 50, 58, 67, 68–9, 85, 106, 182

St Luke's Church, Old Street: 61

St Luke's Printing Works *see* Printing Works

St Margaret's Church, Lothbury: 50, 68–9

Salaries *see* Staff

Salisbury, Lord: 127

Salomons, David: 119, 122

Sampson, George: 58

Sampson, M. B.: 97

Sanderson, Sir James: 74

Sandys, Samuel (1st Baron Sandys): 53

Sarajevo: 130

Saturday, Early Closing on: 102

Savannah, George: 191

Sayers, Professor R. S.: 195

Scawen, Sir William: 13, 21, 23

Schacht, Dr 171

Scotland: 63–4, 96

Scott, David: 57

Scott, Herbert: 150

Seal of the Bank: 17

Secretary of the Bank: 19, 75, 107, 143

Securities Management Trust: 156

Sephardi Jews: 47

Sedgwick, Obadiah: 13

Serbia: 133, 138

Seven Years War: 55–6, 64

Sewers, Access to Bank by way of: 106–7

Sewers, Commissioners of: 107

'Shadow Factories': 177

Shaw, Dr W. A.: 40

Shepherd Bros., Messrs: 19

Sheridan, R. B.: 88

Shillibeer, Samuel: 1

Shower, Sir Bartholomew: 23–4

Siepmann, H. A.: 167

Sinking Fund: 72

Smee, Alfred, FRS: 104

Smee, William: 103, 104

Smith, John: 13

Smoking, Restrictions on: 102

Snowden, Philip, Lord Snowden, Chancellor of the Exchequer: 154, 160, 161, 162–4, 187

Soane, Sir John: 58, 81, 85–7, 99, 106, 107, 150

Soane Museum, the: 107

Socialists: 154, 160, 162–3, 184–7, 192, 194–5, 196

Somers, Sir John: 13

Sons of Clerks accepted for the Bank service: 83

South Africa
  Reserve Bank of: 168
  Union of: 137
  War in: 130

South America: 42, 88, 118, 126

'South Sea Bubble': 41–5, 64

South Sea Company: 41–5, 52, 117

Sovereigns *see* Coinage: 76, 78

Spanish dollars: 76, 78

Specie Notes *see* Notes, Bank of England

Spectator, The: 205

Sports Club, the Bank: 132

Sprague, Dr O. M. W.: 159

Staff
  Clerical—numbers employed: 19, 34–5, 56, 66, 83, 100, 101, 123; salaries: 19, 61, 100, 101, 124, 129; pensions: 61, 124; sons of clerks: 83; conditions for (mid-nineteenth century): 123–4; women clerks: 130
  Advisers *see* Advisers
  Bank Annuity Society: 104
  Bank Provident Society: 103–4
  Clerks Widows Fund: 103–4
  Leave of Absence *see* Leave of Absence
  Library *see* Library and Literary Association
  Rules and Orders for: 60, 69; on Bill transactions: 102; on betting and gaming: 102; on smoking: 102; on moustaches: 102
  Welfare of: 103, 205
  Porters, Messengers, Watchmen: 34–5, 83–4; Robes and Liveries: 34, 83–4; Arms: 34, 68, 83

Stamp Duty: 99

Stamp, Sir Josiah (Lord Stamp): 153

Stanley, Sydney: 193

Statistics Office: 200

Statutory Rules and Orders: 174

Stephenson, George: 87
Stephenson, Robert: 87
Stepney, Bishop of: 182
Sterling: 168
Stevens, Anthony: 20
Stock Exchange: 101, 102, 108, 126, 128, 134, 135, 137, 161, 173, 190
Stock Exchange Association: 105
Stock Transfer Offices: 69, 101, 105, 184, 189–90, 193
Stockbrokers: 62, 69, 105, 184
Stothard, Thomas, RA: 82
Strand, the: 125
Strikes and labour disputes: 145–6, 163
Strong, Benjamin: 157
Stuckey, Vincent: 93
Subscriptions to Capital see Capital of the Bank
Sun Fire Office: 57
Sundays, work on: 61
Sunderland, Earl of (Charles Spencer, 3rd Earl): 39–40
Swansea Branch: 92
Sweden, Bank of: 2
Swinton, Lord: 188
Switzerland, National Bank of: 138, 171
Sword Blades Company: 37, 44

Tallies, Exchequer: 21, 32, 42, 71
'Tap' loans: 177
Tariffs: 163, 164–5, 166
Taylor, Sir Robert: 57–8, 85, 86, 106, 189
Teesdale: 114
Telephones in the Bank: 139, 178
Telford, Thomas: 88
Tench, Nathaniel: 13, 23
Tenniel, Sir John: 129
Theory of the Foreign Exchange: 118
Thompson, Sir John: 53
Thompson, Thomas: 62
Thornton, Samuel, MP: 74, 82
Thornton, Mrs Samuel: 82
Thorneycroft, Peter, Chancellor of the Exchequer: 196
Threadneedle Street, Premises in: 49–51, 57–59, 66, 68–9, 85–7, 149–50, 178–9, 184
Three Nuns Court: 58
The Times: 84, 97, 128, 134
Tite, Sir William: 7
Tivoli Corner: 86
Tokenhouse Yard: 85
Tories: 9, 28, 39–41, 97
Tower of London: 7, 83

Trades Union Congress: 163, 197
Tradesmens' Tokens: 78
Trafalgar, Battle of: 83
'Transfer by Deed' Offices: 190
Transportation of criminals: 89–90
Treasury, the Bank: 58
Treasury, Committee of: 60, 95, 107, 141–2, 143, 149, 153, 170, 180
Treasury, H.M.: 37, 71, 116, 135, 139–42, 148, 156, 174–5, 176, 186, 187–8, 190, 202, 204
Treasury Bills: 179, 204
Treasury Notes see Notes, Treasury
Treasury Solicitor, the: 186
Trotter, H. A.: 167
'Tunnage Bank': 12
Tyneside: 114

Unclaimed Dividends: 72–3, 80
Unemployment: 146, 169
Unemployment Insurance: 146, 162–3, 169–70
Union Joint Stock Bank: 128
Union of London Bank: 128
United States of America: 66, 79, 96–7, 113, 118, 137, 140, 144, 151–3, 160, 165, 171, 190–2, 203
Usury Laws: 4–5, 94–5, 107
Utrecht, Treaty of: 42
Uxbridge House: 122

Versailles
  Treaty of 1783: 65
  Treaty of 1919: 154
Vickery, Abraham: 62
Victoria, Queen: 106
Vienna: 161
Vinson, Mr: 190
'Volpone': 39
Volunteers
  Bank: 81–3
  for the Cape: 131–2

'Wage Restraint' Policy: 196
Wall Street: 161
Walpole, Sir Robert: 45, 51–3
Walpole and Ellison, Messrs: 65
Walpole, Clarke and Bourne, Messrs: 65
War
  of 1914–18: 133–46
  of 1939–45: 173–84

War Loans
  1914: 138–9
  1939: 176–7
War and Lombard Street, The: 138
War Memorial, the Bank: 149, 182
War Office: 148
War Savings Certificates: 138–9, 177
War Stock Conversion 1932: 166
Ward, John: 13
'Warehouse, The': 47–8, 57
Washington, D.C.: 191
Watchmen *see* Staff
Watson, Sir Brook: 53, 76, 82
Waterloo, Battle of, 79
Waterlow Bros. & Layton Ltd.: 136
Ways and Means Advances *see* Advances
  to Government
Welfare Organization: 103, 205
Wellington, Duke of (Arthur Wellesley):
  94, 106, 110
Western Branch: 122, 125, 157
Wheeler, Sir Charles, PRA: 150
Whigs: 10, 26, 38–9, 41, 76

Whitchurch, Hants.: 56, 177
Whitehead, P.: 81
Whitmore, John: 79
Whitworth, Arthur: 189
Widows Fund, Clerks *see* Staff
Wilkes, John: 67
William III, King: 8, 12, 22, 36, 51
Willis, the Rev. Sherlock: 68
Wilmington, Lord (Spencer Compton,
  Earl of Wilmington): 53
Winthrop, Benjamin: 74
Withers, Hartley: 137
Wolverhampton: 114
Women Clerks *see* Staff
Wood, Sir Charles: 109
World Crisis, The: 133

'Young Plan', the: 154, 165, 187
Youngson, A. J.: 159

Zoffany, John: 62